CENSORSHIP 1917

A Da Capo Press Reprint Series

CIVIL LIBERTIES IN AMERICAN HISTORY

GENERAL EDITOR: LEONARD W. LEVY

Claremont Graduate School

CENSORSHIP 1917

By James R. Mock

DA CAPO PRESS · NEW YORK · 1972

Library of Congress Cataloging in Publication Data

Mock, James Robert.
  Censorship 1917.
  (Civil liberties in American history)
  Bibliography: p.
  1. European War, 1914-1918—Censorship—U.S.
I. Title. II. Series.
D632.M6 1972   940.4'05   74-37864
ISBN 0-306-70436-6

This Da Capo Press edition of *Censorship 1917* in an unabridged
republication of the first edition published in Princeton,
New Jersey, in 1941. It is reprinted by special arrangement
with Princeton University Press and reproduced from a copy
of the original edition in the Library of the Ohio State University.

Published by Da Capo Press, Inc.
A Subsidiary of Plenum Publishing Corporation
227 West 17th Street, New York, N.Y. 10011

Manufactured in the United States of America

Censorship-1917

By the Same Author
(with Cedric Larson)

WORDS THAT WON THE WAR
*The Story of the Committee on Public
Information, 1917-1919*

By James R. Mock

Princeton University Press, Princeton, New Jersey
London, Humphrey Milford, Oxford University Press

To Bonnie and Louise

Preface

A NATION EMERGING FROM A MAJOR WAR IS NOT THE SAME nation it was when it entered the struggle. The hostilities release forces that cannot be brought under control by a treaty of peace.

In no phase of life in a democracy is the threat of lasting harm from war greater than in the realm of personal liberty. Those wounded in battle eventually die; relatives of the slain pass away; economic losses are replaced in one manner or another; but the wartime repressive measures are like dead hands that do not relax their grasp upon the republic after the occasion which created them has passed. The true test of a democracy is the rapidity and thoroughness with which it throws off those restraints that were necessary for the waging of a successful war.

The main purpose of this volume is to show the extent to which the First Amendment to the Constitution was set aside during the greatest crisis through which this nation has passed up to the present time. A second aim of the book is to reveal an evil more dangerous to the continued existence of a true democracy than World War I censorship. That evil was the danger of carrying over wartime repressive measures into an era of peace for the sake of stifling political, economic, and social reform when reconstruction should have been the all-absorbing effort of this nation.

Few books are the product of a single person, and this work is no exception. The efforts of a great number of individuals made possible the writing of this volume. First of all, the author is indebted to Mr. Cedric Larson with whom he collaborated in producing *Words That Won the War*, a study of the Committee on Public Information. Only the present national emergency prevented Mr. Larson from taking an active part in the preparation of this book. Mr. Larson, however, has made available the material he gathered concerning censorship of soldiers, the cinema, and books.

Second only to Mr. Larson's assistance has been that of Evangeline Thurber, Helen Hunter, and Bess Glenn. Without the tireless aid of the first it would have required many additional months to complete this book. Miss Hunter read the manuscript, and made invaluable suggestions from the standpoint of reader interest. To Bess Glenn the author is indebted for the index.

For their assistance in making available research materials and resources of the Library of Congress and The National Archives the following deserve special mention: Henry Danilowicz, W. H. Flanagan, Charles Keyser, Frank E. Louraine, David C. Mearns, Harry C. Shriver, E. Stratford Smith, John Thaxter, Leo Tighe, Robert E. Ballantine, Dr. Henry P. Beers, Stanley K. Carter, Meredith B. Colket, Jr., John H. Dethman, Maxcy R. Dickson, Jesse S. Douglas, David C. Duniway, Edward S. Epes, May E. Fawcett, Dr. Philip M. Hamer, Lyman Hinckley, Harold E. Hufford, Dr. Dallas D. Irvine, Arah D. Mallison, Dr. Charles L. Stewart, Elizabeth Stillwell, Jerome Thomases, Philip J. Thompson, Karl L. Trever, and Edna Vosper.

Correspondence and interviews with persons who played a part in World War I censorship, as well as conferences with individuals who have been in positions to study the control of civil liberty have added greatly to the contents of this volume. Those individuals include George Creel, Paul Fuller, Jr., Dorsey W. Hyde, Jr., Captain Henry Hyde, Dr. Harold D. Lasswell, Isaac McBride, Major General Frank McIntyre, Marcus W. Price, Edgar Sisson, and Eugene White.

Finally, without the editorial guidance and the friendly interest of Joseph A. Brandt and Datus C. Smith, Jr., of

Princeton University Press, this book could not have been written.

The National Archives   J.R.M.
July 1, 1941.

Contents

Censorship-1917

Our Censorship Heritage

DEMOCRACY FACES A DILEMMA IN WARTIME. FOUNDED UPON the belief of citizen participation in government and of freedom of speech, press, and assembly for all citizens, when war comes those freedoms must be subordinated to the winning of the struggle, if the very government that guarantees civil rights is to continue to function, and thus assure to the citizens their constitutional privileges. In a democracy in peacetime, individuals or groups may select as many enemies as they please and struggle against them. During a war, these domestic enemies—for example, nicotine, indecent dress, vested interests, labor agitators, corrupt politicians, and many others—must be forgotten in the fight against the wartime enemy, namely, the foreign power or powers.

With this necessary concentration upon one object, divided counsels are dangerous to the life of the democracy. While in peacetime individuals could have different ideas of what the evils were that impeded the progress of the democratic way of life, in wartime the evil has to be reduced to one, the nation or nations with which the democracy is at war. If citizens persist in acting upon their several beliefs as to the way the enemy is to be defeated no united war effort can be made, and the democracy will be conquered.

Too much individualism in time of crisis may force the government of a democracy to restrict civil liberties. The individualism may not be in opposition to the war: for example, groups of citizens, disturbed at the real or fancied activities of enemy agents in their locality, and feeling that the proper authorities do not have the power to deal adequately with the danger, may organize vigilante societies, armies of "volunteer unofficial spy chasers," or resolve themselves into mobs, and without too much evidence of the guilt of the suspects deny them their constitutional rights. It was this feeling that there was no law to punish disloyal persons that was given as one reason for the Illinois lynching of Prager—an incident treated in the following chapter. Thus, in time of crisis, to prevent citizens from taking power into their own hands, a government may be forced to pass laws restricting the liberties of its people.

There are two risks, however, that a democracy must take. First, some freedom of criticism must be allowed to enable the citizens to object to bureaucratic or military inefficiency that may be endangering the nation's war effort. A democracy is primarily a peacetime organism to whose officials war is an evil but necessary avocation upon occasion. And with officials trained for administration in normal times, they may be wholly unfitted to perform the tasks of waging successful war. It will lie largely with public opinion to bring about the necessary changes of personnel and policy. The second risk democracy takes is in the possible carryover into the post-war era of the restrictions upon citizens' constitutional rights. If wartime federal repressive laws are aped by states, municipalities and even unofficial groups of citizens to suppress meetings, speeches, and publications of dissident groups after the war is over, then democracy has received that which on the surface seems to be a scar, yet, with the passage of time, may prove to be a mortal wound.

Consider the dilemma facing a democracy in wartime from the standpoint of the citizen. In war the individual as surely as the nation is facing a crisis, and in a crisis individual rights are subordinated to the welfare of the group and nation. For instance, in an overcrowded lifeboat a man may desire to flex his muscles, stand erect, and move about, but he will have to relinquish those ordinary rights for the sake of the lives of his companions. Or a person's rights may be curtailed in order to prevent a crisis, as Mr. Justice Holmes pointed out in the famous 1918 case of *Schenck v. United States.* In this decision, in which the Supreme Court upheld unanimously the conviction of Schenck and his companions charged with violation of the Espionage Act, Holmes held that "The most stringent protection of free speech would not protect a man in falsely shouting fire in a theater and causing a panic."

That it is possible, however, for the people of a democracy to enjoy the Bill of Rights even in wartime is being demonstrated again in Great Britain. There, the government, although possessing emergency power to suppress any publication inciting opposition to the war, has tried to allow generous freedom of criticism of the conduct of that struggle. From the beginning of the war until the latter part of January 1941, only one newspaper, the Communist *Daily Worker*, had been suppressed. Even with Britain almost in a state of siege, British censorship authorities are said to have no mandate to impose any intellectual blackout of the type which would result from the curtailment of the freedom of speech, press, and assembly.

It is interesting to note, incidentally, that in World War I, Britain did not deal with the dissenter so harshly as did the United States. For example, conscientious objectors in England received sentences of not more than two years, while similar persons in America received sentences ranging from fifteen to twenty years.

These harsh penalties were but a twentieth century phase of American life that has flamed in crisis, and smouldered in peacetime, at all times practically unnoticed since the nation began. And the story of that phase needs to be told in order that Americans can see how far and how rapidly they have travelled on the road of censorship.

Federal law gave, in 1917, reality and legality to the belief that it is better to preserve the United States without the Constitution than the Constitution without the United States. Specifically, the guarantees of freedom of speech and freedom of the press, offered all citizens, began to slip away from the American people on April 6, 1917 when war was declared. The provisions of the Selective Service Act, the Trading-with-the-Enemy Act, the Espionage Act (and its amendment, the so-called Sedition Act), during our turn in World War I, made the federal government, for the first time in 119 years, the thoroughgoing legal restricter of our constitutional liberties; what is even more significant, however, is that for the first time in the history of the United States, the executive, legislative, judicial, civil, and military forces were all empowered to set aside these and other guarantees of the Constitution.

Our entry into the European struggle changed the emphasis in American thinking from life, liberty, and the pursuit of happiness, to subordination of the feelings and desires of the individual to the winning of a war. Life, liberty, and the pursuit of happiness, for many of our citizens, took their places beside wheat, meat, gasoline, and other commodities that the people denied themselves. The nation as a whole was organized for war, and in war human life itself is cheap; consequently, those things that made for the good life lost their significance; the war became the vital interest. Had the authorities seen fit to use their powers to the utmost, an American's boasted liberty would have existed only in his memory.

In times of crisis, our liberties have always disappeared to some degree. Freedom of speech and freedom of the press have been the sectors in which the greatest losses have occurred. Just before the beginning of the Revolution, spoken or printed expressions of opinion had to agree with the prevailing taste of the neighborhood or suffer restraints amounting, in many instances, to mob violence.

During our War for Independence, minorities had few privileges. In regions controlled by Americans, Tories were driven from their homes, were deprived of their votes, and were prohibited from holding any public office. Regions dominated by British sympathizers saw English generals having the mails searched for rebel matter, or even forcing prominent rebels to flee the neighborhood.

The conscientious objector suffered for his beliefs in those days. The largest group in that class was the Quakers, who have always opposed war. They were attacked by mobs. In some instances, they were compelled to join the militia. Many of their schools were closed. Their quarterly religious meetings were prohibited. Finally, state authorities in Pennsylvania deported a band of them to the hills of Virginia in the winter of 1777-1778, the winter of Valley Forge.

Opponents of the ratification of the Constitution occasionally knew what it was to be denied their liberty of action. A quorum of the Pennsylvania legislature in the state convention seeking to act on ratification of the Constitution, was effectively obtained when a crowd of men broke into the lodgings of two anti-Federalist legislators, dragged them to the State House, and held them in their seats.

With the supporters of the Constitution, the Federalists, in power, and with the nation at peace, personal liberty had to fear only the Indians and the English common-law principle of seditious libel. This doctrine rendered King and Parliament immune to criticism. Despite the fact that in the United States the people were the government, political factions invoked the doctrine on this side of the Atlantic to punish their opponents.

This guerrilla type of politico-judicial warfare was brought into the open by the Alien and Sedition Acts of 1798, when war with France threatened. The Alien Act was not enforced by President Adams, but the Sedition Act was used against editors and others whom he and his party wished to silence. It provided:

"That if any person shall write, print, utter or publish . . . any false, scandalous and malicious writing or writings against the government of the United States, or either house of the Congress . . . or the President . . . with intent to defame the said government . . . or to bring them . . . into contempt or disrepute; or to excite against them . . . . the hatred of the good people of the United States . . . he shall be punished by a fine not exceeding two thousand dollars, and by imprisonment not exceeding two years."

Armed with this legal instrument, the Federalists, with Secretary of State Pickering in the vanguard, used the courts to put to flight their political opponents. Under that short-lived statute—it expired March 3, 1801—not more than twenty-five persons were arrested and ten were found guilty of violating the law. Of that ten, possibly one of the greatest sufferers was David Brown. He had brought about the erection, in Dedham, Massachusetts, of a liberty pole bearing sentiments that opposed, among other items, alien and sedition laws, stamp and land taxes, and tyrants of America. Also, at the time of his arrest, he had in his possession a number of manuscripts that were termed seditious because they contained such ideas as that it was wrong that "a few men should possess the whole Country and the rest be tenants to the others." For his activities and sentiments he was kept in jail for two years.

The storm of protest these measures aroused has not been obscured by the passage of time. Madison accused the federal government of exercising a power not delegated to it, and one which, "more than any other, ought to produce universal alarm, because it is levelled against the right of freely examining public characters and measures, and of free communication among the people thereon, which has ever been justly deemed the only effectual guardian of every other right."

Opposition to these acts led to the passage of the Virginia and Kentucky Resolutions in 1798, which declared that a state had the right to nullify an Act of Congress. This question of states' rights continued to trouble the nation until the Civil War provided an answer.

Those odious Federalist measures brought about the downfall of the party and the election of Jefferson. In fact, it is said that it was the vote of the first victim of the Sedition Act, Matthew Lyon of Vermont, "that broke the tie in the House of Representatives in 1800 and elected Jefferson President."

Never again has a political party attempted to destroy its chief rival by a sedition law patterned after that of 1798. No matter how sorely tempted a political party was to resort to such measures, growth of sectionalism, the rise of the slavery issue, and America's absorption in American affairs after 1815, together with the memory of the fate that overtook the party championing the Alien and Sedition Acts—all these factors worked against the reenactment of such measures.

When our next great crisis came after 1798, mobs and a general accounted for the negation of individual liberties during the War of 1812. That there were so few instances of repression in the Second War for Independence may have resulted from the fact that public opinion about the struggle differed from section to section, but only rarely within a given section.

In New Orleans after the defeat of the British there, Andrew Jackson was upon one occasion more than censor. *The Louisiana Gazette*, on February 21, 1815, announced that Jackson had received word of peace between the United States and England. The General demanded that thereafter the editor secure his permission to print news of such nature; and the bickering began. It ended with Jackson imprisoning a writer who protested the censorship, turning out of the city a judge who issued a writ of habeas corpus in favor of the imprisoned writer and therewith trying the offender by a courtmartial. The incident was closed when peace was proclaimed on March 13.

Various sections of the country took unkindly expressions that failed to agree with the opinion of the majority. Editors and speakers in New England were applauded for sentiments that were censured in Baltimore. In that city, when the editors of *The Federal Republican* declared the War of 1812 unnecessary and attacked the motives of Madison in advocating its declaration, the Administration ignored the paper, but a mob wrecked its printing office and destroyed its presses. When publication was resumed a month later, another mob killed one of the principals.

Freedom of speech and of the press is measured by tolerance of the public, not of the law. For instance, in 1812, a person could safely object to the war with Britain only if he lived in

New England, rather than in regions where the struggle was popular. This was likewise true during the Mexican War; expressions that would have brought punishment in 1798 were applauded half a century later. On Sunday, June 7, 1846, the noted minister, Theodore Parker, preached "A Sermon of War" in Boston; referring to the heads of the government, he said, "the political authors of a war on this continent, and at this day, are either utterly incapable of a statesman's work, or else guilty of that sin. Fools they are, or traitors they must be." Try to imagine what the officials of other times would have done with Parker for uttering these words: "In regard to this present war, we can refuse to take any part in it; we can encourage others to do the same; we can aid men, if need be, who suffer because they refuse. Men will call us traitors, what then? . . . We can hold public meetings in favor of Peace, in which what is wrong shall be exposed and condemned."

Fortunately for Parker, he lived in a time when no sedition acts were in force and in a place where many others also had misgivings about the Mexican War. Moreover, in his section of the country, the danger of a Mexican invasion was slight.

The Civil War saw the first great threat of destruction of the Republic and of personal liberties. With a nationwide struggle involving nearly all citizens as fighters or as producers of material, with a long, shadowy, and fluctuating boundary between the rival factions, and with southern sympathizers in the North and northern sympathizers in the South, freedom of speech and of the press was greatly curtailed. To all intents and purposes the Constitution was placed in cold storage. After all the successful efforts of Marshall to assume powers for the judiciary, that part of our government did not assert itself effectively until after the War. The writ of habeas corpus was suspended in the North and in the South.

Inroads upon personal liberty from 1861 to 1865 were not made wholly under statutory enactments. One must look to sources other than the results of the application of the Confiscation, Conscription, Indemnity, and Treason Acts, in order to explain the great number of cases in which arbitrary arrest, imprisonment without trial, and release without explanation were meted out to individuals. The number of persons treated in this fashion is variously estimated from 13,000 to 38,000.

Those citizens lost their liberties at the hands of Army officers, United States marshals, and State and local authorities acting under instructions from federal officials. Although the President, according to the historian James Ford Rhodes, did not direct a single arrest, "he permitted them all." Lincoln would have had time for nothing else, had he attempted to keep watch against the raids upon constitutional guarantees that his Secretaries of State and of War, and his generals were making. The War Department established a censorship over telegraph lines, while the Postmaster General denied the use of the mails to newspapers charged with being disloyal. In some instances, newspapers reached towns for which they were destined only to be confiscated by the authorities there.

Of the cabinet members whose duties touched upon restrictions of the individual, Edward Bates, the Attorney General, was the least aggressive. His general attitude was indicated in two communications to James O. Broadhead, United States District Attorney at St. Louis. In one he stated: "I would use indictments for treason sparingly especially against small men." And again, "It is not desirable to try many treason cases nor any one in which you have not a great probability of success. Better enter a *nolle prosequi* than be beaten. . . . As to minor offenses such as conspiracy, plunder of public property, obstruction of the mails and the like you must judge for yourself."

The Secretary of War suffered no such misgivings. He ordered the arrest of members of the Maryland Legislature and of any other persons whose detention was necessary in order to prevent the secession of that state. Acting upon those orders, General Banks and General Dix took into custody nineteen legislators, the Mayor of Baltimore, two editors, and a Congressman. To make sure that they did not do any more mischief, they were finally sent to Fort Warren in Boston.

A Washington paper incurred the displeasure of Stanton by publishing information of military movements. On March 7, 1862, the day following that violation, Stanton ordered Brigadier General Wadsworth, the military governor of the District of Columbia, to take immediate military possession of the printing office in which the paper, The Sunday Chronicle, was printed, to destroy all the papers that could be found there, "and hold the parties in custody that they may be dealt with according to the rules and regulations of war."

Federal marshals and Army officers were the greatest direct restricters of the freedom of speech and of the press. They informed their superiors of the disloyal activities of citizens in all parts of the North, and they executed orders from those superiors. Preachers, editors, politicians, and ordinary persons were arrested arbitrarily, and had their activities circumscribed by those agents.

In one instance, the provost marshal at St. Louis took no chances that the Lord or three Missouri counties should hear one local troublemaker. He directed the commanding officer at Glasgow, Missouri, that one Caples, whose teachings and example had been productive of much trouble, and who had decided to preach at Glasgow, was to be forbidden "his exercising in any manner the functions of a preacher or public speaker in the counties of Saline, Chariton and Howard until further orders."

The open season on preachers shifted to Virginia where General Butler arrested a Norfolk clergyman. He placed the divine at hard labor for "disloyalty in belief and action." The President, however, changed the sentence to exclusion from the Union lines.

Editors, more than preachers, seemed especially to suffer loss of their constitutional rights. Again Missouri provided the setting for such an occurrence. Although it was not among the eleven seceding states, southern sympathizers and supporters, under the leadership of Claiborne F. Jackson and

General Price, had necessitated the continued presence and the active intervention of Union troops. In that state of affairs, Edmund Ellis had published, in his *Boone County Standard*, from October 1861 to February 1862, pro-Confederate articles under such headings as, "Root, Abe, or Die!", "News from General Price," and a pamphlet, "To the Patriot Army of Missouri."

A military commission convened at Columbia, Missouri, and found Ellis guilty of publishing information for the enemy and of encouraging resistance to the government and laws of the United States. He was ordered to be placed outside the lines of the state of Missouri for the duration of the war, and the presses, type, furniture, and material of the offending editor were ordered confiscated and sold for the use of the United States. The finding and sentence were approved by command of Major General Halleck.

The fate of the *Boone County Standard* was harder than that which overtook the *Chicago Times* and the *New York World*. The Illinois paper was suppressed by General Burnside, the commander of the Department of Ohio, "On account of the repeated expression of disloyal and incendiary sentiments." In spite of an injunction issued by Judge Drummond of the United States Court restraining the military forces from carrying out the order of the General, a captain and his men seized the office of the *Times*, and prevented the morning issue of June 3, 1863.

This procedure, far removed from the threat of rebel armies, caused articulate opposition. In Chicago, a meeting of prominent citizens, presided over by the Mayor, sent a request to Lincoln to rescind the order. A resolution by the State Legislature at Springfield denounced the action. In response to these expressions of public sentiment, Lincoln rescinded that part of the order which suppressed the *Times*, and the Secretary of War informed Burnside that he was to arrest no more civilians and to suppress no more newspapers, until the President had been consulted.

Less than a year after the Chicago paper had been penalized, a similar fate befell the *New York World*. It had published a false proclamation of the President, "gloomily recalling recent disasters, setting a day for public humiliation and prayer, and calling for 400,000 men." An order, signed by Lincoln and countersigned by William H. Seward, Secretary of State, directed General Dix to arrest the persons involved and to imprison them until they could be tried by a military commission. Three days later, however, they were released, and the military forces were withdrawn from the printing establishment.

Just prior to his action against the *Chicago Times*, Burnside had triumphed over one of Lincoln's political opponents who had transgressed the General's Order Number 38, a decree that stated, in part, "The habit of declaring sympathy for the enemy will not be allowed in this department." Persons committing such offenses were to be arrested, tried as spies or traitors, and, if convicted, were to be put to death.

At a Democratic mass meeting at Mount Vernon, Ohio, on May 1, 1863, Clement L. Vallandigham, Member of Congress and candidate for the Democratic nomination for Governor, made a speech that appeared to violate General Order Number 38. Burnside had him arrested and tried by a military commission that sentenced Vallandigham to close confinement for the duration of the war. The President changed the sentence to banishment. According to James Ford Rhodes, the "mischief of the procedure lay in the precedent." A Lincoln, he feared, might not be in the presidential chair when another such threat to personal and political liberty occurred.

When the notion struck him, Stanton was not above suppressing a song. In 1862, the ever-cautious McClellan had been replaced by Burnside, who was soundly thrashed at the Battle of Fredericksburg. Almost at once there arose a clamor for the return of McClellan to his old command. When this was at its height, Septimus Winner of Philadelphia, who wrote "Listen to the Mocking Bird," happened to be in

Washington where he is reported to have heard Union soldiers shouting "Give us back our little Mac!" He returned to Philadelphia and wrote the song entitled *Give Us Back Our Old Commander: Little Mac, the People's Pride.*

According to Claghorn, Winner's biographer, "The piece swept all through the North. More than 80,000 copies were sold within a few days after its issue. It was sung by nearly every soldier of the Army of the Potomac, during their day's work and at the campfires in the evening."

Stanton called singing the song treason, and ordered the arrest of Winner. At the same time the song was suppressed in the Army, and any soldier caught singing it faced arrest. Winner was brought before a military tribunal and charged with treason, while "Stanton ordered all existing copies destroyed, and notified Mr. Winner that further publication of his song would result in his confinement in Fort Lafayette. Upon his promise to discontinue the sale of the song, Mr. Winner was released."

That song was to come into momentary prominence later. When Grant ran for a third term, there was much opposition, but a band of 306 delegates stuck with him to the end. Whenever Grant's name was mentioned, they all sang in unison, *Give Us Back Our Old Commander*—the song written about McClellan now being applied to Grant. Times and men had changed, for those words, "when applied to McClellan, meant treason, according to the Lincoln Administration, but became the highest proof of patriotism a few years later when applied to Grant."

Opposition to these Civil War attacks upon our constitution guarantees has been largely ignored, as much by the historian as by the agents who made the attacks. The attitude that the military took toward Judge Drummond's injunction in the *Chicago Times* affair was typical. In most instances in the North, a clash between civil and military jurisdiction resulted in the civil giving way. Army officers refused to answer writs of habeas corpus, and the courts, seemingly, could do nothing to carry their writs into effect. Seizing and holding persons without trial was condemned by more than one judge, but it was "carried on with a nonchalant disregard for either courts or constitution."

Several powerful voices were raised in protest against the curtailment of free speech and free press. Wendell Phillips said that habeas corpus, the right of a free meeting and a free press were annihilated in every square mile of the republic. And Senators Trumbull and Hale voiced their opposition to the arbitrary arrests.

Such outbursts were mere whispers drowned in the roar of popular approval that greeted the extra-legal silencing of the dissenters. About such manifestations, Lord Lyons, in Washington, wrote Earl Russell, "The applause with which each successive stretch of power is received by the people is a very alarming symptom to the friends of liberty and law." And Count Gurowski observed, in January 1862, "The thus called arbitrary acts of government prove how easily, on the plea of patriotic necessity, a people, nay, the public opinion, submits to arbitrary rule. . . . Here every such arbitrary action is submitted to because it is so new, and because the people has the childish naïve, but to it honorable, confidence that the power intrusted by the people is used in the interest and for the welfare of the people. But all the despots of all times and of all nations said the same."

Thus, in the final analysis, the people themselves, by their own inattention, if not their downright approval, made it possible to set aside the Constitution during the Civil War and in the era that followed. Our liberties were not to undergo another potential threat on such a scale for more than half a century after Lee's surrender.

In the years that immediately followed the Civil War, the First Amendment to the Constitution had little meaning for a large minority of our citizens. The southern states were reconstructed by their enemies in and from the North, who saw to it that generations of intelligence and leadership were penalized in favor of the ignorant and the amenable. For the first few years after Appomattox, the States that had seceded were divided into five military districts with a general at the head of each. With them in control, constitutional guarantees existed only at their whim. With so much power in their hands, and with Civil War animosities still rankling, the wonder is that more acts of oppression were not committed.

As it was, numerous outrages were charged against those officials. Military authorities at Memphis were accused of levying fines upon citizens for offenses without granting trial. At New Orleans, during the first four months of 1866, the Governor informed President Johnson that General Canby had assumed the right to control the civil affairs of that city and its administration.

And in South Carolina, General Sickles was accused of ordering the rearrest of an eighty-three year old man who had been convicted of murder by military commission and whose sentence Judge Nelson had set aside. Calling the man an escaped convict, Sickles sent him to prison at Charleston. When United States Court Judge Bryan issued a writ of habeas corpus to bring before the court certain men held under the sentence of another military commission, General Sickles declined to obey the writ.

The Reconstruction period over, freedom of speech and of the press were not directly endangered for several years. If, however, one includes economic and political liberty as fundamental aspects of a democracy, then our country lacked many truly democratic characteristics for many minorities. Voting qualifications or poll taxes kept the Negro in the South and the poor white in the North from using the ballot. Although no federal laws interfered with the bill of rights, so-called Socialists, labor unions, and other groups have been restricted in their activities by being accused and found guilty of violating such city ordinances as disturbing the peace, or for not obeying the sign to "keep off the grass."

As far as the federal government is concerned, however, no liberties, except economic, were threatened again until World War I. In fact, during our War with Spain, the public at large was hardly aware that any censorship existed. The

yellow journals of the time had played their part in bringing
on the struggle, and they were not going to be denied any
news that could be secured in any manner. The methods
they used, which in some instances included their own dispatch boats, made it almost impossible for the government
to withhold any information relating to affairs in Cuba. This
situation was partly met by General Greeley of the Signal
Corps, who succeeded in securing the cooperation of the
Western Union Telegraph Company in Florida. As a result,
by May 1898, censors were employed at Tampa, Miami, and
Jacksonville. This meant that any confidential information
correspondents might learn in Cuba could reach the newspaper only by dispatch boat or by mail. By the time the boat
or letter could get to New York or to other places outside
Florida, the news was stale. Seemingly, the only protests about
that censorship were lodged with the Secretary of War by the
St. Louis Post Dispatch and the *Pittsburgh Dispatch*.

In the meantime, similar arrangements had been made in
Porto Rico. At Ponce, in August 1898, General Miles received
word from the War Department that telegraphic censorship,
liberally administered, was to continue at the telegraphic
centers he controlled. Messages detrimental to the welfare
of the United States were forbidden.

Thus matters stood when peace was concluded, and we
received the Philippines from Spain. In those islands, "the
little brown brother of William H. T." (William Howard
Taft, Civil Governor of the Philippines) did not look with
favor upon a change of masters. More than two years of fighting were to ensue before the United States gained complete
control. Although war with Aguinaldo and his followers did
not break out until February 1899, the situation was so
strained that in the preceding month the Secretary of War
had directed General Otis, the commanding general, to censor
press dispatches. Complaints arose from the American press
almost at once, not because of the suppression of news, but,
according to the *New York Herald*, because of discrimination.
On January 31, 1899, the *Herald* carried a cable from London

to the effect the censorship at Manila was giving an opportunity for Spaniards abroad and the anti-expansionists at home
to promulgate the wildest kind of fairy tales about deplorable
conditions under the Otis régime. When the Associated Press
representative at Manila also charged that preference was
being given to other press representatives, the War Department informed Otis that there was no desire to interfere
with his censorship of matter sent from there, but that it
was necessary for all to be treated alike.

Otis's activities continued, and the criticism of the press
for his handling of the news of our operations in the Philippines went on. The newspapers soon were charging that the
General's reports of the military situation were misrepresenta-
tions. He was not conscious, however, of sending misrepre-
sentations. In fact, Otis thought his dispatches at times were
too conservative. When he informed the correspondents that
they had defied military authority and were liable to punishment, the General found that they courted martyrdom, which
he thought it unwise to permit them. This controversy finally
led him to the point where he was willing to remove the censorship and let them cable anything.

According to some of the newspapermen at Manila, the
whole trouble was that the government had left a small man
to deal with the most delicate problems, requiring broad
statesmanship.

If the man could not be changed, the requirements could.
And Otis was informed that the censorship might be entirely
removed, "only continuing the requirement that all matter
be submitted in advance, that you may deal, as you may deem
best with any liable to affect military operations or offending
against military discipline." The instructions continued, "For
reasons that are obvious, this should be done as of your own
motion, and without making any general or formal order or
announcement. Do it without announcing that you are going
to do it." That procedure evidently was followed, for, on
October 10, the New York Times carried the news that press
censorship had been removed, and that the Manila corre-

spondents had been unrestricted since September 9. The *Times* stated that General Otis was responsible for the change.

Although there were charges of mail censorship at that place, F. W. Vaille, director of posts at Manila, informed the Postmaster General that no letter for the States had been opened by anyone after it had been mailed there and before its dispatch to its destination.

The Philippines were to receive the attentions of a censor during the time of the Military Governor. On December 18, 1900, censorship instructions were given to the Manila office of the Eastern Extension of the Australasia and China Telegraph Company. All messages to and from Europe and America could be accepted without being censored, press included, but in the latter case, a copy had to be telegraphed to the censor. All messages for the Visayas, with the exception of three islands, were to be censored. These regulations were in force when Aguinaldo was captured in March 1901, and the backbone of the insurrection was broken.

Beginning with 1914, some form of censorship of communication and of news existed in this nation under the sanction of the United States government, until such supervision had been recognized by a formal legislative enactment during the time that we were at war with the Central Powers.

When this country sent troops to Vera Cruz in 1914, some news that the War Department thought unsatisfactory was printed in our papers. The Secretary of War asked General Funston at Vera Cruz if he had a censorship over the cable from that city. Funston replied that the censor was Captain Charles W. Wells who had succeeded Naval Constructor Gatewood at that job. To the General's suggestion that a cable censorship be established also at Galveston, Secretary Garrison said at that time, May 11, 1914, he could not act upon that suggestion.

The presence of a censor at Vera Cruz was brought home to Robert H. Murray, the correspondent there for the *New*

York World, later the Mexico Commissioner for the United States Committee on Public Information. During May 1914, he had tried to send to his paper a cablegram in which he made an attack upon Rear Admiral Cradock of the British Navy. The censor refused to pass it. By May 19, however, both parties had their triumph, for the message had been stopped by the censor and Murray informed Funston that the article had been sent by mail. But no derogatory mention of the Admiral appeared in the World during that period in May.

By March 13, 1916, some members of the Fourth Estate who had heeded the request of the War Department to refrain from printing information of use to the enemy in Mexico began to feel that they were losers. James Keeley, editor of the Chicago Herald and later European head of all of the Creel Committee propaganda against the Central Powers, asked the War Department to define the limits of censorship. The evening before, he had received a dispatch from the censor, Major Ryan, to kill the story that General Pershing had arrived at Columbus, New Mexico. Keeley did so, only to be informed from New York the next morning that some of the papers in that city carried the very information the Herald had suppressed.

The Chicago Tribune had obeyed the letter of the censorship order by omitting the Associated Press dispatch regarding the arrival of Pershing at Columbus. It had, however, published a similar account written by Floyd Gibbons, Tribune correspondent there.

The Judge Advocate General could offer no suggestions. He observed that under the circumstances the patriotism of newspaper editors and their cooperation for the success of the expedition in Mexico had to be relied upon with respect to such matters as Keeley had pointed out.

Brigadier General Macomb, Chief of the War College Division of the Chief of Staff, held that censorship of the press functioned only in theaters of operations or where martial law existed, and he had no information that the latter had been declared anywhere in the United States. The General pointed out that the way to handle a problem of the type that Keeley had raised was through the exercise of forethought, that all steps should be taken before the occasion arose for the application of censorship. Nothing was done with that recommendation. Instead, the commanding general of the Southern Department appointed a censor with whom copies of all dispatches sent out by correspondents were to be filed.

Through all this controversy, the people at large had been concerned only indirectly, and had been interested even less. Their attention was centering more and more upon America's connection with the European struggle. Aroused by stories of German frightfulness in the occupied regions of France and Belgium, and of their nefarious activities and plots in the United States, our people, in 1916, were beginning to think of the Allied cause as their own. Fear of what might happen to this country in the event of a German victory overseas made us willing to accept any measures that would prevent that eventuality. At the same time, by April 1917, most Americans had evolved a simple pattern out of the complex European situation. There were only two sides, one black, one white, the former pro-German, the latter pro-Ally. And we were resolved that in this nation we would be all white.

In our excited state of mind, in 1917 and 1918, divided counsels or opinions were discouraged. The demand was for a united nation, and to achieve it the American people cheerfully surrendered—sometimes knowingly, sometimes unknowingly—their constitutional liberties under a stream of city ordinances, and of state and federal laws.

Of all rights guaranteed citizens of the United States, the World War was to abrogate all but those concerned with property. And even property rights were to undergo certain limitations when the War Industries Board, the Food, Fuel, and Railroad Administrations began to function. This abrogation was to be expected in any nation engaged in a life-and-death struggle. But in the carryover of these necessary wartime suppressions, these deviations from the normal life of a democracy—in that carryover into the post-war era lay the real threat to our democracy.

The Seed of Censorship

DURING THE FIRST WORLD WAR, EFFORTS TO CURTAIL CIVIL liberty in the United States came from so many different directions the citizen failed to realize how close he came to losing civil liberty entirely. Some states resurrected Civil War statutes to deal with opponents of the draft, while other commonwealths enacted legislation to take care of disloyalty in almost any form. Mobs or citizens' committees took matters into their own hands, and dealt directly with unpopular persons, or with individuals suspected of not being good Americans. And in the economic phase of man's activities, citizens' liberties were held in abeyance by state and local food and fuel administrators, when the need arose.

Before the federal government could get any censorship bill through Congress, seven states and the Territory of Alaska had enacted statutes looking in that direction. The day after we declared war, Vermont passed a sabotage law, and from then until long after the Germans had been defeated, state after state passed restrictive laws that bore directly upon the negation of civil liberties. Massachusetts, for example, made its governor a potential dictator, and authorized him to take possession of any property that was needed for public use. At the same time, showing its attention to detail, the Bay State defined the manner in which the "Star-Spangled Banner" was to be rendered.

In Delaware, if a man had too much leisure, he was given opportunity to regret the fact. That Commonwealth decreed that every able-bodied male, with certain exceptions, between the ages of 18 and 55 had to be usefully and lawfully employed, or he would be subject to assignment to some job by the State

Council of Defense. The Council and the employer were to determine the compensation of the late loafer.

In addition to musicians and loafers, syndicalists, saboteurs, alleged seditious persons, aliens, and displayers of red or black flags soon discovered that many states had new laws for them.

Pennsylvania, however, relied upon a statute of 1861 to silence a preacher. The Reverend William A. Prosser was jailed in Pittsburgh because he urged attendance at an anti-draft meeting and said, "Let our prayer be that if we are drafted we shall solemnly refuse to go."

Theodore Cossman, also of Pittsburgh, suffered under the same law. He made a street speech against enlistment, and distributed handbills inimical to the interests of the United States by advertising a picture that was to have been shown at his theater. The picture in question was, "*Infidelity* with Anna Q. Nillson," according to the newspaper advertisement. The theater was closed by the police.

As state followed state in passing laws to restrict the individual, the press in those commonwealths paid little attention to the measures. For example, on April 24, 1917, Iowa enacted a statute against insurrection and sedition. It was advertised in the *Des Moines Register* eight days later, but no editorial comment was forthcoming in that paper. The only restrictive legislation the newspaper noticed were the various proposals in Washington, D.C., which, according to a quoted remark from Iowa's Representative, Cassius C. Dowell, were dangerous to liberty of the press, as well as to the individual.

Nor were there many outbursts against the economic regimentation imposed by such agencies as the United States Food and Fuel Administrations. Those agencies, through their local, state, and federal organizations imposed restrictions upon the American people with respect to the kind and amount of food and fuel commodities they could possess. Persons and firms violating the orders of the Food or Fuel Administration had their businesses closed for lengths of time that varied from one day to the duration of the war. Other violators were forced to contribute the amount of their fines to the Red Cross, and still others had to remove fuel from their basements, and give it to the poor.

In Georgia, for instance, failure to use the required amount of substitutes in bread and rolls cost the Atlanta Baking Company $1,000, which it donated to the Red Cross. The license of A. P. Treadwell & Company, Atlanta brokers in cottonseed cake and cottonseed meal, was revoked, and the firm was ordered to suspend operations for the duration of the war because it had failed to answer two summonses to explain its failure to make delivery on a number of cottonseed contracts. The Federal Food Administrator for Georgia gave the company instructions for winding up its business. In New York, because Swift & Company was found to have assisted the seller to profiteer in eggs, Swift, the purchasers of the eggs in question, was ordered to suspend dealings in that commodity for thirty days from midnight of April 10, 1918.

Profiteering in matzoth, the unleavened bread eaten by the Jews in their celebration of the Passover, virtually put L. Stern of Boston out of business for thirty days. The Food Administration issued an "unfair order" against him, prohibiting all firms licensed under the Food Control Act from buying from, selling to, or dealing with Stern for thirty days after April 20, 1918.

Charging exorbitant prices for sugar, and forcing combination sales, caused the Food Administration to close the doors of Louis Hoffman, a wholesale grocer of New York City. This information was released for the morning papers of January 28, 1918, and the order was to take effect three days later. In the meantime, to make sure that Hoffman did not again charge 17 cents a pound for sugar, his business was administered under the direct supervision of the New York Federal Food Board.

County food administrators could, upon occasion, punish food violation and disloyal speech simultaneously. John Sattler, a wealthy farmer of German birth, who lived near Emporia, Kansas, was taken to Topeka for internment for just that reason. When a food administrator protested against the feeding of wheat to Sattler's pigs and chickens, instead of conserving it for the Army and for the Allies, Sattler made disloyal remarks, and was haled into court for revocation of his first naturalization papers, on the ground that he did not take them out in good faith. This contention was upheld by the court.

In its sphere, the Fuel Administration exercised similar restrictive measures. For example, J. M. Lieberman, Detroit, was informed that on the evening of October 28, 1918, he had lights burning in his show windows in violation of the "lightless night" order. He was instructed to appear before the Fuel Administrator for Detroit and pay the penalty, or the Detroit Edison Company was to be told to discontinue his lighting service. Lieberman paid the fine of $5.

Because E. L. Moore of Albion, Michigan, had made application to three different coal dealers for anthracite coal, and in each case had stated that he had placed no other orders for that commodity, Moore ran afoul of the Fuel Administrator for that state. At the hearing of his case, Moore was told to take the hard coal out of his basement, and deliver it to the government representative in Albion, to be used for the benefit of the poor, and for which he was to receive no pay. In addition, he was ordered to send to the office of the administrator, within forty-eight hours after the hearing, a receipt from his local Red Cross for the sum of $200 that he had given it for war purposes. Finally, Moore was directed, "Take your medicine in the way that you should."

Different World War agencies often collaborated to restrict the activities of individuals. This was true of the work of the United States Housing Corporation in conjunction with the Fuel Administration. The former was created to take care of the housing problems of war workers, and one of those problems was rent profiteering. In at least one city, Philadelphia, an attempt was made to keep rents from becoming exorbitant. There, when the Housing Corporation found a landlord attempting to force a renter to move by raising his rent, the Fuel Administration counsel was notified and saw to it that no coal was furnished the landlord.

During 1918, "gasless Sunday" regulations were enforced by the Fuel Administrator, and many motorists were made aware of those measures. Consider the case of Louis A. Koch of Detroit, who, with his wife and another couple, prepared his Haynes automobile for a "tour to Cleveland." They had planned to start early one Saturday morning, but rain that day kept them home until noon. By steady driving, the tourists reached Toledo, and spent the night. Seeing other cars on the streets next day, Koch decided to set out for Cleveland. At Lorain a member of the American Protective League, spotted the foreign license, and stopped the car. The League, a citizens' auxiliary of the Department of Justice, was described by John Lord O'Brian, special assistant to the Attorney General for war work, as the largest division of American Secret Service. It was said to have had about 260,000 members. It was from the report of the League agent that Koch was summoned before the Michigan State Fuel Administrator, and was fined $15 for driving his car on a gasless Sunday.

All the numberless instances in which American civil liberties were circumscribed by governmental agencies for the winning of the war, show that the imposing of such limitations did not occasion any noticeable, articulate, or prolonged opposition on the part of the public. Perhaps, after all, the people were willing to have the liberties of some individuals restricted. The many instances of citizens denying other citizens those rights, lend support to that contention. Fear of spies and enemy agents caused, or served as a pretext for, many violations of the Bill of Rights.

And persons in various communities were taking the law in their own hands. An editorial of the *Anaconda* (Montana) *Standard* was indicative. On February 25, 1918, it held that all persons should unite to prevent I.W.W. activities, and continued, "Let no one be afraid of hurting anyone's feelings or interfering with anybody's liberties. The feelings and liberties of those who are fighting against America behind our own lines are not worthy of consideration."

The *Nebraska State Journal* of Lincoln foresaw that such a wartime situation would be portentous. It observed, "We are in for some lively times, no doubt, in deciding what obstructing the war shall consist of, and whose obstructing is to be interfered with." The paper believed that the difficulty arose from the fact that each person had his opinions as to the best way to promote war operations. Whoever preferred another way, therefore, was proposing a less effective way, and so was virtually obstructing the war. This idea reduced itself to the general proposition that whoever opposed anyone's political or economic conception of what ought to be done, in his eyes, was obstructing the war, and was subject to prosecution for disloyalty.

Ordinary courts, however, moved too slowly, and the punishments were too light and too uncertain in the opinion of many impromptu judges in 1917 and 1918. Those human instruments of extra-legal procedure preferred language restriction, mobbing, whipping, tarring and feathering, persecution, and lynching. There were many spokesmen for that school of thought. For example, L. B. Foley of the Merritt and Chapman Derrick & Wrecking Company, New York, wrote George Creel, chairman of the Committee on Public Information, "When our Government shall have *shot* [red ink underlining] or *hung* [same] the men who are spreading anti-American propaganda, the way will be cleared for more immigrants to become citizens of our country." Mr. Foley left his correspondent the task of defining "un-American." And in that same vein, Myron T. Herrick, former Governor of Ohio and our former Ambassador to France, was quoted in the *Daily Patriot* of Concord, New Hampshire, to the effect that, "This is no time for leniency. We should lock up all those who utter words that prejudice our cause."

The extra-legal group would have received its greatest inspiration from a speech by the Reverend Charles A. Eaton, pastor of the Madison Avenue (New York) Baptist Church. He was quoted as having advised workmen at the Port Newark shipyards, "If you get a spy, don't wait; don't be gentle with him. You have plenty of rope and lots of steel girders to string him up. If he comes with a bomb, don't say, 'let us pray'; don't slap him on the wrist, don't tell him he's a bad man. Take him out on the marsh, truss him up, put the bomb on his chest, light it and step back and watch him blown to hell and his kaiser."

Suppression of spies and traitors was not enough, however. The citizens realized that to win the war, a gigantic positive effort was required. Money was of paramount importance, and many measures were taken to ensure maximum contributions. The city Council of Topeka, Kansas, for instance, sent a questionnaire to city officials and employees. Each recipient had to state the amounts he had subscribed to war needs, or give reasons for his failure to subscribe.

If, in some instances, control of one's own money was taken out of the hands of the individual, freedom of assembly was denied even more frequently. In Oakland, California, the mayor refused the municipal auditorium for a demonstration designed to prevent the sending of American troops to European trenches. The meeting had been planned by the Women's Home Protective League, whose activities, according to the mayor, bordered on treason. In Scott County, Minnesota, the rôle of the Oakland mayor was played by the county Safety Committee. At a meeting on January 21, 1918, it called attention to the danger of disloyal or inflammatory utterances. Because of the seriousness of the situation, the Committee resolved that during the period of the war the Nonpartisan League was to hold no meetings within the county. That resolution had the sanction of the law, for, five days later, the sheriff and his deputies prevented an advertised meeting of the League, and prohibited the scheduled addresses.

This political party was to have such a stormy career during the war that it deserves special attention. The Nonpartisan League, founded in North Dakota by A. C. Townley in 1915, was but an agrarian protest movement which was gaining converts rapidly in the spring wheat area by 1917. Its growth caused it to be feared by the Democratic and Republican Parties, and by the conservative interests of the Dakotas, Minnesota, and Nebraska, namely, the bankers, millers, railroads, and owners of line elevators. Taking advantage of the national crisis, the League's enemies charged its leaders with disloyalty, with obstructing the draft, and with trying to array class against class. Of this last charge, Judge Amidon said it was at least 3,500 years old, and was repeated in every instance where an attempt was made to change an existing condition. This sentiment was noticed in the *New York Times* in connection with a ninety-day jail sentence Townley served in Jackson, Minnesota. Seven months after the Armistice he was found guilty of violating the Minnesota espionage law by making speeches in behalf of the Nonpartisan League. In an editorial the *New York Times* praised the sentencing and stated that the League made war directly on the institutions and traditions of the United States.

In wartime, anyone with a sense of hearing could be an informant. For sneering at the Liberty Loan, Henry Schneider, a New York waiter, was sent to jail for six months, while in Yorkville, New York, Adam Loris was sent to the workhouse for sixty days for shouting "Hurrah for the Kaiser."

And notice what happened to Perry C. Miller, a streetcar conductor in Topeka. One of his passengers was reading his son the newspaper account of the valorous deeds of an American machine gun company in France. Miller, uninvited, contributed the remark that he did not believe it, and was said to have continued with, "The newspapers print these stories of the war just as it suits them best." Expression of those opinions resulted in a request for the conductor to appear at the office of the United States marshal. There, it was suggested to Miller that he apply for work in the harvest fields. He was quietly informed that he was not fit to mingle with the public. When last seen, the former conductor was making an application for farm work at the Federal Labor Office in Topeka.

Equally serious was the offense of talking to a parrot in German, if the conversationalist happened to be an unregistered enemy alien. In Chicago, June 15, 1918, detectives passing a hotel heard raucous voices using German expletives issuing from an upper window. They slipped up to the door of the room, listened, and finally entered. There was Leo Deringer conversing with a yellow-headed parrot in the tongue of the enemy. The detectives learned that Deringer was an enemy alien and not recorded. The man was jailed, and the German-speaking bird was remanded to the custody of a loyal bird store.

Distrust of the German language led to widespread efforts to eliminate it from all phases of American life. According to *School and Society*, it was gradually being excluded from the public schools of the United States, principally through the efforts of the National Security League, which was carrying on a crusade against the teaching of the Teutonic tongue or ideals. Such efforts resulted in many cities in dropping the subject from the schools' curricula, and in legislative enactments to that effect in a few states. Among these were Delaware, Indiana, Iowa, Montana, Nebraska, and Pennsylvania.

This action was in direct opposition to the advice of P. P. Claxton, United States Commissioner of Education, and to the 1918 report of the British Committee, appointed by the Prime Minister to inquire into the status of modern languages in the educational system of Great Britain. Claxton hoped that the war would not affect in any way the policies in regard to the teaching of the German language in American schools. He stated, "The fewer hatreds and antagonisms that get themselves embodied in institutions and policies the better it will be for us when the days of peace return." And the British Committee came to the conclusion "that it is of essential importance to the nation that the study of the German language should be not only maintained but extended."

While the National Security League was crusading against a language, other groups were eliminating from their faculties professors suspected of disloyalty. One body, a Minnesota Safety Commission, decided that Professor William A. Schaper, chairman of the Department of Political Science in the University of Minnesota, was disloyal to the government because he had opposed the entrance of the United States in the war. Upon the Commission's request, the University's Board of Regents dismissed Schaper, September 13, 1917, without informing the alleged disloyal professor of the specific charges against him. The member of the Board who was said to have led the attack upon Schaper was Pierce Butler, later a Justice of the Supreme Court of the United States.

Faculty members of other institutions were treated in the same manner, but Schaper's case differed from the others in its final conclusion, two decades later. On January 28, 1938, the Board of Regents of the University of Minnesota exonerated Schaper, a member at that time of the University of Oklahoma faculty, and granted him $5,000 remuneration, including the salary for the school year in which he was dismissed.

Not only was the German language removed from most curricula throughout the United States, but whole towns banned it. In Menard, Texas, the citizens' loyalty committee issued a public proclamation prohibiting the private or public use of German as long as the war was in progress. Germans were warned not to use their native tongue in their homes or elsewhere. A similar measure adopted by an Iowa town was said to have been so all-inclusive that one's old grandmother, just over from Germany, and unable to speak a word of English, could not use her native tongue, even to talk to herself.

Sterner methods than moral suasion were sometimes employed.

In Elk City, Oklahoma, April 9, 1918, William Madison Hicks, ex-minister and Socialist lecturer, at the time under federal indictment for promoting the "World Peace League," was taken from the police by a mob of 100 citizens, given a coating of tar and feathers, and ordered to leave the country. He had been jailed for alleged propaganda against Liberty Bonds.

A similar incident, with a different setting, was reported by the *Vicksburg* (Mississippi) *Daily Herald*, April 17, 1918. It related how, charged with disloyalty toward the United States government, failure to buy Liberty Bonds, and as being an undesirable citizen, Walter A. Hunter, wealthy Louisiana planter, was ordered to leave the state forever. The charges and order were made by a committee of citizens of Newellton, who tarred and feathered him before placing him aboard the Vicksburg train. According to the *Herald*, "He was marched about the streets with a large placard on his breast which read: 'Disloyal to the U.S.' He was made to salute and kiss the United States flag, while a committee composed of ladies sang patriotic songs."

On the same day that the Vicksburg paper reported that incident, the convicts in the State Penitentiary at Santa Fe, New Mexico, stripped, tarred, and feathered Major John M. Birkner, a federal prisoner charged with the violation of the Espionage Act. After the coating had been applied, the prisoners led the Major around with a rope around his neck. Birkner was born in Germany, but had served in the American military forces more than thirty years. He was alleged to have made disloyal utterances, such as, "You can't beat the Dutch," and, "The Germans will sink American transports as fast as they are sent over."

While tar or yellow paint made the mobs' work more noticeable, some of those groups resorted only to whipping the objectionable person. This punishment was visited upon the Reverend Herbert S. Bigelow, a pro-war radical who, later, was a member of the Cincinnati City Council and a member of Congress from Ohio. On Sunday afternoon, October 28, 1917, he had prayed publicly for the saving of the soul of the Emperor of Germany, and for the men on the European battlefields to throw away their arms. That evening he was kidnapped while on his way to address a Socialist meeting in Newport, Kentucky, and was horsewhipped by his captors. The whipping was administered "in the name of the women and children of Belgium and France."

From Aurora, Indiana, June 15, 1917, came news that exciting scenes had marked the close of Flag Day there. A mob of citizens numbering fifteen hundred to two thousand caused an enforced display of American flags on homes and business houses of pro-German sympathizers. For more than two hours, the town police force was powerless to check the crowd as it marched from house to house, dragging men out of their houses, some in night attire, and forcing them to hoist flags over their homes, others to wave and salute flags. It was estimated that 25 to 30 per cent of the crowd was composed of women.

On February 12, 1918, at Staunton, Illinois, a mob completed a successful tarring and feathering of two suspected of having dealings with the I.W.W. Then, according to the *St. Louis Republic*, "Aroused to a fury of patriotism because a member of the mob had shouted that it was Lincoln's Birthday," the citizens rushed to the homes of suspected pro-Germans, dragged them from their beds, and forced them to kiss the flag.

In this instance the town police force was not powerless to check the mob. Instead of being present to maintain order, the Chief of Police said all patrolmen were busy looking for chicken thieves, and none was available to stop a demonstration again pro-Germanism.

With no police control, hundreds of citizens, including bankers, lawyers, farmers, merchants and their wives, thronged the streets of the town, bursting in doors of suspected pro-German sympathizers, and dragging them to the streets to undergo the test of loyalty. "Bonfires were built and the crowd roared with laughter when a German with a hugh paunch sang." Germans who could play musical instruments were forced to play "The Star-Spangled Banner." The *Republic* added, "Homes of alleged pro-Germans were ransacked for German flags, but none was found."

Next day the *St. Louis Globe-Democrat* observed, "It was a Lincoln's birthday celebration, such as Staunton had never before witnessed."

Of all the mobs that dispensed their peculiar type of precipitate justice, so-called, the Collinsville, Illinois, party occupies a place all its own, for, in that instance, a man was lynched. A registered German alien named Prager, who was said to have tried unsuccessfully to enter the Navy, and later had registered for the draft, after some arguments with labor union officials and miners, put up posters at the Maryville mine, the afternoon of April 4, 1918. Those posters proclaimed Prager's loyalty to the government. According to the *New York Times,* when the workmen left the mine they were incensed by the proclamation, and began to hunt him. The mob idea was said to have had its inception in a saloon on the outskirts of the city, where miners from Maryville and Collinsville gathered. Many of the men were foreigners, who understood little English, and it was believed the remarks of Prager were exaggerated.

The mob swarmed around the City Hall. The size of that gathering was not diminished by the activities of the authorities, if a newspaper account attributed to one of the self-styled leaders was true. The leader, Joseph Riegel, was reported to have said that he was in a saloon about 10:15 that evening, when a policeman came in to close up the place, telling them that a German spy was in the city jail and that a mob was there. At the City Hall, Mayor Siegel made a speech to the crowd, pleading with his hearers to give the prisoner the right of trial. The plea was ignored. The building was searched, and Prager was discovered hiding in the basement.

Barefoot, with an American flag draped around his body, he was taken outside the city limits. The mob stopped at a large tree beside the Old National Road. A small boy was boosted up the tree to adjust the rope, and Prager was hanged. That the charges of disloyalty, sufficient to warrant the death penalty, were open to question, was evident from the fact that he was buried by the Odd Fellows Lodge, of which he was a member.

Eleven men were indicted for that crime, and while many of the newspapers throughout the country demanded that the guilty be punished, the jury was not convinced that those indicted had actually committed the deed. On the other hand, the defense, in trying to prove that Prager had made disloyal remarks, went so far as to try, vainly, to introduce into the record remarks that the deceased was said to have made in another state in 1915. When all the arguments were finished, the jury was out forty-five minutes, and of those only eleven minutes were said to have been consumed in reaching a decision, which was, not guilty.

This news was received with different emotions in various parts of the country. In the courtroom where the accused were tried, the announcement that all of the defendants had been found not guilty was reported to have been attended by wild demonstrations in which the accused men were overwhelmed with congratulations. Among the newspapers, the verdict was not overwhelmingly popular, but here and there the jury's action was, in effect, praised. For instance, an editorial in the *Topeka* (Kansas) *Daily State Journal* for June 7, 1918, said, "Of course we are a law-abiding people, loving justice and the right, but it may have been noticed that there have been no indignation meetings held in protest against the acquittal of the men who hanged a Hun sympathizer at Collinsville, Illinois."

While all the foregoing instances of the inroads upon our liberties were in progress, few condemnatory comments about them appeared in the daily press. All ears, eyes and channels of communication, interested in matters of censorship and related fields, were pointed toward Washington. That a man was whipped, tarred and feathered, his house ransacked, all his buildings painted yellow, or his speech curtailed, all those incidents seemed to mean far less to most citizens than whether or not a censorship law was passed by Congress.

These excesses committed by groups of citizens, and by local authorities in the name of patriotism, showed the necessity for federal legislation. Censorship may be bad, it was reasoned, but the actions of one class of persons who, in wartime, would destroy the government, and the equally harmful efforts of another group of citizens to maintain democracy by resorting to violence are compelling reasons for emergency statutory restrictions. If one seems to have a naïve faith in the efficacy of federal censorship in wartime, it is because of the small choice one has. Between repression by mobs and other extralegal bodies on one hand, and federal authorities on the other, only the members of the mobs and of the vigilantes would prefer the suspension of the Bill of Rights by their method.

"Laws Against Spies and Traitors"

IT WAS A VERY ENGROSSING WORLD IN 1917, WITH SCARCELY A dull moment in which to think about long-term results. So engrossing to Americans was the world scene during World War I that, apparently, they were never aware of piece after piece of federal legislation which, when fitted together, made the mosaic of censorship. In addition to criminal laws already upon our statute books, liberties of persons who would have been untouched by those laws, were circumscribed by at least three executive orders and three federal statutes, all six of which were produced as war measures. Although, as each of the sextet was pending, there was articulate opposition, when the order or law became a reality, there were other incidents, or omens of coming legislation, of much greater news value.

There is another side to this seeming indifference on the part of Americans toward federal restriction of their civil liberties. The United States was at war with a nation whose secret agents in this country, the American people thought, were present in every key city and key industry, striving to hinder the war effort of the United States. Closely related to and explaining the presence of Teutonic spies and saboteurs was the fact that the war was not waged on the battlefield alone, but by the people as a whole. And, as individual liberty was restricted in the combat zone corresponding restriction was necessary with the entire nation a theater of war, "in which," as Zechariah Chafee, Jr., points out in *Freedom of Speech,* "attacks upon our cause are as dangerous and unjustified as if made among the soldiers in the rear trenches." It was for the sake of strengthening the "inner lines" that these six measures were enacted. Also, these federal regulatory laws and orders must be considered as a part of American life itself, a means that this government used to insure its continued existence.

Certain groups in the United States had not waited for our declaration of war on April 6, 1917 before they began agitating for some federal wartime restrictions of freedom of speech and of the press. Foremost in that assemblage were the Army and Navy. As early as 1907, the former was considering "The Press in War" as it applied to (1) Illustrations of the mischievous effect of unrestrained publication, (2) Laws of the other countries restricting publications, and (3) Constitutional guarantee of "freedom of the press." There is no evidence that any measures were recommended for legislative enactment as a result of that study, at least at that time. But the subject was not likely to have been forgotten, since the British were continuing studies of like nature down to the outbreak of war.

In 1915 the War Department considered the subject again. This was a result, in part, of communications the Department received from Americans in England pointing out the weaknesses of censorship there and stating that those weaknesses came about because no provisions for censorship had been made before hostilities began. Another reason for resuming this study was the Mexican situation that has been noticed in the preceding chapter. With Europe and Mexico presenting concrete problems of censorship, our Chief of Staff directed a consideration of legislation "necessary to control the press in time of war," and at the same time ordered a study of methods employed by the English to control the press. To those members of the General Staff who were engaged in this work, the Act of March 3, 1911, "To prevent the disclosure of national defense secrets," seemed too limited in its operation. After considering the expanse of territory our country embraced, the chance of irresponsible publication by periodicals and newspapers in wartime, and the fact that telegraph, telephone and cable lines were privately owned, the officers submitted a tentative draft of legislation that they recommended be sent to Congress for action. The measure they proposed would have conferred upon the President the power to restrict the publication of certain information inconsistent with the defense of the country.

Again, no legislation came directly from this work of the General Staff, but the next year, 1916, saw the Army and Navy working together on the problem of censorship. A joint board of the two services recommended a bill empowering the President, in time of national emergency, to issue a proclamation prohibiting publication of news relating to our armed forces, matériel, or to the means and measures contemplated for the defense of the country. Continuing, the Board recommended that it should be made unlawful for any unauthorized person, within the jurisdiction of the United States, to publish or cause to be published any facts, information, rumors or news prohibited by the Presidential proclamation.

When this measure was proposed by the joint board, it found a similar idea expressed in Senate bill S-5258. This latter was designed to prevent the disclosure of national defense secrets. It did not satisfy the War, Navy and Justice Departments, and a conference of representatives from those three agencies proposed amendments that dealt specifically with control of the press. The Attorney General, however, thought it would not be wise to include censorship in S-5258. And censorship was to wait until 1917 before it became a law.

In the meantime, the Secretary of War, with no prospect of any legislation on the subject close at hand, was trying to prepare for any emergency that might arise in connection with censorship or the need for it. He wrote Daniels, Secretary of the Navy, that in order to establish such censorship of the press, telegraph, cable and other means of communication as might be necessary, and might "now or hereafter" be authorized by law, he requested Daniels to designate a Navy officer to cooperate with an Army officer, appointed for the same purpose, to draft the necessary rules and regulations for the effective control of publications and means of communication. Those two officers were to consult with representatives of the press associations residing in Washington regarding rules and regulations to be adopted. Daniels approved the suggestion.

Secretary of War Baker also foresaw another use to be made of those officers. They were to be required, from time to time, to recommend officers of the Army and Navy, preferably from among those on the retired list, "to act as censors at the various places where such services may be required."

So far as Baker's department was concerned, it may be said to have gone under censorship to the common citizen, June 9, 1916. At that time a temporary division of the office of the Secretary of War was established, to be known as the Bureau of Information with Major Douglas MacArthur in charge. It was to be the only source of information given to the press from the War Department, except that of a routine nature that did not bear upon the contemporary military situation.

To encourage the establishment by law of a more extensive censorship, Secretary Baker wrote Edwin Y. Webb, chairman of the House Committee on the Judiciary, August 11, 1916. He invited Webb's attention to the lack of any law authorizing the President to restrict the publication of certain vital defense information. Baker observed, "In this country the proper legislation authorizing such control of publication should be adopted when, as now, the country is at peace." After informing Webb that censorship legislation had been made the subject of study by the General Staff Corps, by the Judge Advocate General of the Army, and by a joint board of Army and Navy officers, Baker attached the draft of a proposed bill recommended by those investigators. Webb assured Baker that the matter would have his prompt attention.

Although no legislation resulted immediately, the censorship ball had been started rolling. And, on February 5, 1917, Webb is found introducing a bill that proposed to punish with life imprisonment any unauthorized person who, in wartime, should collect, record, publish, or communicate certain military information, or who should communicate or publish reports or statements that were false, or that were "likely or intended to cause disaffection in, or to interfere with the success of, the military or naval forces of the United States."

The next day, opinions that were opposed to this espionage bill began to find their way to Washington. For example, from New York the American Union Against Militarism sent Secretary Baker a telegram protesting "against unnecessary and dangerous censorship of press proposed in bill now being pushed by Army General Staff." The message pointed out that both the military and naval forces already had regulations that gave complete control of military information to those services. The Union held that under the deceptive guise of furthering that control, the proposed bill would give military authorities absolute control of the press in time of war when democracy most needed free discussion of men, measures, and objectives. In the opinion of the Union, the only results of the bill would have been to protect military incompetents from public criticism, to throttle the freedom of the press, and to allow the discussion of war and peace terms only by permission of military authorities. Among the names of those who signed the telegram were Paul U. Kellogg, Oswald Garrison Villard, Ernest Poole, Norman Thomas, and A. A. Berle.

Undismayed by those sentiments, Daniels and Baker continued perfecting their censorship plans. The former was more active than the latter in this respect. On March 1, 1917, he proposed to Baker that the Navy Department continue the censorship of radio stations and to begin to censor all cable stations. At the same time, according to the plans of Daniels, the War Department would look after communications via telephone and telegraph at our international boundaries, "and elsewhere if necessary." Nine days later, he was requesting a voluntary censorship by the newspapers with regard to shipping news.

The ready response to this request caused *Editor and Publisher*, March 24, 1917, to hope that no censorship law would be passed at the extra session of Congress which was to begin April 2. That trade journal judged from the response that such legislation would not be needed for the suppression of news or for censorship of news detrimental to government interests or to the welfare of the American nation.

Before Congress assembled, the press received another check upon its privileges. On March 24, regulations relative to censorship were announced after a conference of the State, War, and Navy Departments. The newspapers of the country were asked to follow them voluntarily, pending enactment of a press censorship law. Five of the six regulations, according to the *New York Times*, had been drawn at the Navy Department. The sixth, presented by the State Department, was the one that the editors regarded as objectionable. It read: "It is requested that no information, reports, or rumors attributing a policy to the government in any international situation, not authorized by the President or a member of the cabinet, be published without first consulting the Department of State."

While these departmental censorship activities were in progress, with War, Navy, Treasury, and State taking the lead, the extra session of Congress reassembled. After hearing President Wilson's war message, the bills began to be introduced, and among them was one by Congressman Webb that was destined to become the Espionage Act of June 15, 1917.

Before that bill became a law, however, the first of three executive orders dealing with censorship, had been issued. On April 13, the Secretaries of State, War, and Navy, in a joint letter to the President, had recommended the creation of a Committee on Public Information in which the two functions of censorship and publicity could be joined. This suggestion followed rather closely many ideas that had been expressed previously to Grosvenor Clarkson, of the Council of National Defense, by leading newspapermen and publishers in response to Clarkson's request for their opinions and suggestions as to the kind of censorship this nation should have in event of war. Among those who had submitted ideas on the subject were, Mark Sullivan, then editor of *Collier's*, Arthur W. Page of Doubleday, Page & Company, Frederick Palmer, William Hard, and Roy Howard. Clarkson had placed all these replies in the hands of the Secretary of War, where he hoped they would help crystallize thought and action. When he had asked for those opinions, it was thought that the Council of National Defense might have charge of censorship.

The day following the joint letter from the three cabinet members, Wilson created the Committee on Public Information. It was composed of newspaperman George Creel, chairman, and the Secretaries of State, War, and Navy. Creel's selection was in accord with the opinion expressed by Frederick Roy Martin, assistant general manager of the Associated Press. Writing in *Editor and Publisher*, April 4, 1917, he stated that censorship should be "administered by trained newspapermen, and not by retired Army and Navy officers, who may suffer from physical or mental gout and antagonize the press at every turn." Martin held that, "Newspapermen cannot command battleships, and military staff officers cannot conduct newspapers."

If the newspapers were a reliable index of public opinion when the Committee on Public Information was created, the American people were either unaware of or indifferent toward the restrictive possibilities of that Committee. For example, the *New York Times* was more aroused over personnel—specifically over the chairman—than it was over the possibility of censorship. In an editorial of April 16, 1917, the *Times* stated that while Creel might have been unjustly criticized for his activities in Denver in 1911 and 1912, the paper was unable to discover in his turbulent career as a municipal officer there, or in his qualities as a writer, or in his later services to the Woman Suffrage Party in New York, "any evidence of the ability, the experience, or the judicial temperament required to gain the understanding and cooperation of the press."

Other papers throughout the nation, however, did not follow the lead of the *New York Times*. The *Idaho Sunday Statesman* of Boise gave the information that a "Censor Board is Appointed By the President." It made no comment, but contented itself with such an editorial as "An Ancient Obligation" on repaying our debt to France contracted when La Fayette came to this country. One of the few papers to voice any opinion, was the *Times-Picayune* of New Orleans. On April

16, it referred to the Creel Committee thus, "It is called a 'velvet glove' censorship, because it is so moderate as compared with the radical and drastic provisions" in other countries.

From page 11, the *Des Moines Register* told its readers that "Cabinet Officials Plan Frank Statements Through New Censor Board." Frankness and censorship are infrequent companions, hence, the statement at least was worth editorial elaboration. The editorials on that day, however, were on such subjects as, Von Bernstorff, "Eat Corn Bread," and "Selective Conscription." The *Register* made the nearest approach to discussing censorship on April 17 when it wondered "why should Americans be deprived of the full knowledge of what is transpiring that they enjoy in times of peace?" But this observation was made in connection with the pending espionage bill, and not with reference to the already established Committee on Public Information with its dual objects of censorship and publicity.

One of the papers to carry on its front page the story of the formation of the Committee was the *Minneapolis Sunday Tribune*. On April 15, it said, "President Gives Body the Power to Censor or Give out Any Facts." The whole idea was not worth an editorial, apparently, for those expressions of the paper's opinion were directed toward such questions as "The National Conscience and the War" (mainly about raising an army), "Important Appointments" (on the State Public Safety Commission), and "Let the Colonels Do It"— this last referring to Theodore Roosevelt's wish to raise a division of troops and take it to Europe, while Bryan was offering to serve in any capacity in which he might be needed.

A different slant was given to the announcement of America's first Committee on Public Information by the *Helena* (Montana) *Independent*. It announced, "Appoint Censor of News, George Creel is Given Important Post." That information was used to urge the formation of a home defense organization, thus, "A censorship has been established in the United States. Rumors instead of facts will fill the air." The editorial continued, "don't you believe for a moment that there isn't

some embryonic treason about! Newspapers, in these cen-
sorious days, do not print all they learn." In this case there
was no objection to the government curtailing American civil
liberties. It served the purpose of the paper to credit a censorship which even theoretically was hardly two days old, with
shutting off news of embryonic treason which, if published,
would have gone far toward causing citizens to create a
home guard.

Editorials in the *State Gazette* of Trenton, New Jersey,
paid tribute to a recently deceased Judge, considered the
preparations under way to fight the food shortage, and took
an interest in "Changing Names." The matter of shifting
nomenclature, it seemed, arose in a Pennsylvania bakery
whose proprietor decided to sell Lincoln rolls instead of Bismarck rolls, although the similarity of content and of taste
was remarkable.

In the Southwest, the *Arizona Republican* of Phoenix,
mentioned that a committee was named to safeguard war
secrets, but two of its main editorials concerned the cost of
the war, and the uncertainties of baseball. While in another
corner of the country, the weekly *Argus and Patriot* of Montpelier, Vermont, was more interested, editorially, in the question of selective service versus the volunteer system, Red Cross
drives, the police raiding a poker joint, and the non-glare
automobile headlight law.

The Committee, in the days following its creation, failed
to elicit editorial comment from the *Cleveland Plain Dealer*,
but "The Field Sparrow" received attention.

If the possibility of liberties slipping away from them did
not interest the rank and file of the American citizens, what
did? The seven billion dollars for our war effort, pending
selective service legislation, the visit of the Allied High Commission, Wilson's appeal to all to cooperate, prohibition, and
looming above everything else in public interest, was the
armed conflict raging in Europe—all of these subjects seemed
more important than the possibility of censorship.

Creel's group merely supervised a voluntary censorship of the press, which left the matter of news suppression up to the newspapers themselves. Of course, the Army and Navy censored the information they gave out, but news, for instance about troops moving from the one camp to another, was at the mercy of the papers in the vicinity of those camps, if they chose to use it. Approximately 99 per cent of the press observed the rules of this voluntary censorship, and since it was voluntary they made little complaint about the denial of the freedom of the press.

The President's second executive order No. 2604 of April 28, 1917, relating to censorship, went into effect four days later. That order related to all cable and land telegraph lines leading out of the United States. Its objects were to deny information to the enemy; to obtain information of value to the government; to prevent the spreading of false rumors and reports likely to interfere with the successes of the military or naval operations of the United States, or prejudice relations with foreign powers, or the training, discipline or administration of the military or naval forces of our country. In 1917, however, the citizens of the United States were only beginning to be interested in commercial or other matters outside this nation. As a result of that situation, personal or business cablegrams or telegrams entering or leaving this country did not concern any great number of our people directly.

With respect to potential official attacks upon our liberties here at home, one would have expected Americans to know when those threats were impending, or when they had become realities. In the case of the more publicized censorship measures, popular interest in them, as reflected by the newspapers, barely lasted until the laws went on the statute books.

Consider the opposition to the espionage bill outside the halls of Congress. As it was introduced April 2, 1917, the only part of it to which the press objected was not its most fundamental possibility of attack upon civil liberties, but rather the third section of chapter II, which read: "Whoever in time of war shall willfully make or convey false reports or false statements with intent to interfere with the operation or success of their enemies and whoever in time of war shall willfully cause or attempt to cause disaffection in the military or naval forces of the United States shall be punished by imprisonment for not less than twenty years or for life."

The press of the nation, while supporting the sections of the espionage bill directed at aliens, was up in arms over the provisions of the above paragraph. Most editorial writers construed it to be a gag-law, and they assailed it in vitriolic editorials.

Anxious days were ahead for the Fourth Estate as amendment after amendment to that bill was offered which had a distinct bearing upon limitation of the freedom of the press. Most dictatorial of all those amendments was one introduced by Senator William F. Kirby of Arkansas. It proposed a press censorship for the period of the war, with the Secretaries of War and Navy as its directors. They were to be authorized to "summarily suspend" by written order for a thirty-day period any newspaper or magazine publishing any information concerning the plans or conduct of any military or naval operations, or other information relating to the public defense which could have been useful to the enemy. If an editor failed to obey the suspension order, he was liable to a fine of not more than $5,000 and a six-month suspension.

During the month of May, the debate on the espionage bill surged back and forth in Congress. Outside, the newspapers kept up an editorial drumfire against the censorship regulations, and hailed as a victory the defeat of the various amendments, especially the one by Senator Kirby. Whenever such an amendment was voted down, the press hailed it as a victory for the Fourth Estate.

When the last specific measure for newspaper censorship had been killed, and the Espionage Act had become a law, June 15, 1917, the papers had lost sight of, or at least showed little interest in, a provision in Title I, Section 3: "Whoever, when the United States is at war, shall willfully make or

convey false reports or false statements with intent to interfere with the operation or success of the military or naval
forces of the United States or to promote the success of its
enemies and whoever, when the United States is at war, shall
wilfully cause or attempt to cause insubordination, disloyalty,
mutiny, or refusal of duty, in the military or naval forces of
the United States, or shall willfully obstruct the recruiting or
enlistment service of the United States, to the injury of the
service or of the United States, shall be punished by a fine
of not more than $10,000 or imprisonment for not more than
twenty years, or both."

Title III of that Act, handled the mail situation. Its second
section read: "Every letter, writing, circular, post card, picture,
print, engraving, photograph, newspaper, pamphlet, book, or
other publication, matter or thing, of any kind, containing
any matter advocating or urging treason, insurrection, or
forcible resistance to any law of the United States, is hereby
declared nonmailable." Violators were liable to a fine up to
$5,000, or imprisonment not to exceed five years, or both.

Here was the first bit of legislation in more than one hundred years that gave officials the statutory opportunity to
restrict freedom of speech and press, yet the newspapers took
little notice of it. The *Chicago Tribune* noticed that an American tanker had been sunk by a U-Boat. On page 5, that paper
devoted about one inch to "President Wilson Signs Administration Spy Bill" saying that the censorship clause was eliminated. The *Tribune's* editorials for those days were concerned
with "The American Army and Its Plight," "The Why and
Wherefore of Pork," and "Whale Steaks."

The *Every Evening* of Wilmington, Delaware, June 16,
made no mention of the act in news or editorial. The Red
Cross drive, the Liberty Loan success, and the pending Food
Control Bill were more important.

The *Des Moines Register* for June 17, in an editorial
"Brainy Censors," criticized some of Creel's censoring, but
had nothing to say about the act that gave his Committee
more power.

Papers and public, during the middle of June 1917 were interested in events affecting them directly, in items appealing to their emotions, or in happenings that called to their spirit of idealism, as they regarded the fight in Europe in the light of a battle for democracy. All those interests were reflected in the space given to the accounts of Liberty Loan and Red Cross drives, a hat-pin attack on police by women of New York, arraigning a taxi driver on a manslaughter charge, and the announcement that "Haig Plans Big Blow."

This same attitude that caused pending legislation and world events to be of paramount importance was evident when the Trading-with-the-Enemy Act became a law, October 6, 1917. Section 3 d of that measure, together with Title VII of the Espionage Act, was the basis for the first censorship board in the history of the United States.

The subsection mentioned above read: "Whenever, during the present war, the President shall deem that the public safety demands it, he may cause to be censored under such rules and regulations as he may from time to time establish, communications by mail, cable, radio or other means of transmission passing between the United States and any foreign country he may from time to time specify, or which may be carried by any vessel or other means of transportation touching at any port, place or territory of the United States and bound to or from any foreign country. Any person who willfully evades or attempts to evade the submission of any such communication to such censorship or willfully uses or attempts to use any code or other device for the purpose of concealing from such censorship the intended meaning of such communication shall be punished" with a fine of not more than $10,000 or imprisonment for not more than ten years, or both.

Six days later, the President deemed that the public safety demanded it, and established the Censorship Board, together with other agencies of a wartime character. Section XIV to XVI of executive order No. 2729-A created the Board, whose personnel consisted of representatives of the Secretaries of

War and Navy, the Postmaster General, the War Trade Board, and the chairman of the Committee on Public Information.

Yet, in the midst of these precedent-breaking measures, the newspapers had their attention focused elsewhere. The *New York Times*, the day after the Trading-with-the-Enemy Act was passed, gave its first page over to such items as, the World's Series, Wilson praising the work of Congress, and decline in losses from U-Boats. On page 2, it mentioned that a War Trade Council was planned, but did not allude to the censorship provision embodied in the same law. Nor was that possibility noticed editorially in the *Times*. In Minneapolis, the *Sunday Tribune* was enlightening its readers upon the fact that the Second Liberty Loan quota for their city had been fixed at $16,000,000, also that the U-Boat menace was not so great as formerly, and that the street car company was stopping all owl cars at midnight. To the *Sunday State Journal*, Lincoln, Nebraska, the important happenings were that Congress had ended, that guns boomed on the Western Front, and that the White Sox won from the New York Giants. The editorials dealt with "The New Army," which was praised, and with "Peace Talk," which was opposed.

Had there been a desire upon the part of the Administration to get the Trading-with-the-Enemy Act by without much public attention, it could not have timed the effort better. The bill became a law the very day that Congress ended, and most papers gave their space over to a résumé of the extraordinary work of that extra session. And where so many significant laws were enacted in such a relatively short space of time, measures dealing with vast appropriations and selective service overshadowed the others and forced them into the class of honorable mention. Congressional news of the last day of the session was focused not upon legislation but upon La Follette's anti-war attitude and his spirited reply to attacks.

There was no Congress in session when the Censorship Board was created, but other matters were more exciting to the newspapers than the possibilities it opened up in a democracy. In New Orleans, the *Times-Picayune* did not mention the executive order for more than a week after the President had signed it. When the information was published, the enemy-trade aspect was stressed, while editorials were concerned with such items as "Registration of Women," and "Getting Rid of Vagrants." Editorials in the *San Francisco Examiner* at that time considered, for example, "Liberty Bonds Will Teach Thrift to Many," and "Our Merchant Marine Will be the Republic's Bulwark in the Future."

But by January 1918, the restrictions upon our liberties already provided were not considered sufficiently stringent to deal with the situation. As a result, on January 16, Representative Webb introduced another bill that exactly four months later was to become the second Sedition Act in the history of the United States. The twentieth century model was but an amendment of the Espionage Act. Offenses under it included the wilful writing, utterance, or publication of any "disloyal, profane, scurrilous, or abusive language about the form of government of the United States, or the Constitution of the United States, or the military or naval forces of the United States, or the flag of the United States, or the uniform of the army or navy of the United States, or any language intended to bring the form of government of the United States, or the Constitution of the United States, or the flag of the United States, or the uniform of the army or navy of the United States into contempt, scorn, contumely, or disrepute." In addition, the Postmaster General's powers were increased over mail violating the Espionage Act.

And once again, when the sedition bill became a law there was no popular reaction against that event, if the newspapers reflected public opinion. The papers showed no antipathy toward the act and little fear of what it might mean to the American people. The leading journals expressed no alarm over this new invasion of their tradition of freedom. They printed no long editorials upholding the sanctity of the Constitution and particularly the First Amendment.

Far from opposing the measure, the leading papers seemed actually to lead the movement in behalf of its speedy enactment. On April 3, 1918, the *New York Times* carried an editorial on that bill headed, "Punishment for the Disloyal," and said, "Tardily but with serious minds the national lawmakers are repairing the astonishing defects in the federal statutes relating to seditious and disloyal utterances." In violent terms it lashed out against those who drank "toasts to the Kaiser," and urged Congress "to put aside all soft squeamishness about inflicting the death penalty."

When the bill became a law there was little notice taken of a measure whose only American counterpart had driven from power the Federalist Party, and whose very name had become a symbol of evil legislation. The *New York Times* stressed such news as heavy German losses, a new German flying tank, and the report that Balfour said the door was open to any serious peace offer. Editorials concerned "Mr. Hughes To Investigate" (the airplane scandal) and "Foch and Pershing." In Boston, the *Christian Science Monitor* noticed the aircraft inquiry, the packer's profits on dressed beef, and German air raids on Paris. Such items filled the newspapers of the United States. The war was the center of national attention, with local problems and accounts of human interest occupying second place. Questions of freedom of speech and of the press were not newsworthy.

As each executive order was issued, and as each restrictive law was written upon the statute books, there still remained the matter of their enforcement. As the Philadelphia *Public Ledger* stated May 6, 1918, in an editorial on the sedition bill, "It is a serious question whether the bill . . . does not go a great deal further than is safe or necessary for a democracy even in wartime . . . everything depends upon the manner in which its somewhat drastic provisions shall be enforced."

And the group of men who had most to do with the matter of enforcement were the members of the Censorship Board to which the next chapter is devoted.

The Censorship Board

On October 12, 1917, a censor's blue pencil might have marked the boundaries of free discussion in the United States and its territories. Five federal agencies were called upon to work together to perform the task of censorship, but with no corresponding appropriation to help them in their effort. The result was that the one member of the quintet whose department had the necessary emergency funds dominated the actions of the group as a whole. But, what was the reason for this Censorship Board? Who were the men composing it? What were their attitudes toward censorship? How did they censor as a group? The answers to these questions will always interest Americans as they come face to face with national crises.

Citizens of the United States had been subjected to federal censorship before October 1917, however. As will be noticed in a later chapter, in August 1914 President Wilson had directed the Navy Department to take over all wireless stations in the United States, while the War Department was maintaining a censorship concerning military affairs with respect to Mexico. On April 28, 1917, an executive order had placed all submarine cables under the control of the Secretary of the Navy with the Secretary of War being directed, at the same time, to exercise similar control over the telegraph and telephone lines leading outside the country. Also, before October, the press had its own voluntary censorship under the surveillance of the Committee on Public Information. After June 15, 1917, the Department of Justice was busy enforcing the Espionage Act which was the main bulwark of censorship. And, under that measure, together with the Trading-with-the-Enemy Act, the Postmaster General had been given the power to declare nonmailable certain classes of mail that were held to be detrimental to the military success of the nation.

Had the war been raging on our own shores, these censoring agencies might have gone their respective ways with no coordination whatsoever, or their separate duties might have been taken over by a unified super-agency. But, in 1917, the war did not strike home to us. We were engaged in a struggle in which we had to transport our men and matériel across three thousand hazardous miles of ocean, and at the same time make sure that the enemy received no help we could possibly keep from him. With the nation so far removed from the scene of military operations, exports and imports were of paramount significance. And thus it came about, rather curiously, that coordination of censorship was achieved not because of communications as such but because of the relation of communications to enemy trade.

It remained for the War Trade Board, a new federal agency, one with no counterpart in American life before 1917, and created for the purpose of making certain that the enemy received no economic aid, to realize the absolute necessity of coordinating all official censorship activities. Brought into existence under the Trading-with-the-Enemy Act, one of the many duties of the Board was intelligence work—determining the friendly or enemy character of consignees and consignors in connection with exports to and from the United States. According to Paul Fuller, Jr., director of the Bureau of War Trade Intelligence, and later the War Trade Board representative on the Censorship Board, it soon became obvious to the observing that the maintenance of an effective blockade was almost impossible without adequate censorship of the channels of communication.

In September 1917, Fuller, representing the Bureau of War Trade Intelligence, and the late Ogden Mills, the representative of the Military Intelligence Section of the Army War College, went before the Joint Conference Committee of Congress which was discussing certain phases of the Trading-with-the-Enemy Act. They showed that an effective censorship was particularly important to the success of the Army, Navy, and the War Trade Board. Also, it was brought out that censorship, as well as the success of these three organizations, was not possible without the cooperation of the postal authorities. Again, it was pointed out, cable, wireless, and postal censorship would provide information about enemy trade and commerce, and violations of the laws and executive orders relating to the control of exports and imports.

This argument was effective. The various censorships already established were brought together, as associates at least, by executive order No. 2729-A which established the Censorship Board. By that order the Board was composed of representatives of the Secretaries of War and Navy, the Postmaster General, the War Trade Board, and the chairman of the Committee on Public Information. Translated into their respective personalities, they were, Brigadier General Frank McIntyre and Captain Frederic Bulkley Hyde, Captain David W. Todd, Robert L. Maddox and Eugene Russell White, Paul Fuller, Jr., and George Creel. Others served instead of these individuals at various times, but the persons named may be looked upon as "the Board."

The work of America's first censorship board was the result of agreements, disagreements, and compromises among its members. That this was almost certain to be so will be clear to anyone who knows even a little about the personalities of the Board.

The chairman of the Censorship Board, Robert L. Maddox, was also Chief Postal Censor. He had worked up through the various grades of the Post Office Department until, before the war, he was in charge of the foreign mail section. After we went into the struggle, he was sent abroad to organize the mail service in the A.E.F. To one member of the Board, Maddox seemed to be "a politician, cool and adroit under a cover of easygoing frankness. Not a dominating type himself, whatever dominance Burleson might aim to get would be expressed through him." After the war, Maddox committed suicide.

Chairman Maddox was on the road a great deal of the time, and upon those occasions his place on the Board was taken by Eugene R. White. Now a businessman in Washington, D.C., White had entered the service of the Post Office Department in 1897. He had risen gradually until he became a chief clerk of one of the divisions of that agency. From there he went to the Censorship Board where he became Deputy Chief Postal Censor.

Brigadier General Frank McIntyre was an army administrator of experience, having been Chief of the Bureau of Insular Affairs. According to a co-worker on the Board, he was a "suave person, as much a diplomat as a soldier" in his dealings there. While active in his relations with the censoring organization, at all times he was, in the General's own words, "on other and perhaps more exacting duties." General McIntyre is now retired, and lives in Montgomery, Alabama.

Judging from the length of the minutes of many of the meetings of the Board, Captain Frederic Bulkley Hyde had no sinecure. He was a good friend of Attorney General Gregory, and when the censorship was established it was agreed among the President, Burleson and Gregory that Hyde should be the secretary. In addition to those duties, Hyde was a captain in Military Intelligence. At present Captain Hyde is in Washington, D.C., where he is connected with the National Youth Administration.

Captain David W. Todd, of Naval Intelligence, represented the Navy Department. In 1916 he had been one of the officers selected by Secretary Daniels to meet with Army officers, and map out a censorship program. On the Board he was quiet, technically minded, and interested only in the complete operation of the censorship.

The forces of economic censorship had as their spokesman on the Board Paul Fuller, Jr. He was a member of the firm of Coudert Brothers, a New York-Paris company that had acted as counsel in many matters for the Allies from 1914 until America entered the war. According to Mr. Fuller, shortly after April 1917, the Secretary of Commerce asked him to organize a bureau of intelligence. When the War Trade Board came into existence, Fuller became director of its Bureau of War Trade Intelligence. Upon the creation of the Censorship Board, he was called upon "to act as interpreter with the Board of the needs and wishes of the War Trade Board." Mr. Fuller is still with Coudert Brothers in New York.

George Creel represented the Committee on Public Information. He was a well known contributor to magazines and periodicals, and the author of several books. He had taken an active part, as a writer, in the reform movement that culminated in the election of Woodrow Wilson. For a short time Creel had served Denver, Colorado, as a member of the fire and police board, but it was primarily as a crusading journalist that he was known at the time that he was called upon to become a member of the first American censorship board.

Although not directly members of that Board, two Texans should be mentioned. Postmaster Burleson was the person whose Department became the dominating force in the administration of the Board. His very close friend, Dr. Otto Praeger, Second Assistant Postmaster General, actually ran the Board. The latter had been a newspaper publisher and correspondent.

It is hard to discover what attitudes the Board members held toward censorship. There were no precedents for them in America's past, and all they could do, consciously or unconsciously, was to bring to their new task the opinions they had absorbed from the various groups or professions to which they belonged. To Maddox, whose life had been spent in perfecting and expediting the postal service, the idea of postal censorship was not pleasant. To him, it was an unavoidable nuisance as well as a necessary evil. According to a member of that Board, Maddox and the Post Office Department realized that they had "to go through the motions" of censorship or there would have been an immediate howl from the War and Navy Departments. Maddox, therefore, had his staff resort to the sampling method. As for his general attitude toward censorship, Maddox and all the other members of the Board knew they had been assigned the task of censoring, and that that immediate duty was more important than any personal feeling about the extent to which their acts might restrict the constitutional liberties of the citizens.

Realizing the connection between neutral and enemy trade and communication, together with the part that mail played in that field, Fuller had views on censorship directly opposed to those of Maddox. No doubt he saw in every foreign mail sack secret information destined eventually for Berlin. White, on the other hand, felt that 99 and 44/100 per cent of all such mail was innocent of Espionage Act violation, and that communications should be intercepted in cases of actual suspects only. McIntyre regarded the problem as a military matter, since the nation was at war, and sided with Fuller. According to one of their colleagues on the Board, Marlborough Churchill (McIntyre's successor) and Todd wanted to censor meticulously every word of every letter. This observer said, in a light vein, that evidently Military and Naval Intelligence "wanted to put the mail in a warehouse somewhere, and keep it there for three or four months until all letters had been thoroughly and patiently read by three or four officers, and perhaps subjected to three or four laboratory tests." Creel, with his newspaper and writing background inclined toward the more easygoing attitude of the postal authorities as to censorship, but sided with Fuller and Todd in the matter of administering the Board.

Before these men had held their first meeting—one week after President Wilson's order established the Board—Praeger had issued an order, by way of starting the censorship, to the postal officials in charge of the foreign mail service, to hold all mail destined for northern European neutrals and Italy (the French and British were censoring all other mails for continental Europe). In order to have some guiding principles for his censorship, Praeger had Ogden Mills draw up a series of censorship rules. They were modified slightly during the ensuing months.

To return to the Board, at its first meeting, October 19, 1917, it received further instructions from the executive "to establish a mail censorship in such manner as the Board shall determine, wherever in its opinion the public safety demands it." That agency decided upon the immediate censorship of all mails between the United States and foreign countries *"which were not already effectively censored by those foreign governments associated with us."* This meant principally that we would censor mails with Spain, Latin America, and the Orient.

Before any steps could be taken in the direction of actual censorship, the question of financing that work arose, and with its temporary solution came the problem that was to give the most vexation to the Board. Congress had made no appropriation for the expenses incident to a mail censorship, so the then acting chairman of the Board, Dr. Otto Praeger, informed the members of that organization that under the emergency Post Office appropriation sufficient funds were available to defray the expenses of a censorship organization in New York. This *modus vivendi* was accepted by the Board. Later, Congress appropriated a total of almost two billion dollars for the censorship, but it left the control and disbursement of this fund to the Post Office Department.

So far as the authority of the Board as a distinct entity was concerned, the damage was done. As the *Cable Censorship Digest* pointed out, employees received their pay from the Post Office Department, and the impression was created that postal censorship was a Post Office function. This failure to provide funds for the Board, thereby making it dependent upon one of the agencies represented in its membership, took from the Board as a whole the authority to establish stations, to handle the personnel, and to direct methods of procedure.

All this was not apparent at the first meeting. That point of friction was to grow until April 1918, when the President was presented a majority report, signed by Creel, Fuller, and Todd, urging the granting of more power to the Board, and a minority report by Maddox upholding Post Office supremacy. On May 28, Wilson wrote Maddox that he agreed with the minority report because it was in line "with what I have originally intended in putting the practical administration of the censorship in the hands of the Post Office Department, under the guidance, of course, of the Censorship Board and in accordance with its conclusions." Articulate representatives of the Army and Navy considered this action by the President made the Censorship Board "a purely advisory body."

There were only faint rumblings of that coming disturbance, however, when the Board organized an executive censorship committee in New York. That committee met first on October 30, and began censoring three days later. After the Board had established the New York office, it opened the following stations: Cristobal, December 1917; San Francisco (with substations at San Diego and Calexico), February 1918; San Antonio (with substations at El Paso, Eagle Pass, Laredo, Naco, Nogales, Douglas, and Brownsville), February 1918; Honolulu, February 1918; San Juan, February 1918; New Orleans, March 1918; Key West, March 1918; Seattle, June 1918; Manila, June 1918. In addition, the Board maintained contact with the French and English censors and, to an extent, with Italian, Cuban, Haitian and Shanghai censorships.

The censorship, as finally established, differed from the original idea. Originally, the New York Executive Postal Censorship Committee was to be the head station with all the others merely substations, subject of course to the review and orders of the Censorship Board in Washington. A later plan of organization and operation was drawn up by the Post Office Department, and it was adopted. Under the latter, each station was independent of the others, and answerable to the Board.

The individual station was controlled by a group known as the "Postal Censorship Committee." This organization had five divisions consisting of representatives of the Post Office Department, Naval Intelligence, Military Intelligence, War Trade Board, and the Chief Cable Censor, with the employee of the Post Office serving as chairman. There was vested in the Committee, and in the individual members thereof, other than the chairman, executive authority to censor, delete, or detain letters and other matter examined and submitted to it or to them. The Post Office Department, through the chairman, had full administrative authority over the Censorship Station, except only as to those censorship functions which were vested in the Committee and its individual members, and except over employees detailed from other departments. Thus, the chairman was in charge of expenditures and personnel, the receipt, examination, custody and dispatch of the mails, and the organization and discipline of the working force.

According to the instructions that the Censorship Board sent the stations, each representative was responsible for looking after a different kind of correspondence or communication. The War Trade Board agent undertook the censorship of registered letters of every description, and commercial correspondence that dealt with trade, banking, money remittances, mercantile documents, insurance, legal proceedings, letters pertaining to shipping, and communications relating to all munitions of war, when the primary object of the letter was commercial. This representative also handled parcel post.

The officer from Military Intelligence censored matters of military importance. These included all information concerning the location, organization, disposition, size, and casualties of our military units. In addition, he was on the lookout for letters relating to the disposition, strength, and location of enemy arrangements for anti-aircraft defense, together with all information pertaining to new inventions and improvements relating to aircraft and aerial photography, as well as other inventions of a warlike nature. Finally, this officer and the representative of Naval Intelligence censored the communications for information about the activities of the enemy's agents wherever located, and all enemy propaganda.

Naval Intelligence officers censored to discover the location or movements of enemy war vessels, and to delete news about those of the United States or other countries. They took care of all matters relating to information about the destruction or attempted destruction of shipping, as well as all new inventions of naval interest.

The Military and Cable Censorship undertook to censor letters or copies of letters containing codes, or messages attempting to communicate a private code or cover name. Also, this unit watched for all information of every nature relating to the improper or secret use of telegraph lines, copies of suppressed cables and telegrams that persons might try to send through the mail, and copies of all letters that showed that firms or persons were acting as intermediaries for the enemy.

The representatives of the various services headed the divisions of each censorship station committee, but did not do the actual censoring. They passed upon the guilt or innocence of material that was considered suspicious, and ordered its disposition. To catch the suspected communications, a "working force" was employed by each station. In the smallest stations that force was composed of deputy assistant censors, examiners and clerks. Where the volume of mail was great, the following offices existed: a supervisor and an assistant supervisor of examiners, a supervisor and an assistant supervisor of mails, assistant censors, one clerk in charge of salaries and appointments, one in charge of the file room, one in charge of lists and mimeograph work, and one in charge of supplies and allowances. It was this working force, paid by the Post Office Department, that gave the impression that postal censorship belonged to Burleson.

This working force had had no preliminary training for its important task. Its membership was principally from the ranks of the Post Office workers who, according to one source, lacked the attitude of mind necessary for a censor. Trained for expediting mail, they could not be expected to like a situation that was the direct opposite of their training. No effort was made to use invalided, university-trained officers, nor were men physically disqualified for combatant service used as they were in the British censorship. In explanation of this failure to use invalided officers and the physically disqualified, the *Cable Censorship Digest* stated that "Few of them could have been persuaded to serve in the Postal Service as constituted with a prevalent, if not predominant, political control."

These Postal Censorship Committees, with their working force to sort and examine the mail, received from the Censorship Board a statement of the aims of Postal Censorship. They are as follows:

1. To stop all postal communications containing information of Naval or Military importance of any kind whatever which was calculated to be directly or indirectly useful to the enemy.

2. To stop all postal communications containing any photograph, sketch, plan, model, or other representation of any Naval or Military work, dock, or harbor work of such nature that such representations thereof were directly or indirectly useful to the enemy.

3. To stop all postal communications containing any false report or false statements concerning the causes or operations of the war.

4. To stop all postal communications constituting a violation of any law or regulation made in connection with the war, or containing information of any kind likely to endanger the successful prosecution of the war.

5. To supply the proper authority with information of special interest or utility, i.e., information in regard to enemy secret service and propagandist organizations or sources and channels of supply.

6. To supply the proper authority with information likely to assist in detecting the channels of enemy trade or the devices resorted to by the enemy for the evasion of the commercial blockade.

7. To intercept all valuable goods or documents of enemy origin or destination, where the transmission of such goods or documents would increase the material and financial resources of the enemy during the war.

All these objects were to be effected with the least possible interference with the innocent correspondence of the citizens of the United States, Allied, or neutral nations. To guide the censors, special lists of suspects were prepared by the Military, Naval, and War Trade Intelligence forces, and by the Office of the Cable Censor. These lists were submitted to the Censorship Board which prepared and printed a consolidated list with a brief summary of all information relating to the names found thereon. By the end of the war, this list contained the name and address of more than 250,000 suspects.

With a decentralized Censorship Board at their head, the division heads at the various stations soon began to break down the lines of demarcation that had fixed. the field each was to censor. New York furnished the best example of that situation. On August 6, 1918, the chairman there wrote the Board that in a single day, out of a total of 140 comments written upon censored communications, both Military and Naval Intelligence demanded 133, so that but seven comments were treated singly. In addition, each intelligence service demanded practically all the information furnished the other, and both requested considerable information of an economic and political nature that seemed to belong to the War Trade Board. Further, Military Intelligence was said to have prepared and to have issued bulletins of information treating political and economic conditions as revealed in the censored mail.

With all this divisional overlapping and duplication, however, the Censorship Board maintained uniformity of procedure among the various stations. The Board succeeded in achieving that uniformity through holding regular meetings at which the members related facts and information, or made any requests they might have with respect to action they thought the Board should take. The following are some of the matters that body considered, and acted upon.

Before the President gave the Post Office Department charge of personnel matters in connection with the censorship stations, such items as the following appeared in the minutes of the Board meetings. April 17, 1918, the Board voted to keep a man of Austrian birth and not to dismiss him, for "It is well known that the Administration is in favor of conciliating Austrians and Hungarians as much as possible, and it is not thought that such a move as dismissing a man on account of his Austrian birth would have a good effect."

While Austrians were receiving kind treatment in the above case, the Spaniards were not the recipients of similar attention so far as their South American contacts were concerned. For instance, on May 22, 1918, the Board resolved to inaugurate as soon as possible control over all Spanish steamers, through bunker license control, or otherwise, to force them to put in at a port where American or Allied censorship was exercised. This was for the purpose of stopping all communication with Germany via Spain. This resolution was left with Mr. Maddox for action.

How those ships and their crews might be treated when they put in at a censorship port, was the subject of another resolution passed by the Board, which read in part "It is the sense of the Board that passengers and crews of incoming and outgoing vessels be subjected to personal search, excepting in such cases as exceptions may be made for reasons of policy or other good and valid reasons; and further, that Colonel Churchill be requested to take up this question with the Chief of the Division of Customs of the Treasury Department, with the view to securing such instructions as may be needed to carry out the sense of this resolution."

While the chief aim of all shipping censorship and regulation was to prevent materials and information getting to the enemy, some restrictions were suggested for news that might have come into the United States. For instance, at a Board meeting on September 19, 1918, the secretary read a letter from Rear Admiral Roger Welles, director of Naval Intelligence, requesting the Censorship Board to take measures to prevent indiscriminate dissemination in the United States of information contained in Canadian newspapers of sailing dates and other shipping news. The Board requested Mr. Creel to take the matter up personally with the Chief Press Censor of Canada, with a view to having such information omitted from the Canadian newspapers. The chairman was requested to write Colonel Van Natta, our liaison officer in the Havana censorship, with a view to having Cuban newspapers do the same.

In general the actions of the Board met with the approval of the Administration, but occasionally the minutes revealed that this body erred. For example, on September 19, 1918, the secretary read a letter to the Board from the Postmaster General stating that the President had requested him to inform the Censorship Board with reference to its resolution of July 19, 1918, prohibiting the passing through the censorship of communications in the German language. Wilson considered it inadvisable for the censorship to base objections to the circulation of communications on the ground of the language in which they were written, instead of on the substance of the statements which they contained. For that reason the President, according to Burleson, deemed it desirable to rescind the resolution in question, and for the future they were to treat communications in the German language on their merits, the same as communications in other languages. The Board, therefore, rescinded the resolution in question.

With the resolutions passed at these meetings went the instructions that guided and directed the various censorship stations in their work. The following are a few of the typical commands the Board sent out.

On May 2, 1918, "All Censorship Stations" were informed: "Your attention is called particularly to the fact that code messages may be contained in, and transmitted by the standard symbols for chess moves. All mail containing chess problems should be handed, for careful examination, to the representative of the Military Intelligence on your Committee."

Personnel matters of peculiar significance were circularized among the stations. An instance of that kind occurred on June 15, 1918, when they had their attention called to the following extract from a letter from the Military Intelligence Branch of the War Department:

"Information has reached this office that some person, whose identity is unknown, has been recommended by either one J. J. Hawes, or by Dr. Martha Huson for appointment at one of the postal censorship offices. These two persons are acting for Germany in this country and if an application is submitted at any of the censorship offices for employment by any person bearing the recommendation of J. J. Hawes, or Dr. Martha Huson, please be kind enough to refer the application to this office." The stations were told to comply with the request.

That the entire personnel of all stations maintained a strict secrecy about their official activities, could hardly have been expected. When reports of "leaks" came to the attention of the officials in Washington, the following circular went to the stations:

"Attention is called to the fact that the local Censorship Stations should not disclose to the public any information relating to the time or place of censorship of mail; the processes of censorship, or the jurisdiction of the several Committees over mail matter, or any other information about the Censorship without specific authority from the Censorship Board."

Orders to intercept, suppress, or forward mail addressed to specified persons or firms, constituted the bulk of the messages sent by the Board to the stations. For instance, on July 30, 1918, E. R. White notified the stations, "The State Department requests that all correspondence to or from the Swedish Consul at San José, Costa Rica, Mr. M. Koburg, be intercepted. Send to this Office any such mail encountered at your station." Closer attention to such letters in connection with personal mail will be given in the subsequent chapter on mail censorship. Before leaving this subject, however, the following circular to the stations is worth notice. One week after the Armistice went into effect, they were informed: "During this period of transition and general unrest, it is important that examiners be particularly vigilant and watchful for all attempts to incite labor disturbances, unrest among workers, statements advocating revolution, anarchy and sabotage or any form of resistance to the present order of our commercial or industrial [system] or to the Government of the United States." Such information, when obtained, was to be referred to the Military Intelligence representative on the Committee at the station.

Weekly progress reports from these stations kept the Board acquainted with the entire censorship situation. For instance, the following is a summary of the report made by the San Antonio Postal Censorship for the week ending October 25,

1918. The total number of letters examined was 75,908. Of those, 179 were suppressed, and 36 were suspended. During that same period, the sub-stations had examined 43,257 letters. For the station and its subsidiaries, 77 per cent of the mail had been fully censored and released, 3 per cent had been partly censored and released, and 20 per cent had been held for the following week. Including the members of the Committee, the enlisted naval personnel, and the force at each of the sub-stations, there were, for that week 247 members on the staff, of which 180 were examiners.

In addition to that check upon the stations, inspections were made repeatedly by Postal Inspectors, and by operatives of the Military, Naval and War Trade Intelligences. Those officials kept the Board informed about the nature and efficiency of the station forces, and the general condition that obtained at those places.

At times, even these precautions did not seem to be sufficient. For instance, the minutes of the Board meeting for August 22, 1918, reveal that the Treasury and Justice Departments had been advised of the Board's action in suggesting a joint investigation of government activities in Nogales, Arizona. Both Departments had replied that their agents were at that time conducting investigations of their own representatives there, and that neither deemed it necessary to have an immediate joint investigation. The chairman stated that he had requested each of the Departments mentioned to advise him promptly of any facts which might be disclosed in the course of the investigations concerning the censorship employees at Nogales, or the Censorship Service.

In the meantime, some reorganization of personnel at Nogales was made necessary by reports from Military and Naval Intelligence. Colonel Churchill advised the Board that the investigation there by Military Intelligence had resulted in the removal of the War Trade Board man at that place. And Captain Todd, Naval Intelligence, presented a more detailed as well as a more disquieting report on the persons employed by the Mail Censorship Bureau at Nogales. According to

Todd's informant, one female employee had been a former accomplice of Maria Haas, who was said to be a proved German agent. Her position in the censor's office had been secured by an intelligence officer at Nogales. The report about her ended, "This woman is pretty and willing sufficient excuse for giving her a position."

The men investigated lacked that glamour. One had been arrested recently as a receiver of embezzled government property. The Collector of Customs claimed that he was a known smuggler of opium and ammunition across the Mexican border, and that his arrest was imminent at any time. A second male had been discharged as telegraph censor of the Western Union for inefficiency and lying. It was later shown that he had disposed of information secured as censor to private parties. The third man investigated was found to have been employed by the Banco de Sonora as confidential man for Max Muller, former German Consul, and reputed head of the Germans on the West Coast. Last of the group was the postmaster at Nogales. It was said of him that before the United States entered the war, he was outspoken in favor of the Germans and against the United States.

Concluding the above report, which Todd submitted to the Board, the agent observed, "Imagine such a bunch passing judgment on our letters, and some of our official mail has been opened at that, and marked 'Opened by mistake.' Shameful condition."

While the Censorship Board, as a unit, acted largely in an advisory capacity, according to the Military Intelligence report of August 5, 1918, yet, there was represented upon it every censoring agency the federal government had created. By exchanging information, and thus keeping each other advised of measures that were being taken to keep the mails, cables, wireless and other channels of communication from aiding the enemy, the members of the Board made it a useful agency.

If it seemed rather powerless in its own right, the same cannot be said for the censoring activities of the agents of the War, Navy, Justice, and Post Office Departments, and for the Committee on Public Information. Specific instances of the manner in which those agencies suppressed, deleted, delayed, and passed messages that went via wireless, cable, telegraph, press dispatch, and mail deserve treatment before the Department of Justice is called in to bring to time newspapers, magazines, books, motion pictures, and speakers who acted as though they thought the Bill of Rights continued in full force during time of war.

Cables and Telegrams

AMERICANS WITH INTERESTS ABROAD WERE THE FIRST TO BE faced with the loss of some of their constitutional privileges. That partial loss, in the form of restriction on communication, took shape when first wireless, then cable and telegraph lines, were placed under the Navy and War Departments, respectively. Businessmen and others objected, but the regulations—some of them had been issued before the first Battle of the Marne—continued in force until long after the Armistice. Most of this censorship fell to the Navy, for the only international land telegraph and telephone lines the Army had to watch were those going into Mexico. And it was not until after hostilities had ceased that plans were made to handle those channels effectively. In the meantime, so far as Americans were concerned, cable and wireless communication with the rest of the world was possible only by obeying the censor.

President Wilson's neutrality proclamation was a day old when American censorship became a reality. The first phase of such rare restrictions in the United States came with executive order No. 2011, August 5, 1914, which took precautions to ensure the enforcement of our neutrality, as far as the use of radio communication was concerned. This order served notice that all radio stations within the jurisdiction of the United States were prohibited from transmitting or receiving for delivery messages of an unneutral nature, and from rendering to any one of the belligerent nations any unneutral service. Enforcement of the order was delegated to the Secretary of the Navy, who at once directed the dispatch of naval officers and, in some instances, wireless operators "with a knowledge of German if possible," to the six leading wireless stations on the Atlantic coast. To these officers, and to the commandants of all navy yards and stations, went instructions that radio messages containing information relating to operations or to matériel or personnel of the armed forces of any belligerent nation would be considered unneutral in character, and would not be handled by radio stations under the jurisdiction of the United States, except in the case of cipher messages to or from United States officials. In addition, no cipher or code message was permitted from any radio station within our borders via foreign radio stations, if destined for a belligerent.

Protests against this censorship came from representatives of the German government, the Marconi Wireless Telegraph Company, and the Federal Telegraph Company. The first protested against the differential treatment accorded by our government to wireless and cable communications. It was pointed out that military information sent over British and French cables was transmitted afterward by wireless to their warships. John W. Griggs, Attorney General under President McKinley, and, in 1914, president of the Marconi Company, asked to be referred to the legal authority under which the Navy Department assumed such right of censorship. He stated that he wished to respect the policy of the government, but when his company's corporate rights and duty, and the rights of the public were involved, Griggs felt he had to respect only the law that governed the case. And from San Francisco the Federal Telegraph Company objected to the censorship of code messages because three-fourths of its regular business was in code or cipher. These protests were duly filed by the Navy Department. An objection to this censorship from the island of Guam, however, caused Secretary Daniels to answer that the rules to which the objection was made "meet with the approval of the Department."

Soon, violations of these orders were reported to the State and Navy Departments. The Collector of Customs at Galveston stated that a British steamer there was receiving and sending radio messages, but no punishment was suffered by the offending ship. At the same time, Daniels informed the State Department that the commandant of the Twelfth

Naval District, San Francisco, reported that the *San Francisco Examiner* was communicating with the German cruiser *Leipsig* off that port. Again, no penalty was exacted.

Other radios received more severe treatment. For a similar violation, and for failure to give assurance that it would comply with naval censorship regulations, the Marconi station at Siasconset, Massachusetts, was closed by the naval censor. It had not explained satisfactorily why it had forwarded a message from the British cruiser *Suffolk*. In January 1915, Siasconset was allowed to reopen, but German-owned stations at Tuckerton and Sayville were taken over and operated by the United States government.

This action was proved to have been wise when the United States entered the war. In the period of nearly two years that was to intervene between the time that these seizures occurred and the date that we went to the aid of the Allies, about 250,000 messages had been transmitted between Tuckerton or Sayville and central Europe. Those messages were a part of the records of the Navy Department, and by September 1918, had been indexed and cross-indexed. The files were very helpful, for they showed not only the transactions of practically every individual and firm doing business with people in Germany before April 6, 1917, but they were so indexed that a list could be given of the names of such persons or firms mentioned in any way in any particular transaction. Thus, the United States had a record of persons and firms among whom might have been enemy agents in this country.

By June 1916, censorship, having taken control of these stations, was next extended to merchant ships of the belligerents whenever those vessels entered our harbors. For instance, the Radio Neutrality Inspector at Norfolk, Virginia, instructed such boats having radio on board as follows: arriving inside the three mile limit, except in case of real emergency, the aerial was to be lowered and coiled ready for sealing; current was to be turned off both the emergency and the main set; the plant was to be available for inspection at any time, day or night; there was to be no tampering with seals after they had been placed, except by a duly authorized person; sets after clearance could be placed in condition for use after arrival at three-mile limit, and after obtaining permission from the Collector of the Port. Ships whose stay was to be less than eighteen hours, did not have to disconnect their radio, but they were not allowed to use it either for sending or for receiving.

Those neutrality regulations were not always observed by ships of foreign registry. The Norfolk Radio Neutrality Inspector complained that the British steamship *Dorset* had required four notices before it followed his instructions. He stated in his report that he was of the opinion that the vessel did not intend to comply with the regulations unless forced to do so. The ship no doubt knew that it was safe in its defiance of the regulations, for no penalty had been provided.

By this time, some Americans were learning that the constitutional guarantee of freedom of speech did not apply to them if they used that privilege in an unneutral manner. On July 14, 1916, Henry Goldman of the New York house of Goldman, Sachs and Company informed Robert Lansing, Secretary of State, that he, Goldman, had tried to send a message by wireless over the Sayville station to a bank in Berlin. It had instructed the bank to use for German war sufferers the 10,000 marks Goldman was sending, as a donation in "admiration of German efficiency shown by arrival of submarineliner [the *Deutschland*, which had recently made a merchant voyage to America, through the British blockade]." Goldman stated he was subsequently notified that the censor at Sayville would permit this message to be transmitted only if the last ten words in the text were eliminated, and in order to have the money transmitted, he was compelled to comply. He closed his communication to Lansing with, "This procedure appears to me a curtailment of my rights as a native-born American citizen."

In connection with the news about that "submarineliner" from Germany, the agent of the Woolf Telegraph office in New York had one of his messages to Germany deleted.

A passage was removed from it in which he spoke of the visit of Mrs. Marshall, wife of the Vice President, to the *Deutschland.*

These instances of wireless censorship caused Bernstorff, German Ambassador to the United States, to ask Lansing if the rules might not be modified so as to let such messages go through without hindrance "as merely drivel and comment upon events known to the whole world and are devoid of any military importance."

At that time there were no such restrictions upon the cables, all of which were controlled by the Allies. To a letter from Katherine Woods of the *New York Times*, asking why the cables were free but the wireless was censored, W. S. Benson, Acting Secretary of the Navy, replied that the reason the cables were not censored was known only to the Secretary of State or to the President.

In October 1916, information concerning submarines again was not allowed on the air. For example, the *New York World* submitted to Sayville a message for Admiral Von Tirpitz, that the paper would welcome a message from him and would publish it throughout America, giving his views of what the arrival of *U-35* signified in regard to general naval possibilities of future years. The State Department was consulted about the message, and Admiral Benson gave orders not to pass it.

With respect to that same boat, the *New York Herald* was made aware of our pre-war censorship. On October 9, 1916, the radio station of that paper broadcast press reports regarding the activities of the *U-53*. In response to a request made by the acting commandant of the United States Navy Yard there, the *Herald* station replied that no further messages of this nature would be sent out pending the receipt of information about the Navy Department's wishes.

There was no way for individuals and firms in this country to know whether their messages had been stopped by the censor. Carter Glass and Franklin D. Roosevelt, then Acting Secretary of the Navy, had some correspondence about that very point. A firm in Lynchburg, Virginia, requested through

Glass, its representative in Congress, to be informed of the receipt by the wireless station of their mutilated messages in order that they could be repeated and corrected. Roosevelt wrote Glass that such privileges would be incompatible with censorship regulations. According to him, messages sent to and from Tuckerton and Sayville were handled at the sender's risk. If a message was received with mutilated words, the sending station was requested to correct it, without reference to the addressee. If such a message when corrected was not understood by the censor, it was not delivered or sent.

With this training of more than two years in censorship, some officers in the Navy wondered whether it would be put to a more extensive use. Thus, on February 2, 1917, William A. Moffett at the United States Naval Training Station, Great Lakes, Illinois, addressed a confidential communication to the Chief of Naval Operations requesting information concerning the time at which radio, telegraph, and telephone censorship should be put into effect. He was not sure whether the order for mobilization should be considered to include censorship, or whether another order to that effect would be necessary.

Although the files of the Secretary of the Navy contain no copy of a reply to that query, subsequent events showed that the order for mobilization did not include censorship. Two days before we declared war, Captain David W. Todd, director of Naval Communications, informed the Chief of Naval Operations about the Captain's interviews with retired naval officers with the prospect of the organization and control of cable censorship in New York, "which," he added, "will be a business of some magnitude." This was no exaggeration, as 90 per cent of the cable business of the country passed through New York.

Todd was in the midst of selecting censorship personnel when war came, and the Navy Department took over all radio stations. The following telegrams from naval officers to the Department show how this move was accomplished. "Marconi Radio Station New Orleans antenna lowered and set sealed." "Puget Sound Wash . . . Commandant has sent Lieutenant (JG) C C Clark to Ketchican and Juneau City Alaska to take over radio station and take general charge of Alaska district." "Goodyear Tire and Rubber Co Radio station Detroit and Marconi station River Rough closed by me no personnel for operation." "Have placed radio operator as censor at cable station San Juan and Ponce P R." When this task was completed, all sending and receiving radio stations not operated by the government, with the exception of stations that were needed for experimental purposes, had been closed "in order to efficiently prosecute the present war," as Daniels wrote a Pittsburgh electric company.

There was some opposition to that repressive activity on the part of the Navy Department. For instance, the officer sent to close the stations around Buffalo informed his superior officer at Great Lakes, Illinois, that United States Attorney Stephen T. Lockwood, in a published statement, questioned the officer's authority to close amateur stations not requiring license under federal law. The officer at Great Lakes requested the director of Naval Communications to advise United States attorneys not to interfere with the carrying out of the provision of the executive order of April 6 which related to the closure of radio stations. The files of the Secretary contained no reply to that request, but neither were there any further messages that indicated that Mr. Lockwood further interfered with this phase of the Navy's censoring activities.

In the meantime, the executive order of April 28, 1917 increased the censoring by the Navy and by the War Departments. It placed telephone and telegraph lines—those leading out of or into the United States—under the War Department and gave to the Navy Department control of submarine cables, although not until midnight of July 25-26 were the Atlantic cables included. There was no censorship along the Canadian border; consequently the War Department's telegraph and telephone censoring was confined to the lines crossing the United States-Mexico boundary. This censorship was difficult to establish and maintain. An example of the difficulty of censorship along the Mexican border occurred at Nogales, Arizona. That town lay half in the United States and half in Mexico. Thus, a person could receive a telegram in the United States, walk across the street, and send the message on to Mexico City or any other southern point reached by a telegraph line.

Leaving telegraphic censorship with the War Department, and limiting it to the Mexican boundary, responsibility for the censoring of messages received and sent via cable or air rested with the Navy. On April 30, 1917, Captain David W. Todd was appointed Chief Cable Censor, in addition to his duties as director of Naval Communications. His headquarters were in Washington, although most of the censoring was done in New York. In addition to that city, cable censors were stationed at Key West, Guantanamo Bay (Cuba), Galveston, San Francisco, Honolulu, Guam, Panama, San Juan and Ponce (Porto Rico), St. Thomas and St. Croix (Virgin Islands), Cape Haitien (Haiti), and Santo Domingo, (Dominican Republic).

The first circular of instructions to all these censors provided a basis for the broadest restriction of speech, had the censoring official felt constrained to give the circular a broad interpretation. After listing the military objectives of cable censorship, the instructions stated that this activity was to prevent the spreading of false reports or reports likely to cause, directly or indirectly, dissatisfaction with the success of America's cause. Subsequent instructions were to clarify that section, but, except for specific rulings by the Chief Cable Censor, and relating to particular events, these instructions served as a guide to the station censor to whom, in most cases, the final decision was left as to what constituted objectionable rumors and reports. Thus, the main possibility of the restriction of speech lay in the ambiguity of the instructions which would have allowed an overzealous censor to see dangerous rumors and reports in nearly every cablegram.

Cable censorship affected directly the freedom of the press. Seventy-five per cent of the incoming traffic was to large newspapers and news associations. The bulk of the outgoing messages was sent by more than forty foreign correspondents who were filing their dispatches in New York for their papers abroad. The Committee on Public Information, in charge of press censorship, and the Chief Cable Censor, in charge of censoring military and naval operations, determined to censor incoming cables largely for the latter kind of information, except when the State Department requested other deletions. This decision was based upon the fact that the British and French were censoring at the other end of the cables, and were watching news that was destined for this country.

This was not true of the outgoing messages. Censorship officials tried to make sure that America was correctly represented to the rest of the world. Their staff was directed to delete interpolated expressions of editorial comment. Deletion or suppression overtook messages which were, or pretended to be, excerpts or quotations from United States papers arranged to indicate domestic dissatisfaction or anti-war agitation. Messages containing pro-German news only, sent by a correspondent to a paper believed to be published in the interests of Germany were of course to be examined with special care.

There was no general tightening of these press cable regulations for outgoing messages, only a relatively few individual cases were treated with an increasing severity as the censors became acquainted with the different foreign correspondents and with the attitude of their papers. For instance, in New York, more than 2,000 words were filed daily to La Union, Buenos Aires, and they were largely pro-German. The correspondent of that paper was informed that his dispatches would be censored for those sentiments. As a result, according to the Cable Censorship Digest, La Union lost from 50 to 80 per cent of its dispatches daily, and all those forwarded were first edited so that they conformed to known facts. "Cease filing" orders went to the New York correspondents of the Mexican papers La Defensa and El Democrata, because of the German connections of those newspapers.

Outgoing dispatches about labor were closely watched by the censors. They realized that many people in other countries had no accurate conception of an economic fight in this country that had been in existence for years before we entered the European war—an economic struggle that, except for hours and wages, had little to do with the attitude of American capital or labor toward our war effort. To make sure that no labor-capital misrepresentation should leave the United States, specific censorship rulings were made that references to strikes, riots, or activities attributed to an anti-war sentiment, as well as reports regarding activities of the I.W.W. or similar bodies, were to be suppressed. For example, on July 13, 1917, a New York message destined for a paper in Havana contained information that in Bridgeport, Connecticut, labor troubles threatened to tie up the industries in the largest munitions manufacturing city in the United States, that big walk-outs had started at the Remington Arms Company, and that the United States expected to operate the Leadville mines because strike mediation had failed. The entire cable was suppressed "as being grossly exaggerated and inimical in tone to the United States."

Censors had to keep in mind also the economic and political factors of any country to which a cable was addressed. Many messages were suppressed even though the news they gave was well known in America. For example, Denmark was worried about the shipbuilding activities of the United States because she feared America's maritime competition after the war. This Danish attitude was known to the censor who, on June 8, 1917, suppressed a cable quoted from the *New York Times* and intended for a Copenhagen paper. The item stated that Germany was beginning, unwillingly, to supply the ships this country and the Allies needed. Two of those seized in our ports had been leased by the United States government to France, two to Italy, and two to Russia. The article said that many more would soon be ready for use, as the time required for repairs necessitated by German sabotage was overestimated. The suppressed message referred to a steamship of fifty-six hundred tons that was to be commissioned before the end of the month, with many times that amount destined for delivery in July.

Our attempts to censor this shipbuilding news did not satisfy everyone, however. Henry Suydam, representative of the Committee on Public Information in the Netherlands, on April 29, 1918, reported that American censorship was still passing telegrams which were most prejudicial to American interests in Holland. He stated that a flagrant example had occurred five days before when a Reuters dispatch from New York to the Low Countries stated that the United States intended to withdraw its offer of three food ships to the Netherlands if the unfavorable comment noticed in the Dutch papers represented the real sentiment of the country. Suydam observed that unless the news was issued from an official source for some reason of which he was ignorant, it should never have been allowed to leave the United States. He added that at the time when Dutch sentiment was being outraged by Germany, the United States had a splendid chance to end the coolness caused by our commandeering of Dutch ships, and yet the field for American information and propaganda in the Netherlands was rendered hostile by such provocative news dispatches passed by our own censors.

At least one member of the Committee on Public Information thought cable censorship could have been improved, judging from the copies of the suppressed Associated and United Press messages sent him for his inspection and comments. Arthur Bullard, director of the Division of Foreign Correspondents and Foreign Language Publications, wrote Creel, June 8, 1917, that he, Bullard, had read the censored messages and that unless one assumed a deep-laid plot on the part of the news associations to communicate by cipher, there was no reason why they should be interfered with. From reading the censored messages, Bullard had the impression that the whole matter of censorship was in a very chaotic condition. Circular No. 6, July 21, 1917, with its specific instructions to all cable censors, no doubt remedied in part the situation of which Bullard complained.

No amount of criticism, however, was allowed to interfere with the business of censorship, especially with respect to outgoing dispatches interpreting political events in the United States. Maurice Low, correspondent of the *London Morning Post*, had cause to know this. For instance, on November 7, 1918, New York had just witnessed the defeat of John Purroy Mitchell for the mayoralty of that city, and that defeat caused Low to submit a cable which began "defeat John Purroy Mitchell for Mayor of Newyork is blow to Allied cause in this country and will give encouragement to every skulking German calling himself american whose doing his best to hamstring american military preparations in interest of Berlin. . . ." The rest of the item had a similar tone, which caused George Barr Baker, Naval Censor at New York, to telegraph the following about the suppressed dispatch: "You and I know Newyork politics well enough to see the ignorance and stupidity of such conclusions but the british public has no such knowledge." Baker suggested that Low should be informed that the rank and file of Democrats who voted the regular ticket in New York were sending their sons to the front and buying Liberty Bonds just as freely as the Republicans and Fusionists.

Low was to encounter the same treatment of his dispatches, whether they expressed his opinions or the opinions of Americans themselves. On March 20, 1918, nearly all of his dispatch to the *London Morning Post* was cut out. The message was a paraphrase of Theodore Roosevelt's remarks in the *Kansas City Star*, in which the Colonel warned against coddling Bolsheviki at home, and declared that the United States had been derelict in making war on Turkey. Of this dispatch, George Barr Baker said, "I feel very strongly that as the London papers quickly reach Switzerland and from there go into Germany, it would be foolish to allow this sort of thing to leave the country, although probably a very good thing to print here."

Two months later, another of Low's dispatches was suppressed. He tried to cable an account of his visit to the Ford works in Detroit where submarine chasers were being built. Worse than this, to the censor, was the fact that in that dispatch Low described a tank Ford was building that was to have a crew of two men. Low was very specific in his description. According to him, the tank was to be no larger than a double bed and no taller than a man. In the specifications it was completely covered with armor plate, and had a cruising speed of twelve miles per hour. The suppressed item ended with, "Ford can turn out thousand of these high speed murderous tanks day."

The process of press cable censorship was partly revealed by the way this dispatch was handled. It was caught at New York, sent to Washington to the Chief Cable Censor, who referred it to Creel with the observation that, as Low had been accorded special privileges, it was believed desirable, if the Committee on Public Information agreed, to call the matter to his attention. The reason for this deletion was that the United States was anxious to avoid embarrassment as a result of overstatement of war preparations. Creel informed the Chief Censor that the deletion was perfectly proper, but that Low should be informed that his matter was cut. Creel said, "Put it squarely on the ground of military information of value to the enemy, and gross exaggeration."

On November 10, 1917, a French correspondent had his dispatches treated the same way. French impressions about America, destined for the *Petit Parisien*, were censored. The dispatch had intimated that the United States would support, only up to a certain point, arbitration among nations in the solution of international conflicts.

Such expressions caused the cable censorship to receive a warning to suppress dispatches containing those opinions. Censors were told, "All incoming and outgoing press messages will be confined to statements of facts. Speculations or predictions as to future events or estimates of the state of public opinion in this or other countries will be suppressed." One wonders what would have been the fate of any of our public opinion polls had they been in existence at that time.

In spite of those precautions about the cables, some incoming information was passed that the Committee on Public Information thought odious. Creel mentioned an instance of this kind in a letter to Captain Roger Welles, director of Naval Intelligence, June 20, 1918. It dealt with the press dispatch sent by James O'Donnell Bennett in Stockholm to the *Chicago Tribune* under date of April 6, 1918. The offending item described critical conditions in Finland where the Germans had landed troops and food. At that time Creel made it the subject of a very vigorous complaint to the editor of the *Tribune*. The CPI head stated that Bennett had been abroad for several years, had been in Germany until our entrance into the war, and was pro-German in everything he had written. Creel ended his missive by observing that time and again he had been on the edge of deciding that Bennett should have been barred from the cables as one who deliberately gave aid and comfort to the enemy.

To the censor, wrong information was as bad as erroneous opinion. While the Germans could not gain much additional information from Bennett's dispatch, the censor was careful to see that the enemy did not get information too easily. For instance, a Key West, Florida, newspaper correspondent learned that the government cable censor at the Western Union Telegraph office there was being sent to Fort Jefferson, Dry Tortugas. News of the official's trip was not objectionable, but when the correspondent tried to inform his paper, the *Jacksonville* (Florida) *Times-Union*, that the former censor would make that port a camp for the interned officers and men taken from the German ships in American harbors, the Key West censor suppressed the message. And other correspondents there were advised not to send out dispatches referring to the camp, while local papers received warning not to publish such information.

Cable and wireless censorship on the Pacific Coast was more severe than in the East, for on the Pacific our officials did not have the assistance of the French and British censors at the other end of the line. A suppressed United Press dispatch from Tokyo, an interview of the Japanese War Minister, suggests one type of message that was censored. In the account of that interview, the Minister stated that because of the Russian turmoil, and because Italian defeat was likely, he questioned the advisability of Japanese mobilization. He held that Japan had fulfilled her obligation to the Allies. The attitude was reflected in another cable from Tokyo that was killed, a Reuters dispatch quoting Kerensky, the latter part of November 1917, as saying that Russia was worn out by the war, and claiming as Russia's right that the other powers should shoulder the burden.

From the Associated Press "day wireless" of November 14, 1917, to the *Honolulu Star Bulletin*, the San Francisco censor deleted word from Washington that the Fuel Administration estimated a coal shortage of fifty million tons, and that the government was planning to curtail nonessential industries.

More drastic measures than a deletion were necessary, however, when, on January 16, 1918, Fuel Administrator Garfield ordered a five-day cessation of those same nonessential industries in order to conserve the fuel supply. At once the press of the United States attacked the Administration, and it was necessary to keep this from the rest of the world, especially from the enemy. The censors were told: "In handling dispatches relative to the coal embargo, pass only (a) exact news; (b) affirmative and constructive comment and criticism. All hastily formed opinions, all conjectures of disaster, should be strictly deleted."

The *Cable Censorship Digest* quoted a censorship supervisor to the effect that Garfield's order presented a type of problem that his group expected to face frequently as the war continued. First, the supervisor stated, there was a storm of hysterical protest; then deliberately malicious comment; and finally, evidence of calmer thinking on the part of editorial writers. He continued, "During the first twelve hours it was

necessary to deal rigorously with usually calm correspondents."
The same men filed material that could be passed when they
had taken time "to obtain the true facts." Censorship considered it equally important to suppress the first outbursts,
and to have the world receive fair and accurate accounts of
our coal situation as rapidly as possible.

The wireless was watched lest other wrong impressions of
Americans get abroad. For instance, the San Francisco censor
deleted from an Associated Press dispatch of November 17,
1917, to the *Honolulu Advertiser* the news from Washington
that an American soldier with Pershing's forces had been
found guilty of the rape and murder of a Frenchwoman, and
had been executed by a firing squad. Also deleted from the
same message was the announcement that the Navy gave up
for lost twelve men on the ship *Rochester.*

Occasionally, the censor must have seen more in a message
than the average person was capable of perceiving. The San
Francisco official deleted from an Associated Press wireless
of November 2, 1917, to the *Honolulu Advertiser,* the fact
that special stalls had been built on the deck of a steamer to
accommodate sixty-six select cows bound for Hawaii. That
censor also held from the *Star Bulletin* of Honolulu the information that at Philadelphia a blizzard had crippled the
railroads and wires, that it had aggravated the coal situation,
and that frozen switches were slowing railway traffic.

Cable censorship to and from Mexico had been in existence,
at frequent intervals, since early in 1914. At that time, as has
been noted, the Army had been in charge of the censoring,
and had not found the task too easy. Many facts the War
Department considered undesirable for public knowledge
were printed in American newspapers as though they had
come from Mexican cities occupied by United States troops.
Especially irritating was the publicity that was given to those
reports that the food supply was insufficient for the civilian
population of the occupied towns. About that point, Funston
cabled the War Department from Vera Cruz that all the
leavings from the soldiers' meals were eagerly devoured by

crowds of women and children "but there is no actual starvation." Differences in the living standards of the two countries explained that condition, it was felt, but such items appearing in American papers were certain to be misunderstood.

Naval censorship of cables to and from Mexico was as much concerned with the information that nation obtained about us, as it was about opinions from south of the Rio Grande reaching the United States. Of that effort, the work of the censor at Laredo was a good example. From the dispatch to a French paper in Mexico City, February 2, 1918, he deleted the news of Secretary of War Baker's impending visit of inspection to France. Again, an official Berlin communiqué for early in February 1918, was passed although it mentioned the breakdown of a strong British reconnoitering attack, but was deleted when it stated that in one trench raid the Germans captured nineteen Frenchmen, and that in two days eighteen Entente airplanes and two captive balloons had been brought down. Also, the news was kept from the *Courrier du Mexique* that Emma Goldman had been transferred from the Tombs prison in New York to one at Jefferson City, Missouri, and that American hotels and restaurants were subject to food regulations. At the same time, the Laredo censor suppressed stories intended for the International News Service and for the United Press that a German alien enemy, arrested at Laredo on arrival from Mexico had been interned in Fort McIntosh.

At no time was there any indication that the censors themselves seemingly questioned their own authority to delay or suppress incoming press messages. As one censorship official informed the New York office, the legality of censorship over incoming cablegrams could not be seriously contested, for, even if it could be shown that such a procedure was illegal, which he denied, it would have required but a few days for Congress to legalize it by special statute.

This observation had been made as a result of the *New York Times's* Carr V. Van Anda's strenuous objection to censorship that he, the managing editor, blamed for slowing traffic to such an extent that parts of London dispatches to his paper came in after the *Times* had gone to press. His greatest complaint was about a section of Philip Gibbs's dispatch from the British front. There were six sections to the story in all, of which the fourth had come to the censor one-half hour later than the end of the story. The censors had considerable sympathy for Van Anda in his predicament. As the New York censor observed, he had made up his paper in the expectation of receiving certain important dispatches which he had been signalled were to arrive. Transmission cost as high as $250 for a single message, and in the case of Philip Gibbs up to $1,000 for a single dispatch. Van Anda was obliged to sell to other morning papers west of New York in order to recover this expense for his publishers—but it became evident in the last half hour that the make-up had to be changed, and the message sent out incomplete or not at all. About this incident, and its settlement, the New York censor informed Creel "Latest Vananda incident apparently happily closed."

In September the managing editor of the *Times* was complaining again, but this time his objections to censorship were not received so kindly. His protesting telegram to the Secretary of the Navy caused that official to inform that *Times* executive that his, Van Anda's, statements were not borne out by the facts. The Secretary stated, "Your critical attitude towards Cable Censorship is not shared by others, and I am sure if you had investigated the matter more carefully you would not have sent me such a telegram."

And the chairman of the Committee on Public Information, when shown the Van Anda telegram, added his observation. Writing the managing editor, Creel said that from the very first Cable Censorship had shown the *Times* every consideration, and that while appreciation was not expected, attack was somewhat surprising. Creel closed with the assurance to Van Anda that "In the future, as in the past, the *Times* will be given the same faithful and ungrudging service, and there is no complaint that you may have to make, fancied or real, that cannot be carried instantly to Captain A. T. Graham, the Cable Censor in New York."

Such delay as Van Anda complained about, when intentional on the part of the censor, was one of the six ways of censoring messages. That means was used in order to have the passage of time destroy the value of information deemed improper. In addition to delay, communications were referred to higher censorship officials for advice and instructions. If the wording of a cable seemed to convey a hidden meaning, its contents were paraphrased. Where a word or sentence was not acceptable, the offending portion was deleted and the remainder released. The censor canceled an entire message when it was incapable of being adjusted to cable censorship regulations. Finally, a cable could be suppressed—which sounds similar but was different from "cancellation." A "suppressed" cable was "held in the files to prevent any information concerning it from being communicated to sender or addressee."

Relatively few press dispatches were suppressed by the censor. This was because of the fact that the great majority of the newspapers and press associations voluntarily censored incoming cables when this was requested by censorship officials. For instance, Edward Bok, while in London during September 1918, made a statement that American soldiers were exposed to vice and were undergoing "moral crucifixion" in London. The New York censorship allowed the message to go through to the New York World, the Chicago Daily News, and the Philadelphia Public Ledger, with a request in each case that the dispatch not be published. Not only was the request complied with, but each of the papers cabled its correspondent to file no more on the subject.

If some eagerly awaited cables were unavoidably held up, other messages went by the censor before that official could ask for instructions. Late in July 1917, for instance, a cable from Japan announced that returned travelers from Vladivostok were telling of an alleged attempt upon the lives of the members of the Elihu Root Mission to Russia by destroying railroad tracks and a station in advance of the train carrying the party. This official mission had been sent to lend moral support to the pro-Ally Kerensky government that was overthrown by the Bolsheviks in November 1917. The message had been passed because it did not seem desirable to hold it until instructions covering such rumors could be promulgated. On August 6, however, the Committee on Public Information instructed Todd to put into immediate effect the rule that conspiracies, disasters and the like, based upon rumor, were thereafter to be barred from cable entrance into the United States.

As one restrictive ruling followed another during our war with Germany, it was natural to suppose that complaints would increase. The New York censor, for instance, had that eventuality in mind when he stated that opposition to the censorship would grow worse as American participation in battle increased, and with it the public hunger for news. As a result, in the censor's opinion, there was the growing likelihood of a concerted newspaper onslaught against the Press Cable Censor.

Although the Armistice might have ended the New York censor's worries, the cable censorship was continued after November 11, 1918, in spite of the objections of American merchants and commercial interests. This continuation was part of the effort to continue the Allied blockade lest the Germans refuse to accept the peace terms of the victors. Of that blockade, the throttling of trade with enemy firms, wherever located, was a feature almost as essential to its success as the prohibition of direct trade with enemy territory. Wartime experience in stamping out enemy trade had revealed the indispensability of censorship. Guided by that experience, President Wilson ordered the continuance of cable censorship for the duration of the blockade.

For seven months following the Armistice, the censors remained on duty. Finally, on June 18, 1919, word came from London that Britain and the United States would discontinue cable censorship one week later, with the understanding that if Germany did not accept the terms of the treaty, a military censorship on her borders and in her ports would suffice. German acceptance of the treaty removed the necessity for that step.

In spite of all the criticisms, the press and wireless censors could look back upon a job well done. No single message of overwhelmingly valuable information had been stopped, but the enemy agent had been greatly inconvenienced in transmitting his findings. American officials had been enabled to learn the identity of many enemies of the United States. And the rest of the world was largely prevented from getting false impressions of this nation, its war efforts, and peace aims.

This was one of at least two fields of censorship in which, after June 1919, there was no carryover, no post-war perversion of a wartime necessity. The other sphere in which, for about 90 per cent of the persons concerned, there was no continuation of censorship was that which maintained surveillance over communications to and from the armed forces of the United States. And it is with the censorship of the Army and Navy that the following chapter deals.

Soldiers, Sailors, and Censors

IN THE ARMY AND NAVY EVEN OF A DEMOCRACY CONSTITUTIONAL rights of the entire personnel cannot be respected—at least not in the way understood in civilian life. If that should be attempted the armed forces would become only uniformed mobs, and would fall an easy prey to the less democratic but better disciplined forces of the enemy. Nevertheless, since the great majority of American soldiers, sailors, and marines had enjoyed the privileges guaranteed them under the Bill of Rights before June 1917, and were to enjoy those rights again after demobilization, the restrictions on their liberties while in service should interest citizens of all ages in a democracy facing a crisis.

The great wartime expansion of our Army and Navy brought the new members of the services into direct contact with censorship. The first large section of our population to have its liberties restricted was composed of the men who answered the draft call. They were summoned to register June 5, 1917, and began entraining for their cantonments September 18, 1917. From the time they reached camp, those men were told what they were not to write and to whom they were not to talk. In addition, their reading matter was controlled and news dispatches about them were censored. While the draftees were in camps in the United States, the censorship regulations were not so all-embracing, but from their port of embarkation, almost until their return to this country, the members of the American Expeditionary Force were to have their actions, words, and letters pass under the surveillance of some censoring organization.

There were two main aims. First, service censorship was instituted to prevent valuable military and naval information

—for example, regarding troop movements—from falling into the hands of the enemy; and second, to help maintain morale both in the armed forces themselves and in the civilian population. Fortunately, America suffered no military setback in the war, or the censorship, for purposes of morale, might have been more severe.

In its sphere, the Navy Department exercised the same restraints over its men that the War Department did over the soldier. Because of its smaller size, and because its personnel was largely limited to the fifteen naval districts in this country and to ships, the problem of censorship in the Navy was not so difficult, nor did it affect so many Americans as that of the Army. That such restrictions in both services were necessary because of the exigencies of war, made them no less real.

To Military Intelligence was assigned the task of censorship in the various cantonments scattered about the United States. With those camps near cities and towns, it was almost impossible for Military Intelligence to have an air-tight censorship of the words and letters of the soldier. A service man could get leave, go to town, and write what he pleased to whom he pleased. It was in that sphere that postal censorship had to be relied upon to prevent the dissemination of information of value to the enemy. Back at camp, however, the censors and military police were on the lookout to suppress any speech, writing, print, or picture, any true or false report likely to be of use to the enemy, or any criticism of persons in the government service to the detriment of any department of the government or to the successful prosecution of the war.

While this censorship was being applied, other restrictive rules were issued directly to the soldiers. Early in January 1918, as the men continued to arrive in camps, to train or to embark, they were forbidden to act as paid contributors to any newspaper, magazine, or other publication. It made no difference whether the article in question was sent direct to the paper or periodical, or whether it consisted of private correspondence which the writer permitted to be published.

In the meantime, the War Department, through the Committee on Public Information, transmitted confidentially to editors relevant suggestions about soldiers' letters. For purposes of publication, they were to be treated as the uncensored correspondence of war correspondents. Even though a soldier's letter was "passed by the censor," that did not mean it was passed by for publication, but only to enable his relatives and friends to hear from him. For the protection of their news columns, it was also suggested that the editors should remember that the individual soldier saw but little, and frequently did not understand what he saw. He usually could not investigate before repeating untruthful and exaggerated stories, and for that reason his statements, while unquestionably made in good faith, were not always to be accepted as facts.

From the standpoint of building military and civil morale, the above regulations regarding publication of soldiers' communications were not satisfactory. To remedy this situation, on October 2, 1918, a General Order provided that, in so far as it did not interfere with the proper performance of military duty and discipline, there was no objection to publication of, or to the payment for, fiction, verse, essays, letters, descriptive or technical articles, pamphlets, books or illustrations. The material, however, had to be submitted to and approved by the Chief Military Censor, Military Intelligence Division, General Staff. That official was to make certain that the matter intended for publication did not relate to the military profession, the war, or to current events.

This order had for its object the satisfaction of the natural desire of the people to keep in touch with the boys in the camps. The folks at home wished to share with them, at least in part, through their letters the experiences of their military service.

So far as possible there was a censorship of the ideas the soldier might get from outside sources. For instance, books were scrutinized, and certain ones were prohibited by the War Department as being unfit for soldiers to read. Apparently there was no effort to keep such a list secret, for Ernest J.

Chambers, Chief Press Censor for Canada, wrote Creel that a French Canadian paper had published a list of books which our soldiers were forbidden to have in their possession or to read. The list consisted of seventy-five books, by October 1918, and included *America's Relations to the Great War* by the historian John W. Burgess, *Bolsheviki and World Peace* by Leon Trotzky, Norman Thomas's *Conquest of War*, and *Can Such Things Be* by Ambrose Bierce. To Guy Stanton Ford, then a leading figure in the Committee on Public Information, and later President of the University of Minnesota, this list of books on the War Department's "Index Expurgatorius" seemed a very curious one. But the story of banned books is told in a later chapter.

Finally, as the soldier was on his way to the port of embarkation, attempts were made to keep unpleasant ideas and thoughts from him. One example was that of the New Jersey citizen who called Creel's attention to a streetcar advertisement which dampened the ardor of thousands of soldiers. The soldiers rode those particular cars daily to and from the port of embarkation. This objectional advertisement consisted of a cartoon of Louis Raemakers entitled "Gassed." While it was an excellent cartoon, according to Creel's informant, the utter helplessness of the doctor and the nurse, and the intense agony on the face of the soldier, all were hardly appropriate for soldiers to gaze upon just before embarking on a transport. The writer suggested that pictures of a more cheerful nature, showing the better side of war, would be more appropriate. He wrote, "an illustration showing one of our boys trying to converse with a French lass thru the aid of a dictionary, or some pictures of soldiers going over the top with a smile on their lips would have a wholesome effect on our boys."

Soldiers were not the only ones subjected to camp censorship. Before the various training cantonments were opened, the Adjutant General told all camp commanders immediately after the division commanders arrived for duty, that the Secretary of War had authorized them to give newspapermen the freedom of the camps. This included the privilege of establishing offices and running private wires into the camps. But the privileges concerning news, and regulations regarding the correspondents themselves, were at the discretion of the individual camp commander.

This led to no uniformity of procedure, and soon the representatives of the press were complaining of a too rigid censorship of news in certain cantonments. To remedy that situation, on September 20, 1917, the Adjutant General issued a statement, approved by the Secretary of War, which dealt with news items relating to camps and cantonments in the United States. The statement provided that the selection of men, appointment of officers, organization, movement to training camps and cantonments, and the daily life and training therein were to be reported and freely pictured by the newspaper correspondents. The only reservation was that actual train schedules and routes were not to be published until the movement had been completed.

Except for experiments in matériel, intrenchments or formations, the correspondents were allowed to set forth the daily life of the soldier, if it was "discreetly described." According to the Adjutant General, honest and timely comment and criticism could, from a military point of view, do little harm. The main prohibitions related to news about the departure of troops from camps. No departure or preparation for departure was to be reported. The same rule applied to movements of troops after leaving training camps by land or water. These restrictions applied to news about large and small bodies of troops, and to individual officers and soldiers.

Although this statement was in the form of a request, as far as the newspapers were concerned, at least one paper learned that the regulations were to be obeyed. In June 1918 when there was evidence that the 85th Division was about to depart from Camp Custer, Michigan, the representative of the *Detroit Evening News*, asked for instructions as to the limits within which he could discuss the matter. He was told, according to the editor of the paper, that if he mentioned no dates and did not claim to have his information from authoritative sources, he could go as far as he liked. He wrote a dispatch indicating the imminent departure of the 85th, and was not criticized. But indications of the imminent departure of the division disappeared.

On July 8 and 9 symptoms of movement were renewed. Martin wrote another dispatch similar to the earlier one. After it was filed he learned that the commanding officer had requested all correspondents to refrain from mentioning the unusual camp activities, and to continue filing the usual training stories. Martin wired the *News* to kill the dispatch, which was done. But, so the editor wrote Creel, not before one edition had been printed, and that happened to be the one which went to the camp, and the commanding officer would not listen to explanations.

Despite correspondence with Creel and with Newton D. Baker, the *Detroit Evening News* was excluded from the camp reservation for the period of a month—the time dating from the date of the expulsion of the correspondent—and a permanent ban was issued against Douglas Martin, the reporter who wrote the objectionable article.

Photographers in the camps were subject to the rules for reporters. Ordinary photographs of military subjects, concerning which no secrecy was required, might be taken freely around the divisional and replacement camps, and officers' training schools. Photographs from kites, airplanes or balloons, as well as those taken at ports of embarkation were forbidden except to commissioned officers with special permits from the director of Military Intelligence.

As the soldiers started on their journey to France, censorship increased. When it was necessary to advise relatives or other private citizens of approaching departure, persons connected with the military service could convey only the barest essential information. This did not include rail routing or the probable time of arrival at any station, or dates, names of ships, ports of departure, or destination.

After arrival in England or France, no information was to be given by any member of the units concerning names of the organizations arriving, their destination, names of the vessels upon which they made the voyage, or any incidents of that trip. Both officers and men were ordered to avoid talk or discussion with reference to military matters while in any public place. Warning had been given the troops while they were on transports that after they had joined the American Expeditionary Forces all officers and men were to "view with suspicion" any person asking questions about military subjects. Nor were the soldiers to discuss such topics where there was the slightest possibility of such information reaching the enemy.

When troops from the United States took their place in the A.E.F. they found awaiting them a censorship that governed mail, cable, telegraph, telephone, and photography. It was not the purpose of that censorship to restrict unduly the members of the A.E.F. from writing about their life and activities. But, word about their location was a different matter, for that might fall into the hands of the enemy and furnish him with valuable information. Unless required to do so in the performance of duty, officers and men were forbidden to carry on their persons or in their kits any order, map, or other paper that might be of value to the enemy. Private papers bearing military addresses were included in that prohibition.

Although all channels of communication were watched carefully, soldiers' mail was the chief worry of the censors working with the army. The company officer was designated to censor all mail of his command (with the interesting exceptions of "Blue Envelope" and other mail described below). It was his responsibility to see that no mail was forwarded until the writer of each letter had conformed to the requirements. If all was in order, the examining officer signed his name and rank at the foot of the letter and across the lower left-hand corner of the envelope. After that, he sent the mail to regimental or higher commanders to be stamped with the censor stamp. The organization or unit of the censoring officer was not to appear on the envelope. This censorship was held to be part of the duty of an officer which he could not delegate to anyone else. In performing this duty, the censor was to have but one letter open at a time.

After the mail had been examined and passed by the company censor, it was sent on to the regimental censorship. There it was added to the correspondence originating in the regimental headquarters, which had been examined and signed by an officer in the same manner that the company mail was inspected, and all the letters were then stamped with the censor's stamp. This stamp was furnished to regimental and other higher commanders. If the regimental censor found that the company control had not been properly exercised, the correspondence was to be returned to the companies concerned.

From the regimental headquarters the mail was sent to the Base Censorship for its final censoring before it left France for the United States. The work at the base was divided into eight classes. The first dealt with letters acknowledging gifts from strangers. The addressor had to inform company officers if these letters were going to strangers, and in those cases the company censors employed the legend "Through Base Censor," and forwarded them to the base without company censorship.

Correspondence with prisoners of war was another class of mail the Base Censor had to examine. He had to suppress any correspondence destined for enemy prisoners of war. At the same time, the Base Censor examined and then forwarded to the American Red Cross, Berne, Switzerland, all missives for American or Allied prisoners of war in Germany.

In order that men could forward personal or family letters without the necessity of having them read by officers known to them personally, such epistles were enclosed in an authorized "Blue Envelope," which was sent directly to the Base Censor. The regulations specified that only one "Blue Envelope" was to be issued to any one man per week. On the outside of the envelope was a certificate that the letters enclosed related to personal or family matters only, and this declaration had to be duly signed by the writer. If the certificate was not signed by the addressor, action upon the letter was left to the discretion of the censor. All letters in a "Blue Envelope" had to be from the person who signed the certificate.

Censoring letters in foreign languages was another duty of the Base Censor. This official sent to the nearest French military post office, or deposited in American Army post offices for transmission to the former, letters in French written by French officers and men on duty with the A.E.F.

The four remaining classes of Base Censorship work were not so extensive—censoring officers' letters, examining letters to Allied and neutral countries, and finally, sealing with a label "Examined by Base Censor" all communications opened at the base.

In its first issue, February 8, 1918, *The Stars and Stripes*, the newspaper of the A.E.F., commented at length upon the censorship. By the middle of January 1918, according to that paper, the Base Censor was handling 8,000 letters a day. That official, said *The Stars and Stripes*, was not concerned with Private Jones's morals, with Corporal Brown's unpaid grocery bills, with Sergeant Smith's mother-in-law, or with Lieutenant Johnson's fraternity symbols. It was actively interested in keeping out of correspondence all matters relating to the location and movement of troops, all items which, pieced together, might have furnished the enemy with valuable information.

After urging the soldiers to desist from trying out their own codes to inform relatives where the unit was located, that overseas newspaper added a modest request addressed to the company and regimental censors. Those officials were asked not to guess too unsuccessfully the language in which letters were written. When a letter in Greek came to the Base Censor with the word "Chinese" written across the lower left hand corner of the envelope, the Base Censor recognized the good intentions of the officer who did the guessing, but it did not lighten the labor of the distributor. The company or regimental examiner was instructed, according to the paper, to "Have the man who wrote the letter state on the envelope the language it is written in. He is generally a better guesser."

Besides soldiers' mail, the censorship with the A.E.F. had the problem of war correspondents. The Intelligence Section of the General Staff, through its Censorship Division, was charged with the general supervision and control of newsmen with the American Expeditionary Force. This supervision and control was exercised directly through the press officer and his assistants.

War correspondents were divided into two classes, accredited and visiting. The former lived permanently with the Army while the latter came for "tours with the army." Members of both classes had to sign an agreement which included the following: the newspaper representative was to submit all correspondence, except personal letters, to the press officer or his assistant (the personal letters were censored at the base); the correspondent agreed to repeat no information he received at the front unless it had previously passed the censor; he was to give neither name nor location of any unit; there was to be no revelation of future plans or of any information that Military Intelligence might have thought of value to the enemy; and, the correspondent agreed to accept the press officer's instructions as to further censorship rules from time to time. The agreement closed with the statement that if the press representative violated any of these rules, he would be liable to suspension, dismissal with a public reprimand, or detention during the period when some operation was in progress.

An order of September 12, 1917, stated that under no circumstances would correspondents be required to make any statement contrary to their opinions or inclinations. And press officers were ordered not to change any article except through deletion, and, unless the occasion was unusual, the newspapermen were to be allowed to see their dispatches after they had been censored.

Prior to April 2, 1918, correspondents with the A.E.F. had to make shrewd guesses as to the kind of news that was forbidden. But on that date more specific regulations were issued. These were based on the principle that all information not helpful to the enemy might be given to the public. All articles submitted thereafter had to meet four conditions, namely, that they were accurate in statement and implication, did not supply military information to the enemy, did not injure the morale of our forces abroad, at home, or among our Allies, and would not embarrass the United States or the Allies in neutral countries. There were specific instructions or rules that dealt with the manner in which personnel and places could be identified. For instance, individuals' names could be used whenever the story was materially helped by using the name. Concerning the identification of places in the Advance Zone, no sector was to be said to have had any American troops in it until the enemy had established this fact by taking prisoners.

Articles for publication in Europe had to be scrutinized with extreme care. This applied not only to items dealing with important military information, but even to emphasis on small exploits of American troops. Those might have been extremely desirable in the United States, but quite undesirable to have printed in Europe, where they would be in the hands of the enemy within twenty-four hours.

Exaggeration of our industrial or military activities, accomplished or contemplated, was to be studiously avoided by the correspondents. This was stressed "because of the bad effect that this would have on the respect which our Allies have for our promises," according to the list of April 2, 1918.

As the Army became aware of the service the press in America was rendering the cause, and as the correspondents with the A.E.F. became better acquainted with army procedure, the press censorship regulations had to be revised and invoked less frequently. Their final important revision was that of November 18, 1918, necessitated by the Armistice. More specific mention of individuals and units was allowed, but many of the previous regulations were continued. In addition, attention was called to the fact that there would be no publication of articles on atrocities unless the facts had been investigated with the greatest care, and would be able to stand the same test as would be applied to them in a court proceeding.

These rules were specific in their prohibition about the news concerning the return of American troops to the United States. There was to be no complaint about the continued maintenance of our troops in Europe. Nor were there to be any statements implying that those troops should be withdrawn sooner than the government planned.

Finally, on January 11, 1919, the last restrictions, as far as they affected the majority of the soldiers, were lifted. By their repeal, photographs could be taken by all members of the American Expeditionary Force, including civilians serving with the Army and authorized civilians visiting the zone occupied by our troops. The photographs or motion pictures taken by all those persons could be forwarded (except to enemy countries), by the ordinary channels and without censorship.

While the soldier had been subjected to censorship, the Navy Department had been engaged with its own aspect of similar problems. For example, the *New York Sun* of March 24, 1918, had an article about an aerial torpedo. The item had been called to the attention of Franklin D. Roosevelt, Acting Secretary of the Navy, by W. L. Saunders, chairman of the Naval Consulting Board located in New York City. Roosevelt wrote the editor of the *Sun* that the Department had been notified of the article about the aerial torpedo invented by Lester B. Barlow, and that the experiments were being conducted by the Messrs. Sperry. In the name of the Department, the Assistant Secretary of the Navy requested that, for military reasons, no further mention be made in the *Sun* of the aerial torpedo or of any experiments being conducted with it by the Sperry's.

One query about a film did not receive the same kind of treatment. From the Chief Censor of the British Admiralty came a communication to the effect that that official would be grateful for the Navy's decision as to the release of the film *Hands Across the Sea*. This question was asked in view of the Secretary of the Navy's reference, in his speech at Cleveland,

Ohio, as reported in the official wireless message of the United States on April 8. The Secretary referred to American battleships in European waters. Our Navy Department replied that it had no objection to the release of that film after it had been censored by the Commander of the United States Naval Forces in European waters. And release was to be on condition that the cinema did not disclose the identity of any of our ships over there.

In some instances, the Navy imposed censorship restrictions at the advice of other government agencies. For example, on May 28, 1918, the CPI informed the Chief Naval Censor that it was in receipt of a motion picture from a company in Chicago showing several submarines in course of construction at Bridgeport, Connecticut. The censor was asked to instruct plants engaged in construction for the Navy Department to permit no photographers to enter such yards except by permit.

Four days later, a circular letter went to all firms engaged in building ships for the Navy. All firms were asked not to permit private photographers to take pictures of ships being built for the Navy, except when such photographers had permits to do so from Daniels. According to the circular, those permits were issued through the Committee on Public Information after careful investigation. They were issued on the condition that such photographs as were taken were not released or made public until censored by the Navy Department. It was to be understood that those permits were issued to cover specific subjects, at specific places, and were good only for the purpose for which they were issued.

Upon some occasions, the Navy Department reversed its own censorship decisions. On September 29, 1917, Secretary Daniels informed the Naval Consulting Board that he had just received a copy of the Board's *Bulletin No. 1*, dated July 14, 1917, in which certain confidential information regarding the detonation of torpedoes was published at the bottom of page 11. The Secretary asked that all *Bulletins* containing the above information be withdrawn from circulation, and that in the future no confidential information concerning mechanisms of the Navy Department be printed without the explicit approval of the bureau concerned.

Before the Acting Secretary of the Navy's closing communication on this subject, the Naval Consulting Board had done some educational work. The Navy Department had been advised about a certain article in the *Saturday Evening Post* of July 7, 1917. This article, entitled "Naval Inventions," and written by Captain William Strother Smith, U.S.N., had an entire section devoted to "Torpedoes in Action." This article gave practically the same information that was found in the *Bulletin*, and upon seeing this, Roosevelt wrote that the article in the *Saturday Evening Post* "makes it entirely unnecessary for a recall of *Bulletin* No. 1 or for any change in the second edition of this *Bulletin*."

Proper censorship and handling of mail for the expanded Navy was a continuous problem. In Paris, for example, it was necessary to have conferences between the United States Postal Agent and the representative of the Navy there before suitable arrangements could be made for handling naval mail in France. In South American waters, the Navy had received its mail through our consulate general at Rio de Janeiro. But with an increased number of ships operating in that area, different arrangements had to be made. The vice consul in charge objected to the unsightly mail sacks, his staff was too small to handle the mail properly, it took much valuable space, and it "possesses a very disagreeable odor from being in the hold of a ship for many weeks."

There was not much danger that spies or other enemy agents could get more than a vague idea as to the whereabouts of a ship from the addresses on letters sent to our seamen afloat. For instance, on May 4, 1918, the Acting Chief of Naval Operations informed the Bureau of Navigation that the address of the Commander of Squadron 2, Cruiser Force was Room 120, Custom House, New York City.

Almost as much trouble was encountered in handling confidential communications as from the successful routing of other navy mail. This resulted from the fact that several stations and ships forwarded the confidential letters in ways contrary to regulations. Whenever possible, the secret mail was sent by courier. For instance, on March 23, 1918, the Navy Department informed the Naval Station at Charleston, South Carolina, that a certain ensign would reach there Sunday morning at 9:30 via the Atlantic Coast Line. The Naval Station was instructed to have an officer in uniform with credentials there to receive the secret mail.

Difficulties similar to those experienced in the handling of confidential communications were encountered in the censorship of mails returned by pilots on board transport and merchant vessels sailing under convoy. For instance, August 30, 1917, Admiral W. S. Benson, Chief of Naval Operations, sent the Commander of the Atlantic Fleet Cruiser Force a communication on that subject. Enclosures with that message included a memorandum from the commandant of the Fifth Naval District, and also the mail delivered outside Cape Henry to the pilot who took out the chartered steamship *Goldshell* on the night of August 27-28. Benson requested the commander of the Cruiser Force to establish a strict censorship of all mails taken ashore by such pilots.

The Treasury Department did not accept a suggestion that would have prevented those pilots from becoming temporary postal employees. In connection with customs inspection, R. L. Maddox, chairman of the Censorship Board, suggested the examination of seamen and passengers on vessels arriving in ports of the United States, to make certain that they were carrying no illegal communications. L. S. Rowe, Assistant Secretary of the Treasury, stated that such proposals had been considered and rejected. He was positive that the results obtained would not compensate for the additional labor, time and expense involved, to say nothing of the ill feeling and even animosity which a proceeding of the kind would arouse in loyal citizens and neutral friends who composed the majority of the passengers and crews of the vessels that arrived in our ports.

Mail to the United States from naval officers and seamen was examined by the Postal Censorship in this country, as well as by the Navy's own censorship. After receipt of the first naval mail from our forces in European waters, the censor stated that he had received mail from the Navy ships *Wadsworth*, *Davis*, *Conyngham*, *Porter*, and *Wainwright*. Judging from an examination of the letters, great care seemed to have been taken by the commanders of the ships, and the officers entrusted with the duty of censoring the mails had discharged it efficiently except in one detail: the name of Queenstown was not always deleted, and when deletion had been attempted, the name was merely scored through with blue pencil, and was easily legible.

In that mail, only two cases of indiscretions came under notice of the Postal Censor. In both instances the writer was an officer—"one of the two had intended to post his letters on shore." Those two letters gave information about the laying of mines by German boats outside Queenstown immediately before the arrival of the flotilla, and in one of them the writer spoke freely about the operations of German submarines off the Irish coasts, and the toll taken of them.

According to the censor, the general tone of the letters was admirable, "calculated to induce in the reader a high opinion of the personnel of the U.S. Navy."

As the United States drifted back to peace, censorship in the services naturally ceased. That it could not cease altogether in the Navy was the opinion of the Naval Judge Advocate General, George R. Clark. That official, March 30, 1921, in discussing censorship of publications, believed that Marlborough was right when he said that he believed in free speech, but not on board a man-of-war.

Censorship of the personnel of the services is to be expected in time of war, but in a nation in arms, even if more that three thousand miles from the trenches, certain forms of censorship modified normal civilian communication of ideas.

One type of that censorship is treated in the next chapter.

Protective Custody in the Post Office

MENTION OF ANY ONE OF TWENTY-ONE DIFFERENT SUBJECTS might cause the delay, deletion, or suppression of a letter if it came within the sphere of American postal authorities. And that censoring process was approached from different angles. In addition to differences of opinion among the censors themselves, exigencies of war caused the inspection of mail that did not come, technically, within the prescribed censorial limits. Only examples of the various kinds of communications censored, and expressions by the censors themselves, can reveal the type of postal custody we had during the World War.

The organization of mail censorship had several handicaps. It started with a comparatively untrained force of censors who, at first, were inclined to sway back and forth between the conflicting impulses of passing or suppressing each letter examined. This would not have been true of a staff trained for that specific task. In addition, if the censor could reach a decision about the communication directly in front of him, there still remained the problem of determining what percentage of the total mail should be censored. Finally, Military and Naval Intelligence wished to examine all letters, while the Post Office Department desired to keep the mails moving as expeditiously as possible.

Postal opinion of mail censorship was expressed by D. H. Macadam, postmaster at Honolulu, in a letter to the United States Postal Agent at Shanghai: "For my own personal sake, I wish to goodness they would either make it an outright military censorship or turn it over wholly into my own or other civilians' hands." He conceived it his duty to get every piece of mail passed without delay, unless there was a definite military or economic reason for its detention or suppression.

Of the "military fellows," Macadam stated that they did not understand that their gigantic structure rested upon civilian shoulders. He, himself, realized that the machinery of the country at home had to be kept in good working order so that it could continue to support its military burden. The Honolulu postmaster closed, "About half of my time is now occupied in rescuing mail I believe to be innocent from the clutches of my own censorship force."

It is hard, however, to guess what even the liberal Macadam would have done in one remarkable case: A steamship from the United States to China stopped at an American port in the Pacific, and discharged mail. Upon inspecting the mail one of the examiners came upon a peculiar situation which she reported to her chief. "What shall we do with these two letters?" she asked. "Both are written by the same man. One is a short, matter-of-fact letter to his wife, while the other is an effusive and affectionate note to his mistress. But the letters are in the wrong envelopes! What shall we do?" The hard-hearted censor left the explaining to the husband, deciding censorship could not take responsibility for righting even so grievous an error, and sent the letters on as received—still in the wrong envelopes.

It would have been difficult for the unfortunate husband to learn the part that censorship played, or failed to play, in his affairs. For, according to a communication from Creel to the *Philadelphia Public Ledger*, November 14, 1917, he and his colleagues on the Censorship Board were trying to say as little as possible about either cable or mail censorship. According to Creel, their reason was that "in mail censorship surprise is an essential of success." With regard to cable censorship, they felt that the less it became a subject of general discussion, the more efficiently it would operate.

That secrecy was necessary for another reason. It prevented the people of the United States from knowing just what censoring was being done. There were indications that sometimes our censors went beyond the bounds of the twenty-one subjects that were to denote their field of activity. That at least, was the opinion of the chairman of the Postal Censorship Committee in New York City. He wrote Maddox of the Censorship Board that the mail censorship handled matters that hardly came under the heading of giving information to the enemy. He advanced one explanation for over-censoring, namely, that the basis for inspecting messages, the suspect list, had been hastily compiled in the first place, and for a considerable period "we were not in a position to determine with any degree of accuracy, just who were our friends in this and other countries."

Those twenty-one subjects of interest to the censor included enough items to catch almost any information of value to the enemy, if one could distinguish between friend and foe. For example, the subject "Communications with the Enemy" had ten sub-headings that included such points as, "All letters referring to (1) Chess problems (2) Chess magazines," or, "All letters to persons with other than Spanish names at Vigo or other points in Spain (examine with care)," and, "Transfer of money between Argentina and Sweden."

Wartime zeal resulting in over-censoring of sealed messages was not confined to examiners of regular mail. Customs officials of the Treasury Department had the task of seeing that no letters were brought into or taken out of the United States via ships, except those which went through the prescribed channels. In several instances this duty was performed more than adequately. Customs officials not only removed the mail from the ship, but in many instances they took from the masters of the vessels their secret route instructions. After correspondence between Franklin D. Roosevelt and William G. McAdoo concerning those highly confidential instructions to masters, the collectors of customs were directed to turn over all such communications, unopened and uncensored, to the naval officers present at the time of search of the vessels.

What classes of messages did the censors detain, delete, suppress, or copy for purposes of information? The following subjects and excerpts will answer that question.

The first subject, entitled "Military and Naval" is not of particular interest to civilians, but the second item, "Criminal," came closer to the average American's interest. Under this heading was censored all information about sabotage, strikes, and labor agitators.

Of greater importance to the censor were the communications that revealed attempts to evade censorship. Persons and firms along the Mexican border were especially restless under those restrictions. For example, the president and secretary of the Eagle Pass, Texas, Chamber of Commerce addressed a letter to newspapers in other border towns urging the organization of commercial bodies along the boundary. Their purpose was to get relief from "hardships worked by embargo and passport regulations." Fear of the consequences of such actions caused the American consul at Eagle Pass to turn over that information to Department of Justice and Secret Service agents.

Other and more evident attempts at evasion were made, and the censor was always interested. For instance, a father of the Marist College, Washington, D.C., wrote to a person in Mexico City, and enclosed a missive from the wife of an American army colonel. In her letter, she stated that her communications to her husband were not opened, and she enclosed some of the envelopes she used when writing to her husband. The wife suggested that the addressee could send his sealed letters in that way. She mentioned that the suggestion came from her husband.

Delay occasioned by the censorship was one reason given for writers telling their correspondents how to avoid that obstacle. A señor of Gazero, Mexico, informed a señorita in Alice, Texas, that he was sending his letter by a friend who was crossing into the United States, with instructions to mail it in that country. He wrote that in the future he would send all his mail that way and requested the señorita to do the same. But the censor, not the girl, received the information.

The same reason was given by the United States agricultural representative in Matamoras, Mexico. The postscript to his intercepted letter read, "I shall mail this tomorrow from

Brownsville so as to escape the delay through Censor." His message had not escaped, however, for it was apprehended as an enclosure in a letter to Durango, Mexico, from C. L. Marlatt, who, the censor stated, was in the United States Department of Agriculture, Washington, D.C.

Descriptions of methods for evading censorship were stopped, even when sent by United States consuls. One man who held such a position at Puebla, Mexico, wrote his wife in California, and complained of his mail being censored. In one delayed communication he was said to have written, "I told you to address your letters to the American Consular Agent and in that way I hoped that they would pass through without being opened." Continuing, Jenkins was quoted as having remarked: "If an American Consular Officer should not be allowed to write to his wife, without having his letters all opened, then I don't see what benefits he gets from his job."

From the office of the Consul General of Costa Rica, in Mexico City, instructions on how to evade censorship went to a Racine, Wisconsin, address. The addressee was instructed to write the letter, seal it in an 'envelope, and then insert the sealed envelope in another addressed to William H. Prestenary, Consul General of Costa Rica, Mexico City.

Knowingly or unknowingly, envelopes of the clergy were used for the same purpose. For example, the censor learned that Pablo Loos, the German Consul at Cartagena, Colombia, had been enclosing his mail in that of the Bishop of Cartagena, whose mail was supposed to be privileged.

Persons or firms whose names appeared on the suspect lists often tried to avoid censorship by using other names or other addresses, known as cloaks or cover addresses. For example, all censorship stations were warned that Post Office Box number 23, Nuevo Laredo, Mexico was rented to one Hermann Reukheim, a German agent. Mail for seven other names was addressed to the same box. It was believed that all of this mail was intended for Reukheim, and all of it that came to the attention of the censor was suppressed. The intercepted communications were sent to Captain J. A. Powell, Military Intelligence, Washington, D.C.

Investigations conducted by censorship showed that mail might have been sent to an apparently innocent person at the post office box of an enemy, and it was evident that such communications might have fallen into the enemy's hands, if it was not really a cover for him. For example, censorship recorded that one A. Gunkel, on no suspect list, of Box 68, Cartagena, Colombia, sent one dollar as subscription to the New-Yorker Staats-Zeitung, and thanked them for prompt deliveries. But investigation showed that Box 68 was that of Pablo Loos, "the dangerous German Consul in Cartagena," as well as that of his cover, Dr. Gaston y Vivilla.

The censor saw another possibility in that situation. To him, it seemed that the Staats-Zeitung had been dealing with the enemy again, and obviously communications, perhaps even in code, might have been sent to Box 68 undetected, and then fallen into Loos' hands, even when addressed to any other person.

Similarly, a letter addressed to "Mr. James Steven, Casilla 911, Valparaiso, Chile," might not have excited suspicion, since neither name nor number was listed. Yet, United States authorities discovered, any letter with that address would have been delivered to Ferdinand Wiebe—Steven being an alias—who was an active German propagandist.

This idea of a cloak was used by government agents themselves to elude the enemy. For instance, on June 29, 1918, the Censorship Board notified all its stations that Military Intelligence had arranged with certain field agents, a cover name and address as follows:

> Mr. C. E. Whitehead
> 1323 Vermont Avenue
> Washington, D.C.

All mail going through the censorship stations to this address was to be delivered to the Military Intelligence representatives, for transmission by registered mail to Captain Henry Osborn

Yardley, Military Intelligence, Washington, D.C. Yardley, author of *The American Black Chamber*, was later head of a Military Intelligence section at the Peace Conference and from 1919 to 1929 was in charge of the cryptographic department—the so-called Black Chamber—of the Department of State. His success at deciphering secret codes and ciphers, during and after the war, gave him the reputation of being one of the greatest code and cipher crackers of all times. On account of the importance of the letters going to Yardley's cover address, the censors were informed, "It is desired that *no information be given to the examiners,* other than that these letters are to be WITHDRAWN FROM THE MAIL AND TURNED OVER TO OUR [Military Intelligence] representative on the committee."

Letters to or from enemy countries or nationals were naturally examined with special care. This fact caused the censorship of the mail of Alexander Economoff of East Tenth Street, New York City. He was a Bulgarian subject who operated a so-called "Russian Restaurant" on East Seventh Street, and was reputed to be in close touch with a large Bulgarian and Greek group in the city of New York. Furthermore, it was said that he corresponded regularly with his cousin, who was the Bulgarian military attaché in the German Legation in Copenhagen. Economoff was suspected by Military Intelligence of gathering information in the interests of Germany in New York, and forwarding the same to his cousin through the open mail, in apparently business letters, which were written on the reverse side in invisible ink.

Another contact with a Scandinavian country was watched by the censor, although the specific objection to that correspondence was not revealed. A person living in Seattle, Washington, had her mail examined because she was "suspected of carrying on indiscreet correspondence with her husband in Christiana, Norway."

At the request of French authorities, an individual with a French name was added to the suspect list, and all his foreign mail was ordered examined. This person conducted an art gallery in New York. About him, Military Intelligence was quoted as stating that he was under investigation by the French military authorities and also by our own operatives, "on charge of being an agent of the German Government, which charge seems fairly well substantiated by the investigation made up to the present time."

Persons suspected of being enemy agents even included the clergy. The Canal Zone censor reported that he had held twenty-two copies of a blacklisted periodical sent from Madrid and addressed to a Spanish priest who was known as an active agent of pro-German propaganda in Panama. Those copies were inserted among sheets of church music. The censor suggested the advisability of conferring with the Bishop of Panama, through appropriate official channels there, to have that activity stopped. No further comments about that priest's pro-German efforts might be taken as indicating that they ceased.

Suppression or long delayed delivery rewarded the efforts of any suspect who attempted to correspond with anyone in Germany. That was the penalty paid by a professor of Rochester, New York, a Military Intelligence suspect. He was corresponding with a woman named Bertha, who was apparently living in Germany. This correspondence was carried on through Bertha's sister, Mrs. Paul Rode, who lived in South Africa, and who was also a suspect. A watch was kept for all mail addressed to Mrs. Rode, and the communications so directed were transmitted by registered mail to Captain L. H. Mitchell, Military Intelligence Branch, Washington, D.C.

Under the subject, "Political information of interest concerning any country," censors examined mail for reports of revolutionary movements, civilian sentiment, financial and commercial developments, and the economic situation. An example of such an informative missive was a letter of October 9, 1918, according to the censor, from the Pierce Oil Corporation, Mexico City, to a vice-president of that company in New York. The addressor, in inter-office correspondence which his letter contained, included the translation of an article on labor conditions from *El Universal*—on the Censorship List. The article stated that a large number of oil companies were dismissing their laborers and taking on new ones, who had recently arrived in Tampico. They were looking for work, and, being in a critical financial condition, were willing to work for lower wages. The companies aimed to reduce the wages paid to labor, according to the article. And this situation was causing the Board of Conciliation and Arbitration of Tampico, the item said, to investigate, "as the dismissed laborers are ready to resort to extreme measure if their demands are not complied with."

Economic information about Cuba was obtained from an intercepted letter from a branch of a New York firm to its home office. The sender enclosed clippings from an insular newspaper attacking the Cuban Railroad. According to the writer, the object of the articles was to arouse the employees and to incite them to a general strike. The branch representative stated that there was a rumor that the strike was to take place in December 1918. He asked the addressee's permission to allow him to handle the employees "as the case might demand."

A letter from San Francisco to a bank in San Salvador was suspended at New Orleans. It contained a clipping stating that the United States could not afford to stand idly by and see the transfer of the Tampico oil fields from British to German hands. How we would prevent that transfer was intimated in the item which said that the United States government had a force of 7,000 marines, fully equipped, stationed at various points, and an army of 2,600 ready at an hour's notice to sail from Galveston.

Some information gained through an examination of the mail was interesting if not wholly accurate. For example, a comment sheet relating to a letter of October 15, 1918, from an Italian in England to the editor of an Italian publication in New York, had information about the Kaiser. The London writer was said to have had as his authority a Dutch correspondent. From the latter it was learned that William II had been reduced by recent events to a state of superstitious fear, and had been led by this condition to choose a strange religious adviser and keeper of the royal conscience. Another letter, censored for the same reason, was from Ironwood, Michigan, addressed to Cuba. According to the comment sheet, the writer informed the addressee that all Spaniards had to leave this country before May 8, 1918, or they would have to go under the authority of the United States, and thus be drafted into the American Army.

This above sentiment was almost in the category "VI— Propaganda" under which a great part of the intercepted and suppressed messages seemed to come. And under that heading, Subsection A, "Encouragement of hostile feeling and spreading of enemy propaganda in the United States in neutral or allied countries," apparently was most frequently violated.

A letter from a Chilean in St. Louis to a newspaper in Santiago, Chile, was held because its publication would have encouraged hostile feeling. The writer said that while most Europeans here had submitted to the order of the government to become Yankee citizens, he was proud to state that no Chilean or Latin whom he had met had denied his country and his flag, and that many of them had preferred to leave and go toward the Mexican border. Lopez, the writer, said that a few days previously he had been detained in the street by a registration inspector who saw that he was a foreigner. A discussion was said to have followed that closed with the inspector saying: "Well, you shall either join our army or leave the country." And Lopez said he replied: "I prefer to leave the country, than to deny my Chilean flag, and Latin race." The censor observed: "In such pompous language the writer expresses his rabid pro-German propaganda."

Letters that might have aroused ill will toward the United States among the Allied nations were of paramount interest to the censor. For instance, on November 7, 1917, Ernest J. Chambers, Chief Press Censor of Canada, wrote Creel that the American papers had printed an offensive letter from Robert E. Sherwood. The playwright, today's most articulate apostle of democracy, was a member of the Canadian Black Watch Regiment. He had criticized the war efforts of the French Canadians, had stated that they were a race "gone to seed," and said that the Canadians received the hardest assignments at the front. Creel wrote the editor of the Harvard *Lampoon*, one of the papers that had published Sherwood's letter, that the Canadian government "has asked us to see if we cannot discourage the publication of such matter." A similar request was made of the *Boston Record*. For this incident voluntary censorship had to be invoked, for, apparently, the letter had not passed through any censorship station.

Canadian authorities obtained more direct action from our censorship officials upon another occasion. Cornelius Martin, referred to as the inventor of the depth bomb, a resident of Albany, New York, wrote a circular letter that was being sent to various papers in Canada. In the letter, Martin complained about the British Admiralty discontinuing its weekly reports of shipping losses, and substituting a different kind of monthly report for them. The new lists gave the losses in tons instead of in the numbers of ships over and under 1,600 tons as formerly. Intimating that this was a concealing gesture, Martin closed his letter with the observation that the latest manner of reporting such losses raised the question as to whether the Allies were to be kept in ignorance still longer about the large and unnecessary British ship losses in order to prevent an exposure of the incompetency of the British Admiralty.

Canadian editors were told not to publish the circular, or any part of it. And Creel asked our Censorship Board to order the examination of any communication of Martin that went out of this country.

Implied criticism of the Allied war effort caused the censoring of one copy of *Moody's Investment Letter*, destined for an addressee outside the United States. According to the censor, this communication, of July 5, 1918, expressed the opinion that the 1918 German drives had won several square miles of territory and many prisoners, and that before our hope could become confidence, we would have to accomplish the actual checking of a German blow at its very beginning. Also, the *Investment Letter* was reported to have said there was still no hope that the enemy would quit from exhaustion. The censor thought that report "understates conditions favorable to the Allies and unduly emphasizes conditions favorable to the enemy."

If there was an absence of censorship along the Canadian border, there was no lack of it for communications with Spain. For example, a letter from Barcelona addressed to New York contained a clipping from a Spanish paper on the Enemy Trading List, and with no comment about the item from the writer. The article claimed that Americans had plotted with the revolutionary elements in Spain to bring about the following: a fleet of American transports was to be attacked by submarines; the troops were then to be landed as shipwrecked refugees; and arms for them and their allies, the Spanish revolutionaries, were ready at Gibraltar to be used in the revolt that was scheduled to follow.

"Very grave charges, prejudicial to the U S (when printed in the Spanish press)" caused the detention of a communication from the Mexican News Bureau, Washington, D.C., to various addressees in Spain. The comment sheet quoted the undesirable passages as having dealt with affairs along the Rio Grande. In part the quotation read: "It is an unquestionable fact that the undisciplined Ranger force is responsible for the enmity and friction existing between Mexicans and Americans —During the so-called bandit raids many lives of good Mexicans were sacrificed by Rangers and other civil officers."

The New Orleans censors prevented the following criticisms of the United States from reaching their destinations. A Los Angeles mother wrote her son in Cuba that she was forced to buy a Liberty Bond in the name of the addressee because, "They keep tab on you and if you do not buy a bond, they tax you more heavily." The second instance occurred in an enclosure in a letter from "Lizzie," Jonesville, South Dakota, to a marine in Santo Domingo. The enclosure was reported to have been signed, "Mother," Artesia, New Mexico. The mother expressed the same sentiment as the Los Angeles correspondent, but added: "We have to mortgage our stock and borrow money at 10 per cent and loan the money to the government at 4¼ per cent interest." Another "Mother" letter was mailed at Champaign, Illinois, and was addressed to Havana. It contained criticisms of the financial condition of the United States and predicted a financial panic.

One letter was held because it doubted the predominant rôle of Prussia in German affairs and stated that Gerard, American Ambassador to Germany, was untruthful. In the offending missive, according to the New Orleans censor, Mrs. C. N. Griffis of Chicago wrote Mr. C. N. Griffis of Lima, Peru, (presumably the CPI representative of that name) that Prussia was no more the dominant state of Germany than Washington was of the United States. In addition, the censor said, she wrote that Ambassador Gerard could not be believed.

Another example of censored criticism was found in a letter from Buenos Aires to a Moline, Illinois, implement works. The writer enclosed a clipping from the newspaper, *La Union* —on the Enemy Trading List of October 6, 1918. This article implied that Americans were distrusted by the English and the French. It minimized the work of the American Army in France, and stated that the merchandise from this country had been so inferior that after the war German goods, cheap and good, would quickly succeed the expensive but inferior Anglo-Saxon merchandise. In addition, the article was reported to have stressed the barbarity of the North American Negro troops, and also to have stated that no one, not even the Allies themselves, looked for victory in the near future.

And a communication from Spain to Cuba was stopped because of an enclosed editorial. The article said that the Yankees had been called the crusaders of 1918. In the opinion of the editorial, they were not crusaders in 1914, 1915, or in 1916. They merely traded on the tears and sorrows of the belligerents. Once they found that the millions lent to the Entente were in danger, they became the crusaders of 1918.

There were many cards concerning Robert Haberman in the Military Intelligence files. He was described as a leader of the Socialists in Yucatan, and was suspected of being a German spy. Because of that suspicion, it was urged that every person in this country who was known to have had any correspondence with Haberman should be carefully investigated by Military Intelligence.

German propaganda was uncovered in packages as well as in letters. One parcel was held because it contained thirty-two copies of various issues of *German America*, described as a New York weekly. Those issues contained stories in German and war pictures, among which precedence was given to photographs of German soldiers and officials. The examiner stated: "These pictures would make good German propaganda, especially one showing Roosevelt and the Kaiser laughing together which was taken on the former's visit to Berlin."

Another package held by the censor contained the following items: *The World In Perplexity*, a book whose circulation in the United States was prohibited, a Spanish grammar with writing on the inside of both covers, three atlases, and a Bronx Zoo guidebook.

Turning once more to letters, those sentiments favoring Irish freedom were liable to censorship, because they were against England. For example, the censor held a circular letter from the national secretary of the Friends of Irish Freedom, New York, to Cristobal, Canal Zone. The censor noted that it contained such expressions as: "The critical moment when our influence can be used to secure justice and liberty for Ireland may come unexpectedly," and "with a united people of Irish extraction in this country of our birth or adoption, we can materially aid in establishing a New Republic on the direct trade route to Europe." A free Ireland and a trade competitor in addition, would have been disturbing ideas to an England already engaged in a death struggle with Germany.

In addition to the above mentioned secretary, another Irishman in New York had his mail censored. He had been discharged from the service of the Panama Canal on account of suspected disloyalty. That discharge, effective June 1, 1918, had been followed by an order to leave the Isthmus on the first available boat, according to a censorship memorandum from an official at Balboa Heights. The subject and his family were passengers on a steamship that sailed from Cristobal for New York, June 10, 1918. Just prior to his departure, however, his person and baggage were carefully searched. Several letters, pamphlets, and newspapers were found, all of which pertained to Irish freedom movements, and they were turned over to the mail censor.

In those days of censorship, a writer might prepare a news item for publication in Latin America, and get on the suspect list because the issue containing his contribution was caught on its way to Spain. Thus, the author of an article in *Diario de Occidente*, a Salvadorean paper, had his mail watched after the newspaper was read by a New York censor. The item, entitled "The Death of an Irish Patriot," was a eulogy of Sir Roger Casement, whom the writer praised for his heroism and piety; and, in contrast, alleged impiety and brutality in the English. According to the censorship examiner, the article showed clear evidence of intent to influence the Catholic sentiment of Latin America against England.

To the examiner, the article was of less immediate interest than its author. He was the correspondent in New York for *A. B. C.*, an Enemy Trade List paper in Madrid, and for a time he himself had been on the War Trade Board suspect list. His name had been removed from that list, however, because his most recent contributions had a suitable tone of loyalty to the United States. The specimen of propaganda under consideration recalled attention to the correspondent's political sympathies. The censor stated that, according to two members of a New York organization, composed mainly of Spanish-American newspaper and magazine men, the former suspect was a furtive German who would go as far in his propaganda efforts as safety permitted.

Intercepted evidences of pacifist activity were held or suppressed by the censor. For instance, a company in Mott Street, New York, was distributing a map of Europe called "A Europe of Liberty and Peace for Every Nation, as sought by Premier Lloyd George of England, Premier Georges Clemenceau of France, and Woodrow Wilson of the United States." Censorship stations were directed that outgoing mail of this company, so far as it was found to contain maps of this kind, was to be placed under censorship, and the maps refused passage through the mail.

Another indication of suppressed pacifist material is found in a comment about a letter from Santiago, Cuba, to a New York address. The offending communication was stopped because it contained a copy of the publication *La Independencia*, of Santiago, Cuba. An objectionable letter in this paper, according to the censor, though ostensibly loyal to the Allies, was turned into pacifist propaganda by the trick of exaggerating sacrifices yet to be made, suggesting doubt as to the outcome, and frequently alluding to the outpouring of blood.

Mail of propaganda agents for Germany, Socialism, or Russian Bolshevism was carefully watched. For instance, a letter from the Pacific Press Publishing Association, Cristobal, Canal Zone, to a resident of Takoma Park, Washington, D.C., received a lengthy comment from the censorship force. The writer stated that "Brother Green" was to leave shortly for Colombia, Venezuela, Porto Rico, and Cuba. The Cristobal correspondent added a sentence that seemed significant to the examiner. It was quoted thus: "We are getting lots of plans for work and will be sending out Spanish letter tomorrow to the field." The censor observed that these "brothers" and "sisters" were ostensibly Seventh Day Adventists, but were believed to be German propagandists. The commentator did not state the basis for his opinions other than to observe: "Their extensive travels in Central and South America are growing very significant."

Narration of socialistic activities caused the suspension of Linn Gale's letter from Mexico City to a person in Green, Chenango County, New York. The comment sheet covering the case mentioned that among Gale's activities were publishing the *Journal of the New Civilization* (suspended in the United States in April 1918), organizing a church of that denomination, and planning to organize a socialist club in the near future. Gale was said to have added that he was no

longer concerned with party politics, but hoped for the
"speedy triumph of the Socialist party."

At least one man whose letters were censored was believed
to be a Russian agitator. Every censorship station was asked
to send to Military Intelligence all mail to or from Nicolay
Bollosuoff, alias John Hessler. That alleged suspect was said
to have been head of a group of Russian Bolsheviki in Denver,
and was understood to have been opposing the war activities
of this government.

Sometimes mail was detained without censorship revealing
the exact reason, and some famous names appear in this
category. For example, on August 1, 1918, all censorship stations were told to intercept, and forward to the Censorship
Board, any mail addressed to A. C. Townley, D. C. Coates,
Arthur Le Sueur, or Charles Lindbergh (Senior). The stations
were told that the last mentioned lived in Minnesota, and it
was believed the others were in North Dakota.

Townley, who has been mentioned in an earlier chapter and
who will be considered in the discussion about censoring
speech, was the organizer of the Nonpartisan League. Coates,
formerly managing editor of the *Nonpartisan Leader*, Fargo,
North Dakota, had been appointed, June 1917, by Samuel
Gompers, president of the American Federation of Labor, a
member of the National Labor Advisory Committee to the
Council of National Defense. Le Sueur had resigned as lawyer
at Minot, North Dakota, for the Great Northern Railroad to
engage in sociological and educational work, and since 1916
had been president of Peoples College, Fort Scott, Kansas.
Charles Lindbergh, father of a famous son, had been a Member of Congress from Minnesota from 1907 to 1917. In the
latter year he was the author of a book, *Why Is Your Country
at War?*, which questioned the motives behind our participation in the struggle.

In another exceptionally interesting case, A. Bruce Bielaski,
chief of the Bureau of Investigation of the Department of
Justice, on August 6, 1918, informed Creel, "This woman is
considered more or less suspicious by the various Intelligence

Services, and a letter has been intercepted which was written some time ago, but which rather indicates that her sympathies are not with us." That woman was Madame Schumann-Heink.

Under "Anarchist and I.W.W. Activity" were censored letters about the efforts, organization and personnel of those groups, as well as the communications concerning the activity of pro-German socialists. One detained letter was from the president of an Italian Bakers' Federation I.W.W. local in New York, addressed to an individual in Buenos Aires. According to the censor, it contained a notice of an increase in dues, and an official letter promising support in the proposed strike of the Buenos Aires union against night work.

From a brewing company in Rochester, Minnesota, came a letter that the censor held because of its pacifistic and socialistic tone. It was addressed to a person in the Canal Zone. The missive stated that the *New Times*, to which the addressee subscribed, had been stamped out of existence by the "iron heel." The letter added that *The Truth* of Duluth was the only paper in Minnesota that still was free. The censor stated that *The Truth* was a socialist paper of extreme views that published at the top of its front page four lines of apology for or explanation of the I.W.W.

To Military Intelligence, nihilists, pacifists and conscientious objectors were almost the same, so far as their mail was concerned. For instance, all censorship stations were requested to hold all mail, pending further instructions, of a nihilist in Minneapolis, and of a woman in Chicago. Of the latter, the request said: "She is an ardent Pacifist and her husband is a conscientious objector."

And articles opposing universal compulsory military training were stopped by the Military Intelligence representative at the Key West postal censorship station. There, copies of an issue of *The Messenger of Peace*, a Quaker monthly of Richmond, Indiana, were destroyed, with the exception of one copy which was sent to Washington, D.C. The comment sheet on this case stated that the issue in question had reprinted an article from the *Journal of Race Development* in 1916, "very definitely opposing Universal Compulsory Military Training." In the article, one argument that attracted the commentator's attention was that conscription did not promote democracy, because it involved a sacrifice of lives, and not a corresponding conscription of wealth. The same issue quoted from the address of Senator John Sharp Williams against the draft.

Correspondence with a person or firm on any suspect list—for instance, the Enemy Trading List, or the War Trade Board List—of course guaranteed that the letters would be held, even if apparently harmless. For example, "Mama," whose address was the Hamilton Grange Station, New York, directed a letter to a person living at a certain number in Tampico, Mexico. The writer enclosed several clippings in regard to recent submarine attacks, and expressed the hope that the censors would not get the letter. They did, for the Tampico address was on the War Trade Board Suspect List.

Suppression was in store for two packages from Barcelona, Spain, to a firm in Cartagena, Colombia. The New York censorship took that action because the parcels contained fifty-seven copies of *La Guerra Europea* of Barcelona, which was on the War Trade Board List, and whose circulation in and transit across the United States was prohibited.

The examination of all postal communications with firms on the suspect lists delayed financial and commercial dealings. As a result the censors had to be alert to any efforts that were made to carry on business except through proper channels. Some banks along the Mexican border tried to evade the rules, but at least on occasions their transactions were delayed more than ever. For example, the San Antonio postal censorship intercepted letters from a National Bank there addressed to a firm in Mexico. The writers enclosed the confirmation of a telegram to the addressee which read: "We credit you one thousand dollars deposited by State National Bank, San Antonio." The censorship held that letter because it showed an attempt was made to send the confirmation direct, and not through the Federal Reserve Board as required.

Finally, there were some letters censored that would have been hard to assign to any one of the twenty-one types of censorable mail. For instance, Richmond Pearson Hobson of Evanston, Illinois, the naval hero and subsequently ardent reformer, wrote Lawrence Mott in Tokyo a letter which the censor deleted. The writer stated that he was back from his Chautauqua season, and that he was in the midst of the last big drive for nation-wide prohibition.

The above part of the letter passed, but the second paragraph was deleted. It spoke about the Department of Justice disclosures of German propaganda financed by the brewing interests. Hobson stated that he was convinced that the German General Staff was systematically using the instrumentality of the liquor traffic within all the Allied democracies for the purpose not only of propaganda but of financing incendiarism, terrorism and the manifold activities of the spy system. The only comment the censor made, other than to record that one of the Intelligences requested the paragraph held, was: "Writer is a noted prohibition lecturer."

And the censor held the following enclosure that had come in a letter from Japan to the home office in New York. The writer of the enclosure said that there was a strange rumor that government officials in the United States sold licenses for prohibited goods. He closed with, "We can't sit still under such conditions much longer. Please give me your views what we have to do."

Censorship also kept from their destinations copies of a following form letter directed to persons in the Canal Zone and in Mexico by the editor of The Truth Seeker. The letter said, in part, that the suppression of three issues of The Truth Seeker led one to conclude "that a deliberate attempt to cause the permanent suspension of The Truth Seeker is being made by the Catholics in control of the New York Post Office."

When mail censorship was discontinued, there was reluctance to see it go in some quarters. The Military Intelligence representative on the censorship committee at Seattle, Washington, wrote his superior that censorship should be continued. According to the representative, nearly all the information received at Seattle was obtained in that way. Through the censorship, particularly of social mail, the station was kept informed of the activities of "the Bolsheviki, Industrial Workers of the World, Socialists, or other organizations whose aims are antagonistic to this government." In addition, he said, it was the source of nearly all the censorship statistics regarding military, political and economic conditions in Japan, China, Russia and other countries, as well as the sentiment of those countries, "which is likely found of interest to the War Department in reaching the conclusion with regard to the military attitude of the inhabitants for which the United States may have to prepare."

Thus with the postal censorship of one struggle barely relaxed, suggestions were being submitted for a continued inspection of private mail, looking toward World War II.

Although this censorship of letters did not affect the majority of our citizens, the authority was there. Judging from some of the communications suppressed or deleted, censorship needed no further laws—but merely extended use of the loosely interpreted twenty-one categories to impose a complete censorship on all personal letters.

But personal letters could carry propaganda or disapproved information only to single individuals. Much more dangerous was the broadcasting of information through newspapers and magazines. And in those cases the offenders could be punished more directly by invoking a form of "economic sanctions."

At the Editor's Elbow

DURING AMERICA'S TURN IN WORLD WAR I, CONSTITUTIONAL privileges were guaranteed only conditionally to some editors and publishers. If they wrote English without a socialistic or radical slant, their chances for protection under the First Amendment were enhanced. Although the great majority of the Fourth Estate qualified under that test, many papers and periodicals suffered suppression of individual issues. How this was done, has been explained in previous chapters. There yet remains to be told the various specific examples of what was censored.

The Fourth Estate had waged a fight against strict censorship, and, by July 30, 1917, they had won a partial victory. On that date, Creel, realizing that there was no chance for the passage of such a law by Congress at that time, issued the Committee on Public Information statement entitled, "What the Government Asks of the Press."

This statement represented a temporary triumph for the press. Commenting upon the situation, Creel wrote Joseph I. Clark of New York City, that the press had no machinery at all for the enforcement of the agreement into which it had entered so gaily. According to Creel, the whole censorship fight was so dishonest that it bred a great disgust in him. He closed with 'The Administration, however, does not intend to press the matter further. The next move must come from the Press, and honest papers have already started the movement."

That fight and the resulting situation made such an impression upon Creel that, twenty-four years later, he was still voicing his disapproval of the arrangement. In *Collier's* for May 24, 1941, Creel stated that censorship of the press of this country in any form, was and will be unworkable. The former chairman of the Committee on Public Information held that secrecy at the source of information was the only workable press censorship plan for a democracy.

But in 1917, a legal remedy was at hand that could be used upon an offending publication. The Espionage Act of June 15, 1917, gave important economic powers to the Postmaster General and to the Department of Justice. Complying with this law, the Post Office Department issued the "Rules of Procedure for Exclusion of Illegal Publications from the Mails under Espionage Act." Among the nine points comprising that statement the following are especially significant in the light of the later suppressions:

"No publication shall be excluded on account of the general tone of either its editorial or news columns."

"Exclusion from the mails, shall be based only upon specific articles which may be violative of the Act."

According to these rules, the Postmaster General was to be informed of such a violation, and he in turn would notify the offending publisher to show cause why his publication should not be excluded from the mail. The party thus notified had the right to a hearing, which in the case of a daily paper was to be given at once; in the case of a weekly, not more than four days from date of request. All hearings were to be held without regard to technical rules of pleading or evidence, and findings were to be made immediately upon conclusion of the hearing.

Frank Harris, editor of *Pearson's Magazine*, described how this procedure worked in his case. Harris, an Irish born member of the Kansas bar, had returned to Europe where he had become editor of the *London Evening News* and *Fortnightly Review*. After residing in England for several years, he again came to the United States and became editor of *Pearson's Magazine*. He was also the author of *England or Germany* (1915), a banned book discussed in the next chapter. Concerning his experiences with the postal authorities, Harris wrote a member of the Committee on Public Information that he was brought over to Washington in the spring of 1918, under the Espionage Act, to show cause why a certain issue of *Pearson's* should not have been declared "nonmailable for sedition." There was a long hearing before a postal official, ex-Governor Dockery. There was no jury. At the hearing he was told that an article on the shortage of coal in New York was regarded as seditious. He was informed informally, however, that his defense had been satisfactory, and was assured that he would hear nothing more about the matter.

Before Harris had been made acquainted with censorship, the press had been requested to refrain from printing certain feature stories or articles, especially those originating outside the United States. These incoming items were watched to keep Americans from getting wrong impressions about the leaders, the public, or significant events in any of the Allied nations.

An example of this suppression dealt with the speech of Walter Hines Page at Plymouth, England, August 4, 1917. The address of the American Ambassador was entitled "The Union of Two Great Peoples." Page proposed that the British should put in their schools an elementary book about the United States, and require that every child read it. He suggested that well-informed Americans be invited to give popular lectures about our country. Page urged the English to come to this country in these words: "A visit to America and to your great colonies is an excursion into the future of human society."

The London Spectator, after praising the speech as "one of the few very great speeches that have been made in this war," said: "It ought to be reprinted in pamphlet form and circulated by the million on both sides of the Atlantic." This suggestion was heeded, but in this country only short references had been made to it, and they did not include any of the statements mentioned above. One explanation for that lack of notice was contained in a letter from Creel to a Boston correspondent. Referring to the Plymouth speech, the communication stated: "It has finally been decided, upon the highest authority, that its publication in this country is not wise. I am sure you will understand." A copy of the speech in pamphlet form had been in the Library of Congress more than a month when Creel wrote.

If incoming material was examined, even more care was taken with newspapers and periodicals leaving the United States. Here again the censorship was for the purpose of preventing articles from going abroad that might arouse the antagonism of Allied or neutral countries, or that might give the other nations a wrong impression about the United States. An idea may be gained of the kind of news that the censorship considered unsatisfactory from a report of the New York officials, June 10, 1918. They held a collection of clippings from American papers, which, they stated: "If given publicity in Mexico, the news contained would increase the tension between the two countries and could only produce ill feeling." Some of the clippings were the following: The *Baltimore Evening Sun*, May 27, "His Imperial Whiskers of Mexico, Monkeyeth with a Buzzsaw"—referring to Carranza; *New York Tribune*, June 2, "Carranza Stirs up 'Another of his favorite teapot tempests,'" and another article, "Say Wood is Held for Mexican or Russian Service." Another clipping detained was from the *Minneapolis Journal*, May 26. In it the offending article, written by Albert Payson Terhune, and referring to events in the 1840's, bore the heading, "Americans in Mexican War Win two battles at once, outnumbered by 3 to 1. General Scott, with 10,000 Drives 30,000 from enemy Capital, inflicting loss of 10,000."

At times, the entire paper was held, rather than a few clippings. This happened to the *El Paso* (Texas) *Herald* for June 6, 1918. It was held at New Orleans because it stated that 1,800 railroad shopmen had struck for higher wages. The censor thought this was not proper reading for the subscribers in Chile to whom the paper was directed.

And at San Francisco, in addition to holding copies of the *Mid-Week Pictorial* and *Current History*, the censor there held the June 8 and June 15 issues of the *Saturday Evening Post* bound for China, Japan and India. When notified of the action, the general business manager of the *Post* had no idea why they were held, unless for articl,es entitled "Gassed" and "War as an Industry" in those respective issues. Later, the periodical was informed that the article "Gassed" had been torn out by the censors, and the remainder of the issue forwarded, while the entire issue of June 15 was censored. According to the general manager of the *Post*, the article "War as an Industry" was written at the request of the Fuel Administration, and the *Post* had a letter of thanks from Garfield's Department for its publication.

Meanwhile the censorship station at Seattle was holding the June 21, 1918, issue of *The Equitist*, published in the state of Washington. It did not reach its Chinese destination because, according to the comment sheet, it was socialistic, advocated the single tax, elimination of the middleman, and contained advertisements of publications by La Follette, Leon Trotzky, and others.

Pamphlets that did not meet the censor's specifications were kept from Latin American readers. A publication of that kind, printed in Pittsburgh in December 1914, was held from a minister in Caracas, Venezuela. It arraigned all the principal countries at war, accusing them of wickedness, and of being anti-Christian in character. Of the pamphlet, the commentator said: "This pamphlet contains false and harmful statements and is fanatically religious."

At times science suffered the same fate as religion. The *Scientific American*, in one of its issues had an article about the invention of a machine for the straightening and checking of the bore of rifle, shotgun, and machine gun barrels. While the item did not give any actual specifications of the machine, it did state its capabilities.

A copy of the *North American Review*, September 1918, was accorded the same treatment. The comment sheet for that action stated that "Mr. Harvey writes a thoroughly yellow-dog arraignment of President Wilson and Secretary Baker as pacifists under whom the present war can never be won." According to the commentator, the publication belittled the part the Americans had taken in France, implied quarrels with our

Allies over the settling of trade disputes after the war, and opposed the President's Polish policy.

The *North American Review's* War Weekly of October 5, 1918, to the extent of at least one copy, was kept from an address in Monterey, Mexico. The censor stated that on page 12 of that issue, under the title "What is the Answer?", appeared information that facilities in France were lacking for the army of four million men we said we were sending. The articles said that an army of that size could be fed to the German guns so slowly as to produce no result other than increased sacrifice of American lives.

In the same issue appeared an item urging that the press must be free. The commentator remarked that "What is the Answer?" proved the necessity of the censorship the other article condemned, for "Such an article in an issue addressed as it is to Mexico, would be largely quoted by the pro-German press there, and give aid and comfort to the enemy."

The most significant story the censorship attempted to keep within the borders of the United States was the one dealing with the Senate report on the aircraft investigation. About two o'clock on the afternoon of August 22, 1918, the CPI representative attached to the War Department received word from the press cable censorship in New York that the United Press had filed a cable on the Senate report on that investigation. The representative called the United Press and got a brief synopsis of the report which he conveyed verbally to the Secretary of War, and asked for instructions upon which the Chief Military Censor might act. The Secretary decreed: "Such portions of it as would disclose information of military value to the enemy should not be submitted by cable abroad." Based upon this, the order which went out was sweeping, and, in effect, sought to kill the report in all foreign channels.

Acting upon those orders, the censorship stopped only the foreign shipments of papers containing the aircraft report. The *New York Times* edition that was held had the following headlines across page 1:

FRENCH CHASE FOE 7 MILES, CROSS AILETTE;

BRITISH TAKE ALBERT, HAVE 5,000 PRISONERS;

PROFITEERING AND WASTE FOUND IN AIRCRAFT

The *New York World* voiced the sentiments of the papers affected, when it said that, as it was, their foreign mail had been held up without notice, whereas, if the censorship had acted in time, the newspapers "could have made over an edition for foreign circulation which did not contain the prohibited matter."

On the Mexican border, however, the censorship regulation had been too slow. According to a Military Intelligence agent there the Mexican newspapers published comprehensive digests of the report, and stressed such features as, $640,000,-000 wasted, no fighting planes at the front, and other similar items.

If our censorship forces failed to withhold objectionable publications from Europe, there was always England. By March 20, 1918, our Censorship Board received from our liaison officer with British censorship a list of 92 trade and technical publications published in the United States, whose export from the United Kingdom to European countries had been prohibited. The following are examples of the publications detained, and the reasons given by the British for that action:

Motor Age, issued November 29, 1917, at Chicago, was held in England. This issue contained illustrations of various types of "tanks," army trucks and armored cars. In addition, it contained an illustrated article with mechanical details on Signal Corps trucks. The addressee in Moscow, Russia, did not receive that issue.

The *Iron Trade Review*, published in Cleveland, issue of January 3, 1918, did not reach its intended destination in Petrograd because of the article, illustrated by photographs, that described the repair work done on the interned German steamships damaged by their crews in the ports of the United States.

The *World's Work* for February 1918 was stopped in England. It gave details concerning output of ships, losses in tonnage, reported failures of the American War Department in several spheres of activity, and an article exposing the German spy system in the United States.

Albert Shaw's *Review of Reviews* for February 1918 failed to reach an addressee in Norway. According to the liaison officer with the British, it contained in its columns, headed "The Progress of the World," several criticisms of the war policy of the British authorities. In addition, it had the plan of a United States government shipyard, with various shipping details.

Some English publications received the same treatment at the hands of our censorship. One such periodical was *The Statist* of London, which had an issue in the spring of 1918 held in New York. The censored number contained an article entitled "Brute Force Once More," in which the British government was severely criticized for dallying over the Irish Home Rule Bill, and failing to make good its promises in that connection. The censoring commentator stated that the offending article could have been easily twisted into a justification of the violent hatred shown toward England by the Sinn Feiner, although the sentiments which it expressed might not have been endorsed by many Irishmen of moderate views.

While the chief attention of the censor was directed toward news and publications entering and leaving the United States, some time and efforts were devoted to domestic news for home consumption. Action depended largely upon the past reputation of the periodical or paper, the motive from which the suspected article was written and, to some extent, the nature of the clientele. The average American publication, serving a domestic market with news and views shaped for the ordinary citizen, could attack the administration and receive little more than a fiery protest from Creel. Foreign-language publications, however, especially those in German, were suspect because of their generally pro-German stand prior to our entry into the war, because of their subscribers, and because of the possibility that they were in contact with espionage agents of the Central Powers. In addition to this group, the radical papers, periodicals and pamphlets published in this country, were kept under close watch because of the character of their readership, their anti-war and supposed anti-government attitude, and their possible international connections.

Although in general the types of publications just mentioned received the greatest and most continuous attention from the censor, any publication might receive a desist request from the authorities if it contained certain kinds of stories. In that category were jokes in which our Army or Navy had an unheroic rôle. Even the *Christian Science Monitor* was made aware of that fact after its issue of January 30, 1918, carried an amusing story that was going the round of the British Grand Fleet, "just the kind of a joke which Jack Tar likes to give and take with his friends."

According to the account, when the American squadron consisting of the U.S.S. *Delaware, New York,* and *Wyoming,* with destroyers and other craft went up the Firth, the British flagship signalled that they were to anchor west of the Forth bridge. But the Americans passed under that bridge and sailed on. Shortly the British Admiral made another signal, "We signaled just now that you were to anchor west of the Forth bridge; why don't you stop?" The American flagship was said to have signalled immediately the reply: "Well, I guess we have only passed one bridge yet!"

Creel wrote the editor of the *Monitor* and asked him if he would give orders "for greater care in the future."

A similar request was made to the *Washington Herald.* An article in that paper for June 3, 1918, entitled, "7 Cars of Hun Propaganda Censor's Bag," attracted the attention of Maddox, chairman of the Censorship Board. He suggested that the *Herald* people be asked to be more careful. Acting upon that idea, Creel wrote Robert Bender of the United Press that "It was very bad stuff and I will be very much obliged if you would write Newell, telling him to lay off." The writer stated that not only was secrecy essential to an effective operation of border censorship, but our relations with Mexico were very delicate.

More drastic measures were taken with the *Metropolitan Magazine's* issue for March 1918. That number had an article written by William Hard, a contributor to other magazines including *Everybody's* and *New Republic*, and later a member of the Republican National Committee. In that number, Hard questioned the honesty of America's and of President Wilson's aims in the war. The *Metropolitan* was barred from the mails so far as that one issue was concerned.

Barring several issues from the mails caused the publisher of the *Internationalist* to object to that treatment, but to no avail. The chairman of the CPI was informed that the barred issues had violated the Espionage Act. Second class privileges had been denied the publication for May and June 1918, and thereafter the publisher had attempted to send out copies by express. Department of Justice agents had such shipments stopped. According to the Post Office Department, all the publication had to do was to convince the representative of that Department that the issues presented for mailing were free from matter objectionable under the Espionage Act or other laws affecting the use of the mails.

Occasionally such exclusion from the mails attracted the attention of the President. This was true when the September 1918 issue of *The World Tomorrow* was suppressed. One of the persons interested in the publication and in the action against it was Nevin Sayre, brother of President Wilson's son-in-law. At dinner on Friday, September 13, Sayre discussed the suppression with the chief executive. Three days later the President suggested to Postmaster General Burleson that he, Wilson, would not like to see the publication held up unless there was a very clear case against it. And on September 19, Sayre wrote the President that the New York Post Office informed the editors of *The World Tomorrow* that the magazine had been released.

Although these measures seemed harsh to the publisher concerned, similar and even worse punishment was the lot of the foreign-language press. To the descendants of earlier immigrants, even in time of peace, a strange tongue was a matter for suspicion in great portions of this country. In wartime, the use of the same languages the enemy employed in his native country, increased many Americans' distrust of them. Nowhere is there more concrete evidence of that situation than in the censoring of the foreign-language press. And it must be remembered that practically all of the German-language papers and periodicals had been in sympathy with the Fatherland before our nation entered the war.

Concerning the editorial policy of the *New-Yorker Staats-Zeitung*, Bielaski, the chief of the Federal Bureau of Investigation, wrote in October 1918 that it was "gradually converting this paper into a 'colorless neutral organ.'"

Two factors contributed to the difficulties of publications. First, there were bitter rivalries among those papers and periodicals themselves, and second, their lot was not made any easier by Theodore Roosevelt's remark of September 20, 1917, that "we are convinced that today our most dangerous foe is the foreign-language press."

The Post Office Department had the task of censoring this class of publications. Under Section 19 of the Trading-with-the-Enemy Act was the provision that the foreign-language press could not publish, without filing translations with the postmaster, "any news item, editorial or other printed matter, respecting the government of the United States, or of any nation engaged in the present war, its policies, international relations, the state or conduct of the war or any matter relating thereto." If there was satisfactory evidence that the material could be published without detriment to the United States a permit was to be issued by the President which freed the paper from such restrictions. A copy of the permit was then sent to the postmaster of the place from which the foreign-language publication emanated. Some 1,600 applications for permits were received within a few days after the passage of the act.

Many foreign-language papers and periodicals, realizing the difficulties of their situation, suspended publication for financial or patriotic reasons. The former was the reason why the *Illinois Staats-Zeitung*, published in Chicago, suspended operations in June 1918, after seventy-two years of existence. That very month, the New York censor had kept an issue of that paper from going to Mexico. The addressee of the detained mail was the central agency for German propaganda in Mexico, and was on the War Trade Board suspect list. This suppressed issue had a large heading across the front page, "The Allies put all their hopes in America."

Commenting upon that copy, the censor held that if that issue was sent direct from the publishing office, the nature of the contents favored the presumption that the paper wished the addressee to take note of the rôle the United States was destined to play as the deciding factor in the war.

Meanwhile, from Columbus, Ohio, came the information that the German-American Publishing Company was discontinuing its three German-language papers, the *Daily Express*, *Der Ohio Sontagsgast*, and *Der Westbote*. The suspension of publication was made for patriotic reasons.

Some non-English periodicals and papers, because of their value in reaching immigrants with pro-American press material, were favorably recommended to Solicitor Lamar of the Post Office Department by the Committee on Public Information. Creel's organization requested a permit for the *American Hungarian Observer* (*Amerikai Figyelo*) published in Chicago. A preliminary investigation by Burleson's department disclosed several matters which caused the entire history of the publication's attitude and editorial policy to be examined. The investigation satisfied the Department that the paper was loyal, and a permit was finally issued.

Other foreign-language publications were not so fortunate in their dealings with the government. This was true of the *New Jersey Frei Zeitung* of Newark, in October 1917, which was deprived of its second-class mail privilege for alleged seditious and disloyal utterances. Its publishers, editors, and advertising manager were charged with conspiracy to violate the Espionage Act by publishing articles that would interfere with the military success of the United States. District Judge Haight charged the jury in the case that "It was the constitutional right of every citizen of the United States to express his opinion about the war . . . provided in doing so, he did not wilfully obstruct the recruiting or enlistment service." After six hours' deliberation, the jury disagreed and was dismissed.

Cleveland was the scene of another example of interference with the foreign-language press. On July 27, 1918, Richard Brenne, editor of the *Waechter und Anzeiger* was arrested for garbling news. Moreover, the publication had received from the Associated Press a Wolff Bureau story of American battle losses. This release had gone to other papers which featured it as an example of German propaganda. The *Waechter* had printed it as straight news. Possibly it should be noted that at the time of Brenne's indictment, two of his former colleagues on the editorial staff of that paper were in an internment camp.

Before Brenne was finally acquitted, March 1919, the paper had been taken over by Alien Property Custodian Palmer. As soon as the editor had been arrested, Creel suggested to Palmer that the publication be continued by a loyal editor, but the Custodian hesitated. Finally, in October 1918, Palmer decided to run the *Waechter*, and appointed George Coulton, president of the Union National Bank, and Elbert H. Baker, president of the Plain Dealer Publishing Company, to represent him in its direction.

The officers of the *Philadelphia Tageblatt* were not so fortunate as Brenne. For several weeks prior to September 10, 1917, representatives of the Post Office and Justice Departments had been investigating the paper. On that day they arrested five of the men connected with the publishing company on charges of treason, and confiscated and removed from its office all books, files, manuscripts, and other properties. Treason lay, according to the warrant, in "The felony of wilfully making and conveying false reports and statements with intent to promote the success of the enemies of the United States. . . ."

In addition, government officers said that since America's entrance into the war, the paper had published daily editorial attacks on President Wilson and the government's war policies.

From September 1917 to March 1, 1920, the *Tageblatt* men (Dr. Morris Darkow and Louis Werner, editors, Herman Lemke, business manager, Paul Vogel, treasurer, and Paul Schaefer, president) were uncertain of their fate. In the meantime, the editors had been acquitted of the treason charge, but they and the other three had been found guilty of violating the Espionage Act. On March 1, the Supreme Court upheld the sentences of five years each to Werner and Darkow, and of two years to Lemke. Sentences of one year each to Vogel and Schaefer were reversed. Three months later the editors and business manager were pardoned.

An editorial urging readers to refuse to perform military service for the United States resulted in the arrest of Jacob Frohwerk and Carl Gleeser, editors of the Kansas City *Staats-Zeitung*. The latter part of April 1918, they pleaded guilty, and received sentences of ten and five years respectively. Frohwerk's longer sentence resulted from his articles criticizing the participation of the United States in the war. Justice Holmes, when he delivered the unanimous opinion of the Supreme Court, which sustained the convictions, held that the First Amendment to the Constitution did not give immunity for every possible use of language. On April 22, 1919, Gleeser's sentence was commuted to one year and a day. Nearly two months later, Frohwerk's sentence received the same treatment, after the Attorney General held that for 1919, the ten-year term seemed excessive.

English-language newspapers and periodicals, having any other object than the dissemination of straight news or American opinion, were likely to attract the attention of censoring officials. Although the Post Office and Justice Departments concentrated upon political publications, religious papers and periodicals were scrutinized also when presented for export. Creel himself asked the chairman of the Censorship Board to bar the anti-Catholic *Menace* of Aurora, Missouri, from leaving the country. Three Irish-Catholic papers that had issues barred from the mails were the *Irish World*, *Freeman's Journal and Catholic Register*, and the *Gaelic American*. The first was excluded for hoping that Palestine would not be a Jewish kingdom; the second "for reprinting Jefferson's opinion that Ireland should be a republic"; and the third for criticizing Sir Frederick E. Smith, prosecutor of Sir Roger Casement, when Smith was making a short lecture tour in this country. Aside from barring certain issues, the religious publications were not molested to the same degree that socialist and radical papers were.

Continuous molestation and many suppressions occurred with respect to the left-wing publications. Two divergent reasons for such action were contained in the utterances of Burleson and Professor S. H. Clark of the University of Chicago. The former said that no socialist paper would be barred from the mails unless it contained treasonable or seditious matter. The trouble, however, the Postmaster General was quoted as saying, "is that most socialist papers do contain this matter." And Clark wrote Creel, "We all know that many public men and many of our prominent newspapers who have always bitterly fought socialism, the I.W.W.'s and even labor unions are taking advantage of the present crisis in an effort not purely patriotic to squelch all of these more or less radical organizations." The international character of those groups, together with the inability or unwillingness of the editors of radical publications to recognize the difference between the popular mind in peacetime and wartime, made Burleson's words seem more accurate.

Postal censorship was on the lookout to prevent such publications from being exported. The New York censor held five issues of *Defensa Obrera* of Chicago en route to an anarchist paper in Spain. According to the censor, the whole newspaper was devoted to proclaiming the tenets of the I.W.W. Censorship also held the issues of two Minnesota newspapers from addressees in the Canal Zone. They were the *Twin City Reporter* of Minneapolis, and *The Truth* of Duluth. The editor of the latter, for his socialist activities, was said to have been arrested, but was out on bail at the time the paper was mailed.

A copy of *The World*, a socialist-I.W.W. organ of Oakland, California, according to the censor, was held from foreign circulation because it contained an article used by the enemy as propaganda. The objectionable item referred to tales of German atrocities and General Pershing's telegram, alleged to have been sent, branding such tales as false.

Ireland was not the only British dependency about which American censors exercised care. The superintendent of railway mail service at Fort Worth, Texas, transmitted a pamphlet entitled, "An Open Letter to President Wilson," drafted by the Indian National Party. It had been declared non-mailable under the Espionage Act. All copies of that pamphlet were suppressed when encountered at any censorship station.

Turning again to the socialist publications that were censored, the following received that ban. *The New Appeal*, published at Girard, Kansas, had at least one copy of its June 8, 1918, issue detained, and prevented from leaving this country. This number gave the reasons for urgent need for a socialist restatement of its position on the war. In addition, *The New Appeal* said there were three courses possible for the party at that time: (1) Restate its position to keep within the law, but continue its disapproval and opposition to the struggle. (2) To restate the position in general terms, and say nothing about the war, thus avoiding telling whether the party was for or against the slaughter. (3) Restate the position of the party and declare in favor of the fight within certain well defined limits of war aims and peace terms in accord with the socialist program and principles.

A copy of Upton Sinclair's magazine en route to Chile was held by the censor. That official objected to an editorial on the conscription of wealth, in which the writer showed the tendencies to create misunderstandings between the labor and the capitalist classes.

Censorship objected to a Cuban getting the June 2, 1918, number of the *Intercollegiate Socialist*. The commentator devoted his space to an article entitled "The Development of the Guild Idea." The writer of the item, according to the censor, contended that the war was helping along this development, namely, that of "Guild Socialism," a socialism in which the consumers and the producers would each carry on their appropriate functions through nationally organized guilds, subject to state control as to capital and prices, but internally autonomous to the utmost extent.

The censor was not favorably disposed toward another idea that had for its avowed aim the betterment of the human race. A pamphlet entitled "A World Government Needed" held that it was absolutely necessary that the control of the armed forces should be taken from the separate nations and centralized and amalgamated under a world government. It was quoted to the effect that "Proper physical culture would do the same thing as military training and do it better," and "Courage and heroism developed by the slaying of other people are not desirable qualities."

This pamphlet moved the commentator to observe that it did not say a word in praise of America entering the war. To the censor, the writer seemed unaware of the consequences that would have resulted from depriving England of her fleet and France of her army.

Another type of pamphlet was suppressed as it went from an Evanston, Illinois, bookseller to the Canal Zone. This booklet presented sayings of Nietzsche, including such quotations, according to the commentator, as "Man is born for war and woman for the joy of the warrior," "The mob are about to play the tyrant, we must invent a stronger one than they," "Compassion is a miserable weakness," and "The most essential and most vital and most momentous of all man's power is his power of making war." The censor stated that these sayings, spread outside the United States might produce the same effect "as they did in the only country where Nietzsche was widely read, Germany, where they undoubtedly tended to the growth of the spirit of Kaiserism and Conquest."

More than four hundred different issues of publications printed in the United States were denied the privileges of the mails by the confidential list of May 10, 1918. Instructions accompanying that list stated that the fact that one issue of the publication had been barred was evidence enough that the publication would bear watching at all times. And this list did not include all newspapers and periodicals that met that fate. The following are instances of censorship acting upon our publications.

The *Milwaukee Leader*, organ of Victor Berger, was refused second-class mailing privileges in October 1917 because of Berger's articles that tended to interfere with America's successful prosecution of the war. This case was argued from court to court until, finally, in March 1921, the Supreme Court affirmed Burleson's right to bar the *Leader* from the mails.

This triumph for Burleson was short-lived. On May 31, 1921, postal prohibitions against that paper were withdrawn. Postmaster General Will Hays was understood to have proceeded on the theory that the previous administration of that Department had erred in withdrawing low postal rates, and yet permitting the papers to be distributed.

The *New York Call* had to wait until June 1921 before its second-class mailing privileges were restored. Beginning in 1917, this case, too, had gone from one court to another until it had reached the highest, and again it was Postmaster General Hays who restored its second-class privileges.

This publication had been denied the mails because of the socialist propaganda it contained. For that reason the censor detained one copy of the *Call* of October 3, 1918, which was addressed to Mexico, and which contained an article entitled "Bankers Hope to use Soldiers Back from War to Cut Wages." The writer of the article was said to have stated that a certain brokerage firm had declared that after the war such competition would destroy the dangerous power of labor.

If prophecies about the rôle of the soldier in the post-war world were open to censorship, certain conjectures about his fate during the struggle were even more objectionable. *The*

Jeffersonian of Thomason, Georgia, was declared nonmailable for its expressed opposition to the war. The censor noted that opposition in its issue of June 28, 1917, which said that men conscripted to go to Europe were virtually condemned to death, and that everybody knew it. For these and similar sentiments, Burleson barred the publication, which appealed for an injunction to enjoin the postmaster from that action. The case was decided before Judge Speer at Lake Fairfield, North Carolina, August 29, 1917.

In denying the injunction, Speer said of the advice the *Jeffersonian* gave to the conscripts, namely, to await the decision of the Supreme Court upon the constitutionality of the draft law, "In such crises in Lacedaemon the Spartan mother, when her son went forth to battle, was accustomed to exclaim, 'Return on your shield or with it!' How dissimilar, how sordid, is the cowardice the *Jeffersonian* would encourage." In September 1917, *The Jeffersonian* suspended publication.

Opposition to the war caused repressive action similar to that taken against the *Milwaukee Leader* and the *New York Call* to befall the *Masses*, a New York publication. Its August 1917 issue, excluded from the mails largely because of four anti-war cartoons and a poem, favoring Emma Goldman and Alexander Berkman, was not permitted to be posted although President Wilson interested himself in the matter as he did when *The World Tomorrow* was excluded. It was not until January 1919 that the status of *The Masses* was determined when indictments under the Espionage Act against persons connected with the publication were dismissed.

Loss of its second-class mail privileges was the penalty paid by *The American Socialist* of Chicago for advertising a leaflet. From the middle of June 1917, the St. Louis postmaster had declined to distribute the paper, allegedly because of the advertisement of a leaflet entitled "The Price We Pay." The federal government banned the publication from the mails on July 6. As for the offending ad, it read:

Leaflets!
Eye Openers

———

"THE PRICE WE PAY"
By Irwin Tucker
Four pages: 20 cents per 100, $1.50 per 1,000
600,000 already sold.

———

The pamphlet itself was not so mild as the advertisement. It had been published as an article in *The American Socialist*, May 5, 1917, before the Espionage Act had been passed. The pamphlet stated an idea that was to gain wide circulation during the peaceful days of 1934, when war was so abhorrent to the American people, and when Senator Nye's committee, as well as many private individuals, was trying to discover what forces pushed us into World War I.

Tucker, who had preached at St. Mark's Protestant Episcopal Church, New York City, had been editor of the *Christian Socialist*, Chicago, and at one time a member of the Louisiana National Guard, stated in "The Price We Pay" that "Our entry into it [the war] was determined by the certainty that if the allies do not win, J. P. Morgan's loans to the Allies will be repudiated, and those American investors who bit on his promises will be hooked."

Upon losing the second-class mail privilege, the editor of *The American Socialist*, J. Louis Engdahl, announced the inauguration of *The Red Express*. Each local group of such subscribers was asked to organize a station of *The Red Express*, and designate some member as "station agent." Papers for all subscribers to the barred publication were to be sent to the "agent" each week by express. This plan did not succeed, however, for the Trading-with-the-Enemy Act prohibited distribution of such matter via express companies.

On February 2, 1918, the grand jury for the United States District Court, Northern District of Illinois, returned an indictment charging that Engdahl, Berger, *et al* had conspired together to violate the Espionage Act. *The American Socialist* was one of the media which the alleged conspiracy employed. More than a year later, these two were found guilty, and each was sentenced to twenty years imprisonment.

The sentence, handed down by Kenesaw Mountain Landis, the future baseball czar, was reversed by the Supreme Court January 31, 1921. The reversal occurred because Landis had not retired from the case after the defendants had submitted an affidavit charging that the judge was prejudiced.

What attitude did the socialists take toward all this interference? An idea of their feelings may be gained from a letter from Mary Marcy of the Charles H. Kerr and Company, publishers of socialist literature, Chicago, to William English Walling, Greenwich, Connecticut. The company had received word from the Chicago postmaster that the *International Socialist Review* for June 1917 could not be mailed, and that the concern would have to send a copy of the July number to Washington for censorship before it could be mailed. After a week no word had been received from the capital.

The writer then went on to state her views on the world situation: "we have always been first—Pro-working class, and second—Pro-ally. We hope the Germans will be licked but we are going to stand on what we think is the right position for international socialists to take, i.e. we do believe that all capitalist wars are only waged because the capitalists fear they will lose something, or fail to gain something—never because they love abstract justice."

To return to the event which caused the shadow of censorship to become a reality especially to socialist publications and potentially to all editors and publishers—the war—one finds that it had ceased more than two years before the Supreme Court had reversed Landis's decision. On December 10, 1918, confidential information was issued by the Censorship Board to all its stations that censorship of newspapers and other printed matter originating in the United States was to be discontinued. For almost a month prior to that date, it had not been necessary for newspapers to route their incoming messages through the stations at New York or San Francisco.

But, consciously or unconsciously, the stage was being set for an attempt at continued scrutiny of publications. In February 1919, a Senate Committee investigating German plots and propaganda in this country was told that at that time there were a great many anti-American papers and periodicals in the United States. And Attorney General A. Mitchell Palmer gave out the information that there were in circulation in this country 222 radical foreign-language papers, 106 radical papers printed in English, and another group of 144 radical publications that were published in foreign countries. To combat those menaces, according to Palmer, the Attorney General asked for a stringent law since the Espionage Act was no longer applicable. His request was not granted. Although, however, even with the horrors of one war too near for anyone to imagine the recurrence of such a slaughter, and with "fifth column" an uncoined and an unknown phrase, the First Amendment apparently did not assume its traditional significance for many of the American Fourth Estate whose dissenting voices had been muffled in wartime.

Banned Books

SOME AMERICANS HAD TO CURB THEIR INDISCRIMINATE READING habits during World War I. Government agencies, as well as patriotic societies and individuals, maintained a close watch over the volumes the American citizen read. This watch included the surveillance of volumes produced in this country, those exported from the United States, and those produced in other lands. The following instances of books under suspicion, books excluded from export or import with respect to the United States, and books banned within our borders will reveal the extent to which this kind of censorship was practised.

Authorities received information about books from many different sources. One such source was George F. Weeks, editor of the *Mexican Review* who wrote George Creel that he was informed from Minneapolis that the Reverend Mr. Morrill's libelous book *The Devil in Mexico* was being circulated in that part of the country. Had the circulation of this volume been great, it would have had a bad effect upon inter-American relations. The foreword began: "Mexico is one-sixteenth of an inch nearer hell than any country I have ever visited in my round-the-world travels," and the remainder of the book developed that theme. Weeks did not know what steps the government may have taken to suppress "this very manifestly libelous publication," but he had been asked to bring the matter to the attention of the head of the Committee on Public Information. There is no record as to the action taken with respect to *The Devil in Mexico*.

From New York another informant wrote that he deemed it his duty and privilege to bring to the Committee's notice a book published in 1918 by a New York house. It was entitled, *Reflections on War and Death*, and had been written by Dr.

Freud and translated into English by Brill and Kuttner. The book was divided into two sections, one entitled *The Disappointments of War*, and the other *Our Attitude Toward Death*.

The objectionable part of this book, according to the informant, occurred on page 14. This passage stated that a nation at war made free use of every injustice, every act of violence, that would dishonor the individual. It employed not only permissible cunning, but conscious lies and intentional deception against the enemy, and this to a degree which apparently outdid what was customary along that line in previous wars. The informant held that if this statement had been true of the United States and its Allies, it might have been justifiable for the author to have made a general statement of such character in relation to all of the nations at war, but in the opinion of the Committee's correspondent, Freud's attempted explanation was an attempt to exculpate the frightful crimes committed by the German barbarians.

Creel informed the writer that the book by Freud had been read by other members of the Committee on Public Information, "and your report seems to be absolutely justified. I am calling it to the attention of the proper authorities."

If the writings of a psychologist were suspect, the same was true to a greater extent where a historian's publications were concerned. The chairman of the Committee on Public Information had his attention called to a publication entitled *Medieval and Modern Times* by James Harvey Robinson, professor of history in Columbia University, published by Ginn and Company, Boston and New York, 1916. Creel's correspondent, Rear Admiral Roger Welles, of the Office of Naval Intelligence, stated that the representative of Naval Intelligence in San Francisco had brought the book to Welles's notice. The Admiral regarded it as extremely friendly to Germany and unfriendly to our Allies. It was the fact that this book was still on sale which made him feel that the volume was working against the interests of the United States, Britain, and France. Welles cited a few examples from the 1916 edition. For instance, Robinson was quoted as having said that "Germany has developed through its schools and its officials, efficiency and prosperity, and the other nations are copying its methods." Again Welles quoted, "Germany sought to localize the conflict between Austria and Serbia. . . . Earnest efforts were made to avert any catastrophe, but in vain." The Admiral also objected to Robinson dwelling upon the fact that Alsace-Lorraine was originally a part of Germany and that following the War of 1870 these provinces were "ceded back" to Germany. Welles observed, "The whole book would have to be read carefully in order to grasp the subtle propaganda which this book contained."

These views were not echoed by the Committee on Public Information. Harvey O'Higgins, associate chairman, submitted a memorandum concerning Professor Robinson's book, stating that the volume had already been before the Department of Justice. Welles was informed that the edition of 1916 had since been recalled and revised in order to overcome any objection that its point of view was not strongly pro-Ally. Any such appearance was of course accidental on the author's part, in the opinion of O'Higgins. Robinson was considered to be strongly anti-German and had written some of the earliest denunciations of German war aims that had issued from university sources. The associate chairman understood that the edition of 1916 was revised with the assistance of Professor Shotwell who at the time that this memorandum was written, September 30, 1918, was working for the House Peace Commission, "whose anti-German feeling is above suspicion."

Creel himself occasionally informed the Department of Justice about objectionable books. For example, he forwarded a volume entitled *The Imprisoned Freeman*, to A. Bruce Bielaski, head of the Federal Bureau of Investigation. In the accompanying letter he stated that it seemed to be German propaganda and should be suppressed.

In addition to action on suggestions of informants, voluntary censorship by the publishers was a means by which books were suppressed. For instance, Horace Liveright of the firm of

Boni and Liveright informed Creel, August 27, 1918, that two weeks previously a captain of the Military Intelligence Branch called at the publisher's office to find out whether the company was strictly complying with the Post Office ruling on the nonmailability of the Boni and Liveright publication *Men in War*. At the same time, the firm was severely criticized for continuing to distribute its publication by Leon Trotzky, *The Bolsheviki and World Peace*. Liveright reminded Creel that the text of this was published in January 1918 "by the *New York World* and other staunch and loyal newspapers throughout the country."

The publisher stated that his firm had been seriously considering the matter of Trotzky's book, and that since the Soviet government of Russia had, according to newspaper reports, declared itself in a state of war with the United States, the publisher was writing Creel to ask whether in the latter's opinion "we should make a public announcement of the fact that we have discontinued the distribution of this book." Liveright assured Creel that the volume was in no way objectionable—that it was, in fact, a strong indictment of Prussian militarism. Nevertheless, the company did not wish in any way to give countenance to the idea that it in any way sympathized with any enemies of the government of the United States. Upon this occasion Creel wrote Tumulty, secretary to the President, that he agreed absolutely with Mr. Liveright's letter. In his opinion the firm was absolutely patriotic. Without compulsion of any kind it had withdrawn the two books mentioned above, the circulation of which it deemed unwise at that time.

Books sent by Boni and Liveright to addressees outside the United States did not always reach their destination. This fate overtook one shipment of books when the New York Postal censorship held a registered package from Boni and Liveright to a private in the United States Marine Corps stationed in Cuba. The parcel contained a book entitled *The Seven That Were Hanged*, by Leonid Andreyev, as well as another story, *The Red Laugh*. The censor commented that the latter was a terrible delineation of the horrors of war and was truly a story of horror and madness which purported to be told by a soldier driven insane by suffering and grief. The same package contained a copy of H. G. Wells's book, *The War in the Air*, written in 1908, a story of world conflict and imagined air attacks on the United States by the Germans and later by the Asiatics. In the censor's opinion, the epilogue of this book, with its dismal picture of strikes, rioting, pestilence, famine, and death following the war in the air, was not the kind for a nation that was stimulated by the speeches of Woodrow Wilson, and was hoping for mankind to rise to a higher level after World War I.

Brentano's of New York mailed certain books to Mexico City, and they also were seized by the censor. These included a volume of *Deductions from the World War*, by a lieutenant general of the German General Staff. An introductory note in the book, according to the censor, stated that the circulation of this volume was promoted in Germany, but that its export had been prohibited, and that it was useful as a warning about the plans being laid at that time in Berlin.

The American News Company tried to send a resident of Havana one copy of *Jean Jaures—Socialist and Humanitarian*, by Margaret Pease, with an introduction by J. Ramsay MacDonald, leader of the Labor Party. This book, however, did not get farther than the censor's office. The censor stated that the author of the introduction gave a brief account of Jaures in which he described the latter's friendship with the German socialist, Frank, who had been one of the first to die for Germany in the present war. MacDonald's introduction to this book contained the statements that France did not want war; she needed peace for the immense work of socialistic change. This will for peace on the part of France, according to MacDonald, was not a wish to humble herself, but it came from her belief in the possibility of peace between Germany and England, and from her desire to work for it ceaselessly. In addition, MacDonald's praise of international democracy and socialism was not welcomed by the censor.

Books from other countries met a rigid censorship when they tried to enter the United States. In this category was *The Thoughtful Hour*, by Vargas Vila, a Colombian writer of violent anti-American books, which was held and thus not permitted to reach its destination in Barcelona. This action was at least in part because of the fact that Vila was on the War Trade Board suspect list.

The Canal Zone censor detained a book *The Barbarians*, by Alfredo Luis Beltrame, and prevented it from going to the addressee in Lima, Peru. This volume was written by a person who was on the Military Intelligence List. The cover of the book depicted France and England pouring gold into a machine similar in appearance to a concrete mixer but with the head of a dragon, out of whose mouth issued Allied Propaganda. The caption read "This is how it is done." The commentator stated that the author, who had been sent to the belligerent countries as a correspondent for the three Argentine newspapers that had been either suppressed or were under observation for their pro-German writings, described his love for France up to the time he was arrested there as a German spy, and his subsequent hatred for that country as a result of his imprisonment and the alleged cruel treatment by his jailors.

Another package from Madrid to Mexico was held in New York because it contained copies of a Spanish book which was a translation of a German's detailed account of the voyage of a submarine flotilla from Germany to Russia. The censor said the book was very pro-German and that its South American editor was on the Enemy Trading List. According to the censor the book was sufficiently detailed and the events described were recent enough for the naval authorities to gain interesting information from it.

A book called *Lord Kitchener's Secret and England's Disaster*, translated into Spanish from the German was stopped in New York on its way from Spain to Nicaragua. It was published by a Spanish firm which was on the Enemy Trading List. The book was held to be anti-British throughout.

New York was not the only censorship station in the United States that detained these books, for all the stations were ordered to be on watch for certain volumes. On October 4, 1918, the chairman of the Censorship Board advised all censorship stations that *The Great War*, written in Spanish and published apparently by the Pacific Press Publishing Company of Mountain View, California, was not only anti-war but pro-German as well, although it pretended to be impartial. The stations were told to issue the necessary instructions "to assure the summary suppression of any copies of the above mentioned book which may be received at your station."

Again on September 27, 1919, Chairman Maddox instructed the stations that Military Intelligence had received a letter from the State Department concerning a questionable book, *Mexico from Diaz to the Kaiser*, written by Mrs. Alec Tweddle. Military Intelligence stated that the book was not so much concerned with the Kaiser as with criticizing the Mexican policy of the United States. And again the stations were told to suppress any copies of that book intercepted in the mail.

The foregoing suppressions had occurred as a result of the Espionage Act of June 1917 and the Sedition Act of May 1918, but one form of censorship affecting some four million individuals had begun to function almost as soon as the training camps had been established. This censorship, largely by orders issued on the ground, was instituted by military officials with respect to the books our soldiers might read in the various camps and cantonments. A list of objectionable books was gradually built up, and the possession of any book on that list was forbidden within the military establishment. Punishment was to be determined by the commanding officer of the camp. Ordinarily when the copies of the forbidden books were discovered, either among donated volumes, or in the possession of the soldiers, confiscation was the result. Subsequent offences were to be visited with light punishment or in extreme cases with court-martial.

This Army Index was built up gradually over a period of several months, and by the time the Armistice was signed there were almost a hundred books on it. The existence of this list was, for obvious reasons, never accorded any degree of publicity. However, in the early autumn of 1918, when it became apparent that Germany could not hold out much longer, the list of banned books was given a discreet circulation, and it was even printed in a few papers. In general the works were by authors of German nationality or sympathy or were of socialist, pacifist, or religious persuasion.

The Index was in many ways a unique list of books, for out of the hundreds of thousands of volumes which passed through the hands of the Army librarians, these were the ones believed to contain "dangerous thoughts." Although the literary censorship within the military establishment was afforded scant publicity, it went on continuously and silently. On a few occasions, these objectionable books were discussed in the press, and it is interesting to note how they were regarded by the newspapers of that time.

Early in 1918, the military authorities were watching carefully for pro-German books. As early as February 18, 1918, the *New York Times* published an article as follows:

Hun Propaganda at Upton
Books by German authors, Sent from
State Library, Halted in Time

"Camp Upton, L.I., Feb. 17—It was learned today, through unofficial sources, that in the recent shipment of books from the State Library Albany to the new library here, three volumes were found that were considered to be works of German propaganda. They were caught in time to prevent them from being placed on the shelves for public inspection.

"One of the books was by Count zu Reventlow and was dated 1916, the second was by Professor Vondewitz and the third by Captain Paul Koenig. The titles of the volumes were not made public. Very little literature of that sort has reached this cantonment and all that has been discovered was very crude."

The three books mentioned above were: *Vampire of the Continent*, portraying England as the vampire, by Count Ernst zu Reventlow; *War's New Weapons*, by Baron Hrolf von Dewitz; and the third was Paul König's *Voyage of the Deutschland*. The first two were included in the October 1918 Army Index, but the König volume was omitted. The latter first appeared in Germany in 1916 under the title, *Die Fahrt des Deutschland*, No. 21, of the popular series of "Ullstein Kriegsbücher," of which 550,000 copies had been sold in Germany by 1917. Hearst's International Library had brought out both an English translation and a German edition in 1916, and they enjoyed a wide sale.

Dr. Herbert Putnam, Librarian of Congress, and general director of the Library War Service of the American Library Association, collaborated closely with the War Department in suppressing volumes of an alleged harmful character. On August 9, 1918, he directed all camp librarians or supervisors, upon instruction from the War Department, to remove from camp libraries the following books: Anonymous, *Free Speech and Free Press*; Mach, Edmund von, *What Germany Wants*, Little, Brown & Co.; MacManus, Seumas, *Ireland's Case*, Irish Pub. Co., New York; Nearing, Scott, *Open Letter to Profiteers*; Wilson, Theodora W., *The Last Weapon*, J. C. Winston Co.

All of these titles, except the first, were included upon the October Army Index. The *New York Times* made an allusion to Dr. Putnam's letter of instructions to the camps. This was in the issue for Sunday, September 1, 1918, but the article was to be found in the Sports Section.

The same month, the writers of the books banned by the Army attracted the attention of various editorial writers. The weekly department, "The Librarian," appearing in the *Boston Evening Transcript* for September 4, 1918, expressed one sentiment with respect to the banned volumes. The *Transcript* listed about thirty of those books, and then lashed out at them with the following: "Here is a group of old friends! The pro-German whose motive was money, and the pro-German whose motive may have been less selfish, though none the less sinis-

ter. The addle-headed pacifist, working hand-in-hand with the
paid servants of absolutism and militarism, and playing—inno-
cently or not—their game for them. The German-born professors, obedient to Potsdam, and ready to snarl at England. The
American-born professors, their opinions warped and their historical judgment corrupted by a luncheon with Wilhelm II—
and a ribbon to stick in their coats. The professional Irish
patriot—always remaining safe in New York or Boston, but
very warlike against England, and eager to ally himself with the
Hun—in the name of liberty! What a crew they are!"

Among the titles listed by the *Boston Transcript* of September 4, was *Approaches to the Great Settlement*, by Emily
Greene Balch, professor of civics at Wellesley College and
later the founder of the Women's International League for
Peace and Freedom. This work was published by B. W.
Huebsch of New York for the American Union against Militarism, and listed all peace programs that had been put forward
to that date.

In contrast with the attitude of the *Transcript* concerning
the use of such books as those on the Army Index, Edward H.
Anderson of the New York Public Library, was quoted as saying, "If Satan wrote a pro-German book we should want it for
our reference-shelves. It might be of use to future historians.
But in the circulating department we exclude all pro-German
books, and have done so since the beginning of the war. We
go over the books from time to time and take out those that
are objectionable."

The old *New York Tribune* on Thursday, September 26,
1918, published a list of about seventy of the books on the
Army Index, which some enterprising reporter had secured
from the Department of Military Censorship. The bibliography was headlined as follows:

The *Tribune* said of these "improper books" that they were
barred from every Army camp and from every post where
American soldiers were located because their influence tended
to make the soldier who read them a less effective fighter
against the Hun. The article added that the books had been

carefully read by military censors, and that every one contained some objectionable matter, either of a nature to give information to the enemy or calculated to disturb the morale of the American soldier. According to the paper, many of the volumes, as their titles indicated, were the most vicious kind of German propaganda, while others were declared either salacious or morbid and unfit for reading by anybody, but more particularly by soldiers.

Various papers noted with considerable satisfaction that one of the books banned by the Army, *Two Thousand Questions and Answers About the War*, had a preface written by George Creel, chairman of the Committee on Public Information. This banning resulted despite the fact that the material in the book had been passed by British censors, as it had been appearing semimonthly in an Australian publication since the beginning of the war. For the banned book, this material was edited by Julius W. Mueller, a well known New York newspaper man, and American staff correspondent of *The Stars and Stripes*. The volume was then published by the George H. Doran Company for the *Review of Reviews* whose editor, Albert Shaw, obtained Creel's consent to write the introduction. The chairman of the Committee on Public Information closed that introduction with, "The 2000 *Questions and Answers*, in my opinion, constitute a vital part of the national defense."

In June 1918, within two months after he had written the foreword, Creel was worried about his connection with the book. He wrote Shaw, June 26, that while he had glanced through the proof, he had relied less upon his hasty reading than upon his absolute faith in him, Shaw. Creel continued, that after more careful reading he became aware that he could not find "the fundamental truth that Germany was entirely responsible for this war."

As soon as this letter was received, the Review of Reviews Company revoked the order for the trade edition and began a revision of the book. J. Salwyn Schapiro, professor of history in the College of the City of New York, directed the revision which was just completed, September 9, 1918.

More than two months after the book had been withdrawn for revision, the attack upon it began. According to an official of the Review of Reviews Company, almost the very day the revision had been completed, and Army officials had found no objection to the volume, the National Security League informed the company it was about to publish a bulletin warning against the book. Dr. Claude H. Van Tyne of the Department of History in the University of Michigan, then serving as educational director of the National Security League's Bureau of Education, after reading the book, reported in the press that the volume was a masterpiece of German propaganda. In the same manner, the *New York Times* editorialized to the effect that "a vicious and seditious book was sold to and bought by the American people."

The second and revised edition of this book seemed to arouse the opposition of no one. And Creel's introduction in the meantime, at his own request, had been omitted. A prefatory note by "The Publishers" replaced it.

After noticing the fate of a volume whose introduction was written by one member of the Censorship Board, it may be well to pay attention to other censored books. As has been said before, they were mainly works by authors of German nationality or sympathy, or by writers who were socialists, pacifists, or religiously inclined. Many of the volumes, however, were written by persons who tried to attain an attitude of impartiality toward the European struggle.

Under Fire: The Story of a Squad, by Henri Barbusse, was a volume with a curious history. Originally, the book had appeared in Paris in December 1916, and was an instant success. It came out in an American edition in New York in August of the following year, and by that November had gone through seven printings. Yet it was singled out for special censorship by the military authorities. The offending volume, since 1917-1918, has become a recognized literary work of the first World War. The book was included in two editions of Everyman's Library (1928 and 1933) and won the coveted Prix Goncourt.

However, its merits were lost on the military mind in 1917-1918, as it was held to paint a too lugubrious picture of war.

The chief of the Military Morale Section of the Army, writing to Dr. Putnam, Librarian of Congress, on July 16, 1918, stated, that *Under Fire* had recently been removed from a camp library as objectionable. The chief informed Putnam that the book had been exploited by pro-German papers and that radical publications were advertising it. The Germans were said to be publishing the book serially in their propaganda organ *Journal des Ardennes*.

Behind the Scenes in Warring Germany, by Edward Lyell Fox, provoked much discussion. Fox was a newspaperman who had been a special war correspondent with the German armies where he had represented various papers and news services, including the *New York American*. In the testimony about the famous motion picture serial *Patria*, starring Mrs. Vernon Castle, it was brought out that Fox was suspected of being a German agent. These hearings were conducted by the Senate Judiciary Committee after the conclusion of the war. Fox was said to have written stories of Russian atrocities against Germany so realistic in the *New York American* that the German Ambassador to the United States cabled Berlin to find out the details. And *Behind the Scenes in Warring Germany* was believed to argue the efficiency and invincibility of the German army in too favorable terms. One chapter eulogized Von Hindenburg for his military exploits.

Understanding Germany was a book of essays from the pen of Max Eastman, onetime professor at Columbia University, and editor of *The Masses*, whose postal and legal difficulties have been noticed in the preceding chapter. In these essays he showed an extremely pacifistic viewpoint and held all war unjustifiable. He called the Monroe Doctrine "stereotyped egotism," and "an astounding peace of sophomoric cheek," and the English "Mistress of the Seas" tradition "a monumental swagger."

The War and America was written by Dr. Hugo Münsterberg, Harvard psychologist, in 1914. The author was a prolific writer on a wide range of subjects, and this particular book was a defense of his native Germany. He wrote, "Germany's pacific and industrious population had only one wish: to develop its agricultural and industrial, its cultural and moral resources."

War and Waste: A Series of Discussions of War and War Accessories, by David Starr Jordan, was published by Doubleday, Page and Company, in 1913. "The movement of civilization is toward a new conception of the State, not as a 'power' but as a center of jurisdiction," was the thesis of the famous peace advocate. He pleaded for the banishment of all war, and advocated a federation of the European states for settling disputes.

Jesus is Coming was an anonymous volume which had appeared periodically since 1878. Some issues included on the title page "by W. E. B." (The Reverend William E. Blackstone). Revisions appeared in 1908, 1917, and 1932. The second edition announced that the total circulation of this book was 386,000 in twenty-five languages, a figure that had changed to 1,000,000 in forty languages in 1932, despite the Army Index. The book taught the religious doctrine of pre-millennialism regarding the second advent of Christ to establish His rule. The book, by means of diagrams and elaborate and detailed Biblical references worked out the history of the world to the climax at the battle of the nations at Armageddon. The volume advocated pacifism and denounced armaments and militarism as "the suicidal policy" leading to absolute bankruptcy.

The Outlook for Religion, by William Edward Orchard, was published in 1917 by Funk and Wagnalls, and printed in England. The author could not reconcile war with Christianity. He stated, "If only there could dawn upon Europe at this time the idea that the war means the crucifying of the Son of God afresh, and the putting of Him to an open shame, we might see the fruition of His great sacrifice and the ending of His travail." The author spoke of the "false imperialisms" of the nations and stressed the need for the Christian to renounce war and lay down arms.

Songs of Armageddon, by George Sylvester Viereck, the famous German propagandist, was a small book of verse in which the German side received most favorable attention. For example, on page 3, the author presented a poem entitled *Wilhelm II, Prince of Peace.*

The Other Side of Death by C. W. Leadbetter, published in Chicago, 1903, was another book suppressed by the Army. To men in camps and cantonments pages 36-38 had special significance for they contained information about "The Death of a Soldier." This section stated that the very fact that the soldier had developed sufficient heroism to die for "what is to him an abstract idea means very great advancement from his previous position." Leadbetter asked the reader to observe that it was in the last degree unlikely that the type of man from whom our private soldier is drawn would in his ordinary home life have had any opportunity of developing such magnificent courage and resolution as he gained on the battlefield. For that reason, the author thought that in spite of its horrors, "war may nevertheless be a potent factor in evolution at a certain level."

Another class of books which discussed the horrors of war was blacklisted because it destroyed the morale of the troops. For instance, the military censors excluded Ambrose Bierce's books *Can Such Things Be?* and *In the Midst of Life: Tales of Soldiers and Civilians.* Both volumes have appeared in various editions, and the latter, in a 1927 edition, was included in the series Modern Library of the World's Best Books. These works, especially the latter, however, reflected a pessimistic attitude toward war. Many passages in the book, *In the Midst of Life*, would not have been conducive to soldier or civilian morale. One in particular spoke of a Union private viewing a group of Confederates and considering "where he could plant his shot with the best hope of making a widow or an orphan or a childless mother—perhaps all three" for the private "was not without a certain kind of ambition."

If Bierce's stories reminded Americans of the Civil War, the very name of another author whose work was censored should have recalled that struggle to the minds of a great many more citizens. This writer was Major (later Colonel) George B. McClellan, son of General George B. McClellan of Civil War fame, who has been mentioned in the first chapter of this volume. The author of the censored book, *The Heel of War*, which consisted of reprints of articles in the *New York Times*, had served five terms as a member of Congress, had been Mayor of New York for six years, and, in 1915, when the book was published, was professor of economic history in Princeton University. In *The Heel of War*, the author described his trip through Europe in 1915, and pointed out the great resources of Germany in comparison with the more limited resources of the Allied nations. Speaking of France, he said, that in that nation there was no real hatred for Germany "except among the American colony and a small section of unrepresentative French." Turning to England, McClellan quoted the German saying: "Great Britain will never surrender as long as there is a single Frenchman left, or a single American dollar unspent."

At the time this book was banned its author had been promoted to lieutenant colonel and was serving in the A.E.F.

Why War?, by Frederic C. Howe, commissioner of immigration at the Port of New York, was published by Charles Scribners' Sons, 1916. It was dedicated "to Woodrow Wilson whose sympathies for weaker nations and recognition of the rights of struggling peoples have shielded Mexico and China and saved us from the consequences of financial imperialism." According to Howe, surplus wealth seeking privileges in foreign lands was the proximate cause of the war, just as wealth seeking monopoly profits was the cause of the civil conflicts that had involved our cities and states. The author was certain that as a result of the European war the United States was confronted with the same forces that had drawn Europe into that conflict. Ambitions and fears had been aroused that had united the privileged classes in a movement for financial imperialism, for a great naval program, for colossal expenditures for preparedness, and unless some hand interposed to prevent it, Howe thought that the ideals of America and the democratic traditions of a century would be submerged in the new imperialistic program that had no place in our life. He believed that the foes within were responsible for the foes without. The author called attention to the fact that "after eighteen months of conflict, there is no agreement as to what the war is about." The book ended with the observation, "War will remain the agency of privilege and the inevitable outcome of its ambitions until the powers and profits of privilege are taken away."

Belgium and Germany, by J. H. Labberton, translated from the Dutch by William Ellery Leonard, the Wisconsin professor, subsequently famous for his curious book, *The Locomotive God*, was published in 1916. The reasons for its publication were: first, it was a study of philosophic ideas; second, it was a study by a citizen of a neutral country; and third, it was a study by a foreigner well read in German literature. This work attempted to be impartial. Concerning the fate of Belgium, it held that the first impression of that fate was unfavorable to Germany, "and England has left nothing undone to strengthen and confirm that impression." Labberton stated that England's statesmen, excellent and clever judges of human nature, knew well enough that for most people first impressions were lasting impressions, that the mass of mankind could neither see nor think, and that nothing was so sure to take effect as an appeal to its ethical instinct, "at least in the business of shaping that usually rather external phenomenon known as public opinion."

England or Germany?, by Frank Harris, New York, 1915, stated that some of the best heads in the world had written about that war, and yet no one stood out as having approached impartiality. Harris said that both he and Heine condemned the English oligarchy, English snobbishness, and English hypocrisy. According to him, they were both struck with horror by the incredible cruelty with which the English treated the poor, and the unimaginable savagery of their laws, mainly directed against the weak. Harris hoped for a social revolution in Great Britain as an outcome of the war. According to him, this war was a proof, if proof were needed, "of the bankruptcy of Christian morale and of the weak hold the unselfish teaching of Jesus has on the modern world."

The question of the blacklisted books was vexatious at times. Some responsible federal officials saw the need for revising the Army Index, if not for abolishing it, toward the closing weeks of the war. On October 3, 1918, Dr. Frederick P. Keppel, Third Assistant Secretary of War, wrote Guy Stanton Ford of the Committee on Public Information that there was a good deal of discussion as to the Index Expurgatorius of the War Department, "for which, of course, Mr. Baker gets personal credit." Keppel asked Ford if it would be fair to have the latter's office inform the Third Assistant Secretary of War the books, "which it might be profitable to have someone read with a view to their restoration to respectability. Fred Howe, for example, writes more in sorrow than in anger on the subject, and books like Ambrose Bierce's come fairly near being classics."

Carl Byoir of the Committee on Public Information voiced his opposition to the censoring of one book. On August 14, 1918, he informed Creel that the Post Office Department had excluded from the mails Koettgen's translation of A German Deserter's War Experiences. The translator was a member of the Committee on Public Information. From all Byoir could find out the book was anti-German and good propaganda. He said that no one seemed to know why the Post Office excluded it from the mails.

And Creel expressed himself on this matter of censorship when he wrote Joseph Tumulty, President Wilson's secretary, a confidential letter, September 27, 1918. Speaking of the suppression of books by Chesterton (Utopia of Usurers) and Bierce, whose books have been noted above, Creel stated that he regarded the action as utterly absurd, "but no more absurd than other similar actions." He informed the secretary to the President that he was refusing to release the War Department list for general publication. He believed that, even aside from the injustice done, there was the fact that while some books might have been improper for camp reading, there was no reason why they should not have been read by the general public; "and to give these lists to the public is to work grave injustices to loyal people."

The coming of peace should have ended the banning of books based upon wartime conceptions of what constituted a menace to the government and institutions of the United States. In the academic world especially, however, there was a decided holdover of the censorship idea. To make certain that the right kind of knowledge was made available to young minds, states, municipalities, and groups of citizens assumed, in peacetime, powers similar to those the federal government had used for a temporary emergency.

Scissors and Films

PRODUCERS, EXHIBITORS, AND THE MOTION PICTURE PUBLIC HAD
their cinema activities greatly circumscribed during World
War I. By the time that April 6, 1917 arrived, many theater
owners and motion picture producers had become aware of the
type of picture that officials frowned upon. The Preparedness
Campaign of 1916 showed the motion picture world that any
film not conducive to recruiting was looked upon with dis-
favor, at least by those who were interested in preparedness,
and the motion picture world was to be visited with more and
more restrictions as the war continued.

Prior to the 1916 preparedness effort, there were many peace
films, so-called, being exhibited throughout the United States.
The War o' Dreams, released in July 1915, might be considered
in that group. The story told of an inventor who had discovered a new chemical to be used in warfare. He was planning to
sell this secret discovery to the United States War Department
for a large sum of money. He had a dream, however, which
depicted the havoc his invention played in time of war and the
suffering it caused innocent victims. This nightmare was so
terrifying that when the representative of the War Department
came to buy the formula, the inventor tore up the paper, pre-
ferring to remain in poverty rather than to be rich at the
expense of bringing suffering to humanity.

The Battle Cry of Peace, released in September 1915 by
Vitagraph, and starring Charles Richman and Norma Tal-
madge, was claimed to be both a peace and a preparedness film.
In a message concerning that picture, signed by its producer,
Commodore J. Stuart Blackton, stated: "To the fearless patriotism of Hudson Maxim, and the plain, practical, straightfor-
ward truths in his book *Defenceless America*, I owe the inspira-

tion and impetus which caused me to conceive the writing of the silent drama, *The Battle Cry of Peace*. Blackton stated that the aim of the picture was to arouse in the heart of every American citizen a sense of his strict accountability to his government in time of need—and to bring to the notice of the greatest number of people in the shortest possible time the fact that there was a way to insure that peace for which all Americans so earnestly prayed. He held that as a nation we must have the power to enforce and to insure peace.

The plot was, as one reviewer put it, one of "Dantesque horror." The fleet of a hostile European power suddenly attacked the United States, and bombarded New York. Invading forces were landed and soon took possession of the city amid scenes of carnage and horror. The leading characters of the play were all killed.

In April 1917, because of the change in the status of the United States from a peace to a war footing, it was announced that all prints of *The Battle Cry of Peace* had been recalled by Vitagraph and were to be reedited and retitled, so that the picture would stimulate recruiting. Certain of the original titles were deleted because it was felt they might be construed as arguments against war. This renovation, however, did not cause the film to meet with approval of all authorities. In Pittsburgh the proprietor of a motion picture theater was arrested in the spring of 1917 and held for court action under $5,000 bail on a charge of high misdemeanor, after distributing handbills advertising that picture. The authorities held that the handbills alone were calculated to prevent enlistment.

The year 1915 was notable for a number of other films relating to the war. These pictures were satisfactory while we were at peace, but not all of them met the requirements of an America at war. *Court Martialed*, dealing with French military intrigues, was not welcome after France became our comrade-in-arms. Another picture, *The Battles of a Nation*, showed the "actual bombardment of Warsaw." At the same time, the German side of the war was presented in various pictures, chiefly through news reels.

The Battle of the Somme was widely distributed throughout the winter and spring of 1917. It was said to be made up of official pictures of the war, and was to be shown for the benefit of war relief funds. This film was the basis of the previously mentioned pamphlet, *The Price We Pay*, which was banned from the mail because of its denunciation of conscription and because of the heart-rending picture it painted of the horrors awaiting the soldier when he went to war.

Among the last attempts that might be construed as anti-war propaganda in films was the picture, *War Brides*, announced for release November 1916. In this photo-drama Alla Nazimova was introduced for the first time to cinema audiences. The film was made in the record time of two months, and was developed from a stage success in which Nazimova had starred. The plot was that of a young woman whose husband was drafted into the Army shortly after they were married. He was killed in an early engagement of the war, and his widow urged the women of her town not to marry soldiers, so they could escape the tragedy which had come into her life. The military officers endeavored to silence her, but in defiance she finally confronted the king himself.

This film attracted the attention of those who were interested in recruiting. In Seattle, the newspapers for April 8, 1917, carried the announcement that The Moore Theater was presenting one week later Nazimova, the world's greatest emotional star, in *War Brides*, accompanied by a mammoth concert orchestra of thirty pieces. Four days later the advertisement for the film announced that new standards were necessary in the marriage relation when the balance of sex was disturbed by an elimination of able-bodied men. These announcements disturbed a colonel of artillery who was in Seattle, and on April 10, 1917, he wired Washington that a film called *War Brides*, which was very depressing and which conveyed terrible pictures of the horrors that came to the families of men who went to war, was to be exhibited in that town.

The colonel had at least a partial triumph in his efforts at censorship. He was unable to stop the show, but he did per-

suade the exhibitor of *War Brides* to take out many objectionable parts, and to precede its display with a lantern slide
carrying the following inscriptions: "This drama photoplay
will show Mothers', Wives' and Sweethearts' reasons for opposing all wars, but between the lines everyone will perceive
the reason why American homes and American Womanhood
must be adequately protected by a strong army and strong
navy. Young man enlist now. Do your part in the world fight
against Prussian Militarism. Then there will be no such scenes
as this photoplay will portray. This is the time to show your
colors. You will be fighting in the greatest of all wars for the
greatest cause for which any people ever contended. Enlist
today."

And Hinton G. Clabaugh, division superintendent of the
Bureau of Investigation, from his Chicago office notified the
Department of Justice about the picture *War Brides*, on April
28, 1917. He said that an attorney in Watseka, Illinois, who
had seen that picture reported that it could not help influenc-
ing the public mind in a way likely to discourage enlistment,
and it was apt to develop new embarrassments for the government in an already difficult situation. The attorney's request
for censorship of this film was granted by many local censorships throughout the country.

"The serial supreme whose theme is preparedness" was the
advertising slogan of *Patria*. This film, with leading parts played
by Mrs. Vernon Castle, Milton Sills, and Warner Oland, was
released January 1, 1917, through International, a Hearst property. The plot was based upon Japanese government intrigues,
here and on Mexican soil, against America. This serial did not
end until the American forces, under the inspired leadership
of Patria herself, were victorious.

As Japan at the time was technically an ally of the British
and French, this film caused no little embarrassment to the
United States Government after the outbreak of war in 1917.
In testimony after that struggle, before the Senate Judiciary
Committee, Military Intelligence offered evidence to show that
German propaganda might have been at the bottom of the

motion picture plot to divert American attention away from the Allied cause by raising the old fear of the yellow peril.

One of the strongest anti-war films of 1916 was Thomas H. Ince's *Civilization*. This film was a plea against the savagery of war, and was heralded as "a sermon based on the uselessness of war, and emphasizes the fact that in nineteen centuries humanity has failed to accept the teachings of Jesus Christ." With this theme, *Civilization* ran afoul of the censorship laws —once more especially in Pennsylvania. Attorney General Brown of that state wrote identical letters to the producers of this film, as well as to those of *War Brides* and *Patria*. He stated that each film was discouraging enlistment, and that while the Pennsylvania State Board of Censors had the right to revoke the certificate entitling the exhibitors to show those films, he felt sure that the mere reference to the harmful effect of their exhibition would prompt the producers to discontinue them during the crisis. They were asked to acknowledge receipt of this letter, and indicate their intentions regarding it.

With the coming of the war, the *Exhibitor's Trade Review* spoke for the industry when it sounded a note of editorial caution under the subject "War Pictures and the War." This article warned the producers who were bringing out films on war themes to make sure that they were not apt in any way to create "an influence prejudicial to the government's prosecution of the present war." The editorial warned that "unless producers take the utmost care concerning the contents of their pictures in this regard, there is every indication that the federal authorities will suppress such pictures without hesitation."

It was pointed out that the United States had committed itself to war with Germany, the success of which depended upon the full support of the government by the people in all war measures. "Any influence which tends to rob the government, of that support, or to weaken it, could properly and would undoubtedly be put down. This is as true of any other medium of expression as it is of motion pictures. But it is particularly true of the motion picture."

A concrete illustration of a film that was objectionable was said to be one "which dealt minutely and at length with the horrors of war, depicting them on the screen in all their gruesomeness and hellishness," and thereby have a retarding effect upon recruiting. This editorial was undoubtedly influenced by a well defined report that the War. Department was preparing to maintain the closest scrutiny of all motion pictures that dealt with war themes, and would be ready to stop the exhibition of such pictures as were deemed harmful to the conduct of the war. The *Exhibitor's Trade Review* stated that judging from past history, a few daring men would try to squeeze through with pictures as lurid and ghastly as they could be made without actually "crossing the border." The trade journal's advice to such adventurous spirits was, "Don't!"

The warning of this publication was well taken, for with the various executive orders and laws establishing various kinds of censorship, the motion picture industry was watched to make sure that those adventurous spirits were held in check. The Committee on Public Information, through a special arrangement with the War Trade Board, held the whip hand over the export of motion pictures, and thereby was able to exercise a controlling influence on the attitude toward America, so far as the theater was concerned, in all the neutral nations of the world. These films, over which the Committee exercised control, in every case had to be consigned to the United States ambassador, minister, consul or consular agent at the port of destination, and he was instructed to censor the films, equipment or accessories before delivering them or permitting their delivery to the ultimate consignee.

Under the guidance of George Creel the CPI made full use of this prerogative, and soon had a steady stream of American propaganda films going abroad. The heads of American exporting companies met with the Committee's officers and agreed that no American films were to be exported unless a certain amount of American propaganda film was included in the order.

The producers of film for both domestic and foreign consumption were cautioned to observe four elements of censorship in the production of movies during the war to save the CPI and other governmental agencies from suppressing their output. Manufacturers were cautioned against making pictures which represented our life or our ideals falsely. Motion pictures which were derogatory to the United States, or to its Allies or friends, and motion pictures which might give aid and comfort to the enemy, would not be approved. All manufacturers were urged in their own interest in the making of new productions to avoid mob scenes and riots which might have been entirely innocent in themselves, but distorted and used adversely to the interest of the United States. All manufacturers were encouraged to include wherever possible in all new productions, industrial and educational film matter which would aid in conveying a favorable impression of the United States and its people. In all cases of film offered for export, the exporter had to secure from the Committee on Public Information a formal letter of approval, after obtaining a certificate of approval from the collector of customs.

The following are examples of how this censorship worked. A New York company advised a client in Mexico City, October 4, 1918, that a committee had been formed which had agreed not to permit any film to go to Mexico until that committee had decided the purchaser was pro-Ally. The firm said that the film El Automovil Rojo (The Red Automobile) ordered by the addressee was ready to be censored, and asked the latter whether he was willing to receive it under the conditions above stated, or whether he preferred to have his check returned to him. As for the film La Casa del Odio (The House of Hate), the New York firm advised the Mexican concern that it was forbidden to sell a copy of that picture for use in Mexico. This entire message was suspended by the censor; consequently there is no record as to the action of either the New York or the Mexico City firm.

And Courtney Ryley Cooper was informed by Creel that the picture with a Mexican theme that Cooper was planning could not be given blanket approval until it had been seen. Creel stated that the whole Mexican situation was very delicate, and was not being helped by the number of pictures that showed the Mexican as a lawless, ignorant, murderous savage. Cooper was informed that unless he could succeed absolutely in detaching Villa from the great body of the Mexican people, showing him as a mere tool of Germany, new emphasis upon the Columbus raid was bound to be hurtful. The chairman of the CPI closed with the following: "I do not want to tell you not to make the picture, but I can tell you that anything calculated to strain still further relations between the United States and Mexico is unwise and un-American. You will have to guide yourself accordingly."

Probably the most outstanding case of film censorship was that with respect to a picture entitled *The Spirit of '76*, produced by Robert Goldstein in 1917. Goldstein was said to have been an associate of David Wark Griffith in making *The Birth of a Nation*. Seeing the success of Griffith's film on the Civil War and Reconstruction, Goldstein had wished to write a scenario of similar type basing it upon the Revolutionary War period. *The Spirit of '76* was the result, and was said to have been completed before the United States entered the war.

Goldstein's picture was supposed to have been shown first in Chicago in the summer of 1917. After its initial exhibition in that city, it was discussed from every conceivable angle by historians, public welfare workers and government agents. It was then suppressed by Major Funkhouser, the Chicago film "dictator." An injunction against the major was the subject of a trial in the Superior Court of Cook County, Illinois, for two weeks. The court declared that the attack upon the film was invalid, and this caused much sharp discussion. One of the scenes in the film showed the famous Wyoming Valley Massacre wherein British redcoats were depicted slaughtering women and children and seizing young girls.

Goldstein claimed he had left Chicago with a deficit to himself of $35,000. Later in the year, he took the film to Los Angeles and arranged for its exhibition for two weeks, giving bond for $2,000 that its performance would not be interfered with by the police or federal authorities. Furthermore, he had shown the film, previously, to a select committee of Los Angeles citizens, who presided over the subsequent trial in that city, as well as other critics. It was said that some of that committee pointed out certain features which they considered objectionable, and they said they understood these would be eliminated before the film was exhibited. However, Goldstein was said to have restored to the reels the objectionable scenes after that censoring.

The first public showing was on Monday, November 26, 1917, at Clune's Auditorium, and it was advertised in the Los Angeles papers as "A Startling Historical Superdrama." The showing continued only three nights, because the film was confiscated on Thanksgiving night, November 29, 1917. It must have created a favorable impression on the movie critics of that city, for the Los Angeles Times on that day ran the following review of it: "Compressing the eight years' American Revolutionary War into two hours and a half naturally calls for swift and strenuous action. The makers of The Spirit of '76, showing at Clune's Auditorium this week, have accomplished the feat with both honor and adroitness."

In spite of this praise, Judge Bledsoe of the United States District Court (Los Angeles) invested District Attorney O'Connor with a writ and a search warrant for the seizure of The Spirit of '76. O'Connor, accompanied by the district attorney, and B. S. Mills of the American Protective League, took part in the seizure of this 12,000-foot film. There was no excitement attending the seizure, but the officers were delayed owing to the fact that the film of six double reels had to be rewound and carefully packed before being taken to the office of the United States Marshal, where they were locked in a safe.

Goldstein made a motion for the return of the film before the District Court, but Judge Bledsoe in the celebrated case, United States v. Motion Picture Film The Spirit of '76, denied the motion. In the decision of the court, it mentioned in particular the Wyoming Valley Massacre as an objectionable scene. Judge Bledsoe held that it was no time, whatever might have been the excuse, for the exploitation of those things that might have had the tendency or effect of sowing dissension among our people, and of creating animosity or want of confidence between us and our Allies, because "so to do weakens our efforts, weakens the chance of our success, impairs our solidarity, and renders less useful the lives we are giving, to the end that this war may soon be over and peace may soon become a thing substantial and permanent with us."

The case was appealed to the United States Circuit Court of Appeals, 9th Circuit, and the decision was handed down on May 26, 1919, in the form of a judgment affirming the finding of the lower court.

Circuit Judge Hunt, speaking for the court, said in part that the question of the truth or falseness of the act done by the person who, when the state of war existed, attempted to cause disloyalty, was not the essence of the inquiry. Hunt believed that it was clear that an attempt to create disloyalty might be made by showing a picture to the public, as well as by uttering a speech, or publishing a writing. The picture might have been a truthful representation of an historical fact, and yet the nature of it, the circumstances surrounding its exhibition, the time, the occasions when the public exhibitions were held, might well have tended to show whether the picture would naturally, in the light of events, have been calculated to foment disloyalty or insubordination among the naval or military forces. As a result of these court actions the motion picture was forced into bankruptcy, and Goldstein was sentenced to ten years in the penitentiary.

This case has been examined at length here because it illustrates the ease with which refractory motion picture producers could have been dealt with by the courts had they failed to cooperate fully with the government in its war aims. Few, however, cared to run the risk that Goldstein took when the unexpurgated version of *The Spirit of '76* was run in spite of the Los Angeles censors.

Even the famous prototype of the Goldstein film, the picture, *The Birth of a Nation*, produced by David Wark Griffith in 1915, came in for criticism during the war years, because it was held that the film tended to divide the nation. As early as April 1917, the Mayor of Youngstown, Ohio, issued an order prohibiting *The Birth of a Nation* from being shown in that city, fearing it would cause race prejudice, an element so much feared internally in time of war.

On August 12, 1918, Dr. Frederick P. Keppel, the Third Assistant Secretary of War, wrote Mr. Creel asking: "Are the relations of the Committee on Public Information to the moving picture industry of such nature that the Committee could affect the withdrawal of *The Birth of a Nation*? At the present time, it does seem to be unfortunate to play up this film." Keppel enclosed a clipping from the *Charleston* (S.C.) *Messenger*, which was an irate editorial entitled "*The Birth of a Nation*."

The editorial stated that the North, the South, and the Negro had all become united in a common struggle for democracy. For that reason, such a bitter film should not be allowed to keep open the wounds of the Civil War.

Another film, *The Curse of Iku*, is an excellent example of film censorship without suppression. This picture was six reels in length and was released on March 1, 1918, only to run afoul of many censorship boards and government officials. It was produced by the Essanay Film Company, a leading concern of the time.

The plot was laid in Japan in the 1850's when a shipwrecked American was washed ashore and was cared for by a kind-hearted Japanese named Yori. This kind act was against the law of the land. Yori is suspected of this deed by Iku, a grasping oriental who sent his sister to investigate the situation. The sister fell in love with the American, and the enraged Iku married her to a Dutch sailor. From here the plot becomes quite involved, but the ending is satisfactory, for the hero and heroine board a United States cruiser headed for home with the

American flag flying, while the theater organist, or orchestra thundered out the tune of "The Star-Spangled Banner."

This picture was a success and played to crowded houses. One critic of the day said of the film that the story was an unpleasant one and many of the scenes were anything but pleasing to watch. But on the other hand, according to the critic, the acting was splendid, the backgrounds were beautiful, the many scenes of the Japanese customs of fifty years previous were exceedingly interesting, although they were barbaric, and the oriental atmosphere was well carried out. "It is a strong feature and fascinates with its unusual plot while it makes one shudder in many parts."

The picture also made many officials shudder. The State Council of Defense for California wrote a letter to Joseph Tumulty, in March 1918, protesting against *The Curse of Iku* as stirring up racial prejudice in California. The Japanese consul-general for that state was said to have protested in vain over the picture four months earlier. This film was particularly harmful in that it depicted the people of Nippon as unmoral, without business integrity, and especially made capital of the "spy fever" and racial friction which existed so largely in California.

This letter to Tumulty was referred to the CPI, and a print of the picture was ordered submitted to Washington for proper investigation. The print was reviewed on April 29, 1918, by Mr. Hecht of the Division of Motion Pictures of the CPI, Frank P. Lockhart of the Division of Far Eastern Affairs of the State Department, and Captain Sheppard of the War Department. This film was disapproved by all three government officials, and in a letter to Creel, May 8, 1918, Major General Frank McIntyre, Chief Military Censor, said that whether this film was deliberate or unconscious enemy propaganda, it was destructive and wholly vicious. Its sole motif was race hatred, and any other emotional appeal which it may have possessed was subsidiary to that of race hatred. The General thought there was no excuse for its continued existence, "either in its present form or altered at the whim of its producer, and I hope that it may be unconditionally and immediately suppressed and destroyed."

On May 31, 1918, K. K. Kawakami of San Francisco, a special correspondent of Japanese papers, wrote the Division of Motion Pictures of the CPI calling its attention to this film. He stated that when it was shown in San Francisco last summer, at about the time of Viscount Ishii's arrival as a special envoy, there was a strong objection raised by both Japanese and Americans against its public display. As the result of this objection, it was understood that the firm withdrew the photoplay, but, complained the correspondent, the film was being shown again in California and perhaps in other states also.

Creel felt it would be to the best interests of all concerned if the producer, the Essanay Film Company, could be induced to withdraw the film of its own accord and make the desired changes. In the summer of 1918, the Essanay Film Company called in all prints of the offending picture, made all the characters Malays, removed the mob scenes, and changed the title to An Eye for an Eye. Creel was able to write that film company, with some satisfaction, in July 1918: "As the picture stands now, it is no more than a powerful and dramatic representation of individual loves and hates that cannot, in my opinion, be regarded in any degree as the indictment of a nation or slander of a people." Creel seemed to be satisfied with the corrections made in this "mischievous photo-play," and the matter was dropped. However, it is worth noting that the unexpurgated version ran at least three months before it was censored.

Another instance of film censorship was afforded by the 1918 Fox picture The Caillaux Case. This cinema was based upon the life of the French statesman and the celebrated murder trial of his wife and coming trial of Caillaux himself for "plotting against the security of the state abroad." In the April 27, 1918, issue of the Moving Picture World was announced the impending release of the film The Caillaux Case. Across the two-page advertisement was a picture of a serpent bearing the head of the Kaiser, and having four coils, containing pictures of Joseph Caillaux, Mme. Caillaux, Bolo Pasha "secret servant of the Kaiser in America," and Gaston Colmette, the editor of *Le Figaro* slain by Mme. Caillaux.

This immediately caught the eye of the French High Commission stationed in Washington. The Marquis de Polignac wrote Creel protesting such a film and stating: "The film in question has been made in America and it would be advisable to stop its publication which can only hurt seriously France's reputation in the United States." Creel thereupon called for a print of the film for review before it was released to the theaters. The print was sent by the film company with a request for an early censorship as the picture was set for immediate release.

A reviewing board composed of Captain Sheppard, a representative of the French High Commission, and others attended an exhibition of the film on the afternoon of May 1, 1918. The representatives of the State and War Departments passed favorably on the picture, provided it met with the approval of the French High Commission. The latter proved unequivocally opposed to the release of the film, and made representations to the Department of State concerning it. M. Aubert of the High Commission called at the Department and stated that he was disturbed to see newspaper announcements that the film was being placed on the market. Writing George Creel about the subject, William Phillips, Assistant Secretary of State, said that Aubert noticed the production of the picture at that time was claimed to be both timely and valuable from a historical point of view. The Frenchman did not agree that it was timely, owing to the general situation, and could not see how the film could have any historical value in telling the real story of the Caillaux case when the actual trial of that person had not taken place.

Creel wrote the Fox Film Company and explained the situation. That company replied that it would postpone the release date, and make alterations, but protested that $100,000 had gone into the production of the film, which Fox could not afford to lose. A conference of film officials with Creel took place July 24, and the work of editing the film from beginning to end occupied many weeks. The extent to which the revised film was affected may be inferred from a letter of Philip H. Patchin of the State Department to Creel September 5, 1918, as reproduced by Mock and Larson in *Words That Won the War*. Patchin observed, "Now that they have it finished I find myself wondering what they are going to do with it. The only good stuff was objectionable and I am afraid there is not much left."

Creel wrote to Fox, September 19, 1918, and urged them to confer with him in advance when planning a picture dealing with current international problems. In that way, the chairman of the CPI observed, Fox could learn wherein any objection to the proposed film would lie, and in that way the company could save money and be spared much annoyance. At the same time the interests of the government would be tremendously advanced.

The Caillaux Case was finally released on October 15, 1918. The review of it which appeared in *The Exhibitor's Trade Review* stated that the film would attract the public because it was a visualization of one of the scandals with which the citizenry had become acquainted through the newspapers. The *Review* observed that the characters in the picture were selected because of the resemblance to the characters in the real affair, and this would serve to heighten the morbid curiosity of a public always on the lookout for sensations. The publication revealed the effect of censorship upon the film when it said that the feature had been interestingly conceived, but the first half of the picture showed the ill effects of cutting.

Even after the film had been radically toned down by censorship, the French High Commission was dissatisfied with it. Creel summed up this feeling when he wrote a final letter on the subject to the Fox Film Company, October 17, 1918, stating in part: "Quite frankly this has caused us more embarrassment than any other one thing. The French Government is still bitter and insists that we should have ordered the suppression of the film entirely."

The Caillaux Case furnished an example of the portrayal of a delicate subject in wartime. In common with *The Spirit of '76* and *The Curse of Iku*, it aroused ill will against one of the Allies by causing loss of prestige on the part of one of our comrades-in-arms. Censorship operated in each case, although by different methods.

Creel, through his chairmanship of the Committee on Public Information, and membership on the Censorship Board, as well as through having close relations with other governmental establishments, had opportunity to take steps leading to the suppression of any expression, written or pictured, which hindered the war effort. It was to his credit, and to the credit of his associates, that these powers were rarely invoked. Through direct contacts with the leading men of the motion picture industry, cooperation of the film executives was obtained, and the cinema producers were kept in line with the government's war aims.

On their part, the motion picture producers endeavored to use the opportunities afforded by the World War as a means of combating censorship in general. For example, an editorial of May 11, 1918, in the *Exhibitor's Trade Review* demanded a hands-off policy with respect to war pictures. That publication considered those films a part of the fighting forces of the United States. They were units in the Army that was fighting the German peace offensives—more fatal than their military offensives and a hundred times more ingratiating. The *Review* asked the censors who gave them the authority to say what weapons the United States should use, or refrain from using, to combat her enemies. It asked by what right of knowledge, experience, or law the censors presumed to dictate what the United States should tell her citizens concerning her enemies. This periodical warned "suppress any part of any one of these pictured messages and—whether you admit it or not—you are playing the game of Germany as loyally as if you were a paid hireling of the Wilhelmstrasse."

In another instance, also, a censor was rebuked for his zeal. In Chicago Major Funkhouser ordered elimination of scenes from *Hearts of the World* indicting the German officer as an assailant of women. The Major also attempted to prohibit *The Spy*, an alleged exposé of the German spy system, from being shown in Chicago. Such acts as these, and others, by the Pennsylvania State Board of Censors, angered the Hollywood producers and similar authorities. In these cases, charges of "pro-Germanism" were made against each other by the opposing factions.

An editorial battle was kept up, and when Major Funkhouser ordered cuts in the film version of Ambassador Gerard's narrative, *My Four Years in Germany*, the situation reached a climax. Shortly thereafter the Major was deposed and the motion picture industry hailed that action as a victory against the forces of censorship.

The Chicago censor's attitude toward the translation into pictures of Gerard's book was similar to that of President Wilson. To Henry Morgenthau, former American Ambassador to Turkey, the President expressed his distress at the picturization of *My Four Years in Germany*. Evidently the Chief Executive thought enough anti-German sentiment had been aroused, and additional stimuli for that purpose were not needed.

Thus, censorship of motion pictures during the first World War was both by national and local authority. Films would be shown in one city as issued, while the same pictures would be banned in another. This situation finds a parallel today if one examines the case history of such recent films as *The Ramparts We Watch* (censored in Pennsylvania), and *Hitler, the Beast of Berlin*, which was banned entirely in many cities and towns.

But the censorship of motion pictures in World War I was largely a patchwork in which the greatest amount of continued and uniform censoring and suppressing occurred with respect to films entering or leaving the United States. The shortness of the struggle so far as the United States was concerned, and the uniform success of our armed forces, served to prevent an ironclad censorship of the American cinema in World War I

With the passage of more than two decades since that struggle, the motion picture industry has reached maturity and for that reason must be considered whenever censorship becomes necessary. According to some individuals, because of the great audiences that view the pictures, the cinema's power to mold public opinion must be directed in the proper channels in time of national emergency. Other persons believe this is not needed because the rôle of the motion picture is one of entertainment, not propaganda. And some people feel that with the unending and rapid succession of films of all varieties, that very stream may obliterate from the mind of the audience all propaganda efforts, and thus make censorship unnecessary.

"No More Soap-Boxes"

ONE OF THE CHIEF TASKS OF OUR FEDERAL AUTHORITIES DURING World War I was to make certain that eloquence did not set fire to reason. In an earlier chapter we have seen how the individual, the mob, and the various states proceeded against persons who uttered sentiments that were not entirely patriotic. There yet remains the story of the First Amendment in its relationship to freedom of speech, as conceived by federal officials and federal judges during World War I. Whether those authorities made the suspected speaker aware of the Espionage and Sedition Acts depended upon the past history of the speaker, his audience, and the occasion upon which the statements were made. Official action in those instances varied from mild reprimands or requests that certain utterances cease, to penitentiary sentences of twenty or thirty years.

For a speaker who wished to keep out of jail, time and circumstance had to be considered carefully. James Harvey Robinson, the historian, explained this situation in the *Atlantic Monthly* for December 1917. He said that one could always criticize and attack the policy of all government officials. They could safely be denounced as knaves, fools and traitors. According to Robinson, one could even pick flaws in the Constitution, and question the expediency of the state itself—"but one would better not be associating with supposed anarchists when so doing."

And sponsors of speaking engagements exercised precautions in their selections. To safeguard an anticipated audience, the secretary of the Y.M.C.A. of Elkins, West Virginia, wrote Creel to inquire about the patriotism of Mark Sullivan, then editor of *Collier's*. The secretary had heard that Mr. Sullivan was misleading the people and the Elkins' Lyceum Course

Committee was not inclined to secure any talent that would in any way influence the public mind contrary to patriotism, and had no desire "that our people be misled." The representative of the Lyceum Committee asked Creel to inform him at once "as we will be compelled to drop Mr. Sullivan if this be true and most certainly if we fail to secure your recommendation of him." Creel assured the secretary that Mr. Sullivan's purpose was sincere and that he, Creel, would regret any cancellation of Sullivan's lecture.

Other speakers, however, did not receive Creel's sanction. For instance, he wrote Professor Robert M. McElroy, on leave from Princeton and serving with the National Security League, that the Committee on Public Information had been hearing some very disturbing reports about the speeches that were being made by Dr. N. D. Hillis. In every community, according to Creel, Hillis seemed to arouse bitterness and some speeches were "somewhat reckless as to facts." McElroy was requested to write Creel confidentially, and let the latter know if anything could be done. In spite of this correspondence, Dr. Hillis continued to make his speeches.

Addresses of another speaker disturbed the CPI. Professor William G. Ward of Boston University, according to reports from Kansas, put continual emphasis upon the class struggle, and his speeches were responsible for "a good deal of bitterness." Creel urged a member of the Council of National Defense, to use her best endeavors "to have Professor Ward change his tone in the interest of unity." The files of the Committee on Public Information reveal no additional complaints about Professor Ward.

Speeches before restricted audiences occasionally received official consideration. Such an address was delivered at a meeting of the Chemical Alliance, Inc., at the Biltmore Hotel, New York, June 7, 1918, by Horace Brunker, a member of the War Industries Board. He stated that U-boat sinkings during the preceding three months had been three times the total shipping construction; that American troops sent over were barely sufficient to replace the Allied wastage; that those who were on the inside and in a position to know believed the chances at least even that the Channel ports would be lost, Paris captured, and the war, at least for the time being, lost.

Creel forwarded this information to Bernard Baruch, Head of the War Industries Board, and observed "If the statements are true, I think that it might be well to ask for a less pessimistic tone from your speakers."

Edwin Newdick, in charge of the War Industries Board's publicity, explained what had happened. Newdick wrote Creel that the latter's informant had quoted correctly and that the statements made by the speaker were true, and finally, that it came to a question of whether it was warrantable before the audience to speak in the tone which Brunker used. The fact was, according to the publicity director, the Chemical Division of the War Industries Board had been encountering serious opposition in establishing the needed measure of government control over chemical supplies essential to the prosecution of the war. Newdick added "It was important for the progress of their work that the group Mr. Bunker was addressing should be jarred out of its old individualistic, competitive, profit-seeking attitude into a realization of the seriousness of war which demands entire submergence of private and personal considerations."

Mr. Newdick reported that since the meeting a much better response to the call for cooperation to meet war needs had been received from the group at which it was aimed. Also, he stated that Mr. Brunker had been told that "perhaps he went a bit too far in his attempt to bang home a realization of the seriousness of the situation."

Continued exaggeration on the part of a speaker often led to governmental action. Arthur Guy Empey, author of *Over the Top*, should have realized that fact after he had made a speech in New York, April 26, 1918, in which he said that 2,000 mangled American soldiers were in the hospitals of New York. The district attorney was notified and was informed that there were fewer than 300 wounded American soldiers in the entire United States. Creel suggested to the district attorney that such reckless statements should be checked. However, Empey continued speaking, and in September his recruiting commission was revoked. Marlen E. Pew of the CPI Division of News, and later editor of *Editor and Publisher*, informed Creel that this action was taken because Empey was "Too fresh. . . . Persisted in saying that we'd show the French and British how, etc. But the policy has been to say nothing." Officially, Empey's commission was revoked because of the discontinuance of recruiting.

Outright denial of the privilege of speaking was sometimes practised during the World War. One instance of this occurred when the American Protective League demanded that Frank J. Klingberg, suspected of German activities, cancel a lecture scheduled for May 23, 1918, at one of the California universities. The League was under the impression that Klingberg was about to propose a "peace" of some kind, when in reality the address was to have been concerned with the policy that would be adopted by the Allied governments in making the settlement with Germany after that nation had been defeated.

While Klingberg was prevented from delivering his lecture, Senator LaFollette and Theodore Roosevelt were making public statements about the war and the administration that were questioned by patriotic citizens. The former, according to the *Literary Digest*, stated that it was a strange doctrine "that the mass of the people who pay in money, misery, and blood all the costs of this war, out of which a favorite few profit so largely, may not freely and publicly discuss terms of peace." For these and similar sentiments, it was proposed by many that LaFollette at least be expelled from the Senate.

And the *Nation*, November 9, 1918, contained an article "Why is Roosevelt Unjailed?" That periodical asked what would have happened if a humble citizen of the United States had attracted a crowd on the street and then denounced President Wilson by saying among other similar statements "that in the cloak rooms of Congress it is a bitter jest to speak of the President thus: 'Here's to our Czar, last in war, first toward peace, long may he waver.'" The *Nation* believed that if any soap-box orator had used those words of Mr. Roosevelt he would have been given twenty years in jail for "interfering with the draft."

Other speakers were not so fortunate, however, as Roosevelt and LaFollette. Many persons were the objects of federal investigations, if not of more stringent acts of coercion, because of their public or private utterances. At a meeting of the socialist conference of the People's Council in New York in May 1918, government stenographers took down reports of all speeches that were delivered. Among the persons whose remarks were examined was Isaac McBride who had been private secretary to the late Senator Lane of Oregon. Mr. McBride, at present a member of the staff of The National Archives, recalls that although no action was taken against the speakers, the knowledge of the fact that federal officials were present did not encourage over-indulgence in freedom of speech.

Irving Cooke, a member of the Paterson, New Jersey, police force for twenty years, did not escape so lightly for his utterances. While in an argument in a saloon, Cooke was said to have stated that President Wilson was fooling the people, and that American soldiers in Europe were only boys. Cooke was arrested by federal officers, and charged with sedition.

At the same time that Cooke was receiving attention, several persons were punished for shouting their approval of the enemy. One of these individuals was Harry Worbrt, an Austrian whom a police judge of Newark, New Jersey, sentenced to jail for ten days for saying "To hell with the United States." The statement of the police judge at the time of sentencing Worbrt was that the latter should remember that "The best thing to do with men of your kind is to string you up to the nearest electric pole."

Had Worbrt been in the Army, his punishment might have been much more severe. For example, Philip H. Grossner, a private at Fort Banks, on June 6, 1918, was sentenced to thirty years' imprisonment. He had been found guilty by court-martial of making disloyal remarks and encouraging disloyalty among soldiers. Army officials were said to have stated that Grossner had posed as a conscientious objector.

And other sins were noticed as quickly as disloyal utterances. Dr. Carl Muck, conductor of the Boston Symphony Orchestra, was made aware of that fact. In 1915, he had been interviewed by *The Craftsman* on the subject "The Music of Democracy." Muck expressed the opinion that America would have for its latter-day music the great idea of democracy, and of freedom for all the people. But, two years later the music of democracy had taken on new meaning for Dr. Muck. In November 1917, at a concert of the Boston Symphony Orchestra in Providence, Rhode Island, the conductor ignored the joint request of nine women's clubs that the orchestra play "The Star-Spangled Banner" either before or after the program. The incident became front-page news and a subject for editorials. One rendition of "The Star-Spangled Banner" was not too much to expect of a symphony orchestra, although as *The Independent* observed, "one cannot but feel that the playing of our national anthem at *every* concert throughout the season would be a little trying." But for a Prussian or Swiss director to refuse, caused that individual to acquire new prominence. When Theodore Roosevelt heard about Dr. Muck's action the former was said to have declared that any man who refused to play the national anthem "in this time of national crisis should be forced to pack up and return to the country he came from."

This incident marked the beginning of the conductor's troubles. By March 26, 1918, Dr. Muck had been placed in jail on the ground that his presence at large was a danger to the peace and safety of the country. He was arrested and held on a Presidential warrant after the Department of Justice had made an extensive investigation "of his record of pro-German sympathies and utterances." And May 1918 saw the former conductor of the Boston Symphony Orchestra in an internment camp at Fort Oglethorpe, Georgia. It was claimed that before we entered the war Dr. Muck had maintained close relations with Count von Bernstorff, and that he had many meetings with the German Ambassador to the United States.

With regard to those meetings, a contributor to *Musical America* was quoted thus: "As von Bernstorff had no overpowering interest in music, such conferences were not regarded as necessary for purely artistic reasons."

In June 1919, although Dr. Muck was still in the internment camp, plans were being considered for his deportation. The next item about the former conductor of the Boston Symphony Orchestra appeared in March 1921. From the safe distance of The Hague, Muck was able to relate his woes in the United States. He denied disloyal actions in America and was said to have stated "I was accused of espionage because I conducted German music and naturally associated with my German compatriots."

Other compatriots of Muck received far more severe treatment from American judges. For example, according to federal records, in and about Covington, Kentucky, there was a community of Germans which was believed to be disloyal, and steps were taken to ascertain whether this supposition was correct. In the Latonia district of Covington, Charles B. Schoberg had a cobbler's shop. He had been born in Germany more than sixty years before the World War, and had been in the United States since he was a child. From 1872 to 1914, except for four years when he had been out of the state, he had been continuously connected with the Covington city government, and had held positions from policeman to magistrate. He was a leader among his associates, and his shop was used by them for an informal meeting place, for gossip and discussion.

When the war came, the Covington Citizens' Protective League wanted to know "what was going on in this shop." The League employed a detective agency which, in May 1918, found means to install a dictograph in the room where the discussions were held. Wires connected that instrument to a listening post in a nearby building. Employees of the agency took turns listening, and wrote what they heard from the time the shop opened until it closed. This listening continued from May until July, when the testimony contained in the notes was presented to the grand jury, and Schoberg and his friends were indicted.

These indictments all rested upon the Sedition Act of May 16, 1918, which Schoberg and his associates were alleged to have violated by their conversation. Their utterances included opinions to the effect that the Germans in their spring campaign of 1918 were "going through like a streak." The men ridiculed the possibility of the United States taking an effective part in the war. Concerning German sabotage in this country, they said that since the Germans had the name of blowing up munition plants, "they might as well have the game."

To make certain that the jury understood the state of mind of the accused, and for fear that it had been unable to determine that state from six weeks of notes covering every hour that the listening post was in action, Judge Andrew M. J. Cochran allowed to be introduced into the evidence other statements by Schoberg that he had made before May 16, 1918. The jury learned that one of the defendant's associates had been a subscriber to *The Fatherland* and to the *New-Yorker Staats-Zeitung*, and a reader of *The Bull*, three publications the judge considered pro-German. Later, the appellate judge was quoted as having said "if this were true, it would, in connection with his subscription to the other papers, tend to corroborate the charge that he opposed the cause of the United States and supported that of Germany."

In the trial, one important point raised was whether "private opinions privately expressed" even if denunciatory of the United States were permissible under the constitutional provision guaranteeing the right of free speech. But, in his charge to the jury, Judge Cochran declared that the right of free speech did not enter into the case. According to him, "No man has a right to be disloyal or express disloyalty. There is no question of making a man a hypocrite by compulsory silence. If his sentiments are disloyal, his place is not here."

The judge stated to the jury, however, that the Espionage Act, as amended in May 1918, did not mean that one should not take sides against the government as to some particular measure. It was not directed against criticism, "at least all criticism. For instance, no one doubts Col. Roosevelt's loyalty, and yet he is very severe in his criticisms of things that have been done and that have not been done. That is freedom of speech, and nobody undertakes to limit or question his right to do that."

The jury did not require much time to reach a verdict. In twenty-five minutes it returned a verdict of guilty on each of the twenty-four counts with which Schoberg had been charged. The rapidity with which the verdict was reached has two possible explanations. The evidence against Schoberg was so conclusive that there was no doubt about his guilt. Or it might be explained by an observation about the wartime juries made by Judge Amidon, United States District Judge of the District of North Dakota, and later a member of the American Civil Liberties Union, that jurymen believed that in these cases the only verdict which could show their own loyalty was a verdict of guilty.

If a person publicly made any disparaging remarks about the United States or its comrades-in-arms, and a soldier happened to be within hearing distance, the speaker might have faced charges of violating the Espionage Act. Orville C. Enfield, socialist candidate for Congress in the Seventh Congressional District of Oklahoma, on June 6, 1918, was found guilty of conspiracy to obstruct the Selective Service Act. For his efforts, speeches, and for applauding an address against the government, Enfield was sentenced to twenty years in the federal prison at Leavenworth. An editorial in the Daily Oklahoman stated that his conviction had been fairly arrived at, and that he had suffered no injustice. Enfield thought otherwise, since he claimed no originality either as to his views or his phraseology, declaring that he quoted from speeches made by Congressmen.

The judge of the Circuit Court of Appeals, Eighth Circuit, did not agree with the editorial or with the earlier verdict. On October 20, 1919, the judgment of conviction was reversed, and the case remanded to the lower court for a new trial.

In Iowa, a deserter from the British Army felt the effect of the Espionage Act. Daniel H. Wallace, in July 1917, when the administration of the draft act was beginning, delivered a sensational speech "containing lurid pictures of the horrors of war." He was guilty of violating the Espionage Act and was sentenced to prison, where he died.

During the same month that Wallace was convicted, Mrs. Kate Richards O'Hare, "a professional socialist lecturer," delivered an address at Bowman, North Dakota, that brought her a sentence of five years in the penitentiary. Before a crowd of 125 persons she was said to have stated in substance that any person who enlisted in the Army of the United States for service in France would be used for fertilizer, and that was all he was good for. Also, that the women of this country were nothing more or less than brood sows to raise children to get into the Army and be made into fertilizer. She was charged with making these statements with the intention of wilfully obstructing the enlistment service of the United States, to the injury of the service of this nation. Judge Martin J. Wade followed Mrs. O'Hare's appeal to the court with the observation that this was a government of majorities, and that, "the conceited minority must give way to the will of the majority or be crushed by the majestic power which is America. They must yield that patriotism which means obedience to the established law, which is the people, or they must be crushed as traitors."

And in Sterling, Colorado, W. B. Tanner was said to have tried to cause disloyalty, insubordination, mutiny, and refusal of duty in the military and naval forces of the United States. According to the indictment his attempt consisted of statements to the effect that there was no security behind the Liberty Bonds; that the conservation of food was "all bosh"; and that "As soon as the capitalists on Wall Street have all the money they want this war will be over in twenty-four hours."

Similar utterances led to the indictment of H. E. Kirchner at Parkersburg, West Virginia, January 14, 1918. He was charged with making statements to persons, some of whom were subject to the call to service, that the United States government in the prosecution of the war was corrupt; that it was controlled by the moneyed interests; and that the people of this country could never meet the expense of the war.

But the Espionage Act did not apply solely to persons whose speeches obstructed recruiting of the forces of the United States. In the Western Judicial District of Washington, W. E. Mead, an I.W.W. organizer, was convicted of violating that act when his remarks were directed against participation of Canadians or Americans in the service of the British Army. By an act of May 7, 1917, England and Canada had been authorized to open recruiting offices in the various cities of the United States.

Mead, however, was aboard a ship bound from San Francisco to Seattle when his remarks violated the Espionage Act. On board that vessel were several recruits for the Canadian Expeditionary Forces to whom Mead was said to have stated that he could give a thousand reasons why they should not fight. He observed that the slaughter was a capitalistic war, started by England, because she was afraid of Germany "corraling commerce." In addition, Mead held that President Wilson was "in the same swim" with the British in backing up the capitalists. In making and conveying "the said false reports and statements" he was charged with doing so with the intent to interfere with the success of our armed forces. And the judge believed that Mead well knew that his statements were false and untrue.

To many judges, the term "military or naval forces" included more than soldiers and sailors. According to Acting District Judge William D. Evans, of the Western District of Wisconsin, in a republican form of government like ours, with the war conducted as it was in 1917-1918, the forces that actually fought on the battlefield and the forces that produced the food, arms, and munitions at home were so interdependent that it was impossible to say that one belonged to the military forces and the other did not.

Judge Evans voiced these opinions at the time he overruled a demurrer to the indictment of Louis B. Nagler. The latter had been indicted under the Espionage Act for his utterances in Madison when a "drive was on" for the Red Cross and the Y.M.C.A. The indictment charged Nagler with having said he was through contributing to those private grafts, and that not over 10 or 15 per cent of the money collected went to the soldiers or was used for the purpose for which it was collected. The judge held that the term "military or naval forces of the United States" could not fairly be defined so as to exclude the Red Cross or the Y.M.C.A. Thus, by speaking "falsely and with bad intent" concerning them, a violation of the Espionage Act had occurred.

In Oklahoma the Reverend William Madison Hicks discovered that he could not speak of graft in connection with our war effort. In the speech that caused his indictment and conviction, the president of the World Peace League was said to have stated that he represented six generations of Americans, and that he was not going to allow any cheap set of tools and thieves and robbers to bluff him out of anything he wanted to say. Continuing, he was reported as having said that the war was started by a bunch of low grafters; by thieves; by gamblers; by shippers; by a band of thugs, boat builders, trade manipulators; and that there was "not one decent one in the whole smear." Since his listeners included males between the ages of eighteen and forty-five, and subject to military service, Hicks was tried for violating that portion of the Espionage Act which dealt with obstructing the recruiting or enlistment service and related offenses.

At this trial, as in many others, additional evidence was introduced to help the jury determine the credibility of the defendant's testimony. The evidence thus introduced showed that Hicks had been convicted of felonies in Illinois and Kansas and had been confined to the state penitentiary in the former place. The judge instructed the jury that it might consider the testimony relating to his previous crimes and incarceration "in reaching a conclusion whether or not you believe the defendant has told the truth upon the witness stand."

For threatening his local draft board because it did not re-classify him as he had demanded, Troy Deason was convicted of violating the Espionage Act in the Western Judicial District of Texas. Judge Duval West of the Circuit Court of Appeals, Fifth Circuit, held that the lower court had correctly charged the jury that the threats alone, even without direct proof of their success in preventing the board from doing its duty, might have showed to a jury a sufficient obstruction of the re-cruiting or enlistment to have done it injury and thus to have injured the United States. Judge West added that the denials of all the members of the board that they were dissuaded by the spoken threats from doing their duty were not conclusive of that issue, and thus Deason was guilty of violating the law.

Upon at least one occasion, without being informed of what the incriminating reports were, men were convicted of making false reports and false statements with the intent of interfering with the success of our forces. Leonard Foster and his fellow workers were civilian employees for a contractor doing work at Camp Lewis, Washington. For their statements while in the cantonment they were brought before Judge Edward E. Cush-man of the Western District of Washington. The trial was held in Tacoma. Indicted on six counts for the purposes stated above, the jury found Foster and his companions guilty as charged.

But Judge William B. Gilbert of the Circuit Court of Ap-peals, Ninth Circuit, reached a different decision when the case was brought to him. He held that the men had "the con-stitutional right to be informed of the nature and cause of the accusation against them." He stated that the charge was as bare of information as to the nature of their offense as would have been an indictment charging that at a designated time and place they "committed larceny." Gilbert reversed the judgment of the lower court, and remanded the case with in-structions to sustain a demurrer to the indictment.

At Kimball, South Dakota, July 1, 1917, John H. Wolf made remarks that brought about his conviction. Wolf, a mer-chant, discussed the war with three of his acquaintances. In the course of the discussion, Wolf told one of his friends that he should be careful about what he said as his friend might be under the control of the Kaiser before the war was over. Wolf then was said to have remarked that it was an unjust war on the part of the United States; that it was unjust on the part of the United States government to send the boys across the ocean to fight; and that he, Wolf, had advised his own sons not to enlist until they were drafted. The defendant also stated that Germany's attitude in her unrestricted warfare was perfectly proper, both before and after the entrance of the United States into the war.

In that case, Judge James D. Elliott's charge to the jury is worth noticing. He stated that the jury had a right to take into consideration the general purpose and feeling on the part of the great majority of the American people. The judge held that that purpose and feeling was that the war had to be won and that no other result would be tolerated. Interference in any way with enlistment would work against that result. And on that point Elliott stated that it was not necessary, and not practical, that the government should show that Wolf's utterances had caused some particular person not to enlist.

Six months after the Armistice, this case was reversed. In reversing the previous verdict, Circuit Judge Kimbrough Stone pointed out that the defendant had made the incriminating remarks to persons of whom there was no allegation that they were within the enlistment ages. Also, they had been uttered during a conversation between Wolf on one side and three acquaintances on the other. Of that situation Judge Stone said "It is very evident that the sole result which occurred, or really was to be expected, was that each of the four remained firm in his own conviction." Stone observed "It is natural, in time of war, when patriotic sentiment is high, that it is particularly difficult to secure a fair trial for men accused of crimes connected with the war."

After the fighting ceased, other members of the bench were aware of the danger there had been to free speech. For example, at Greenville, South Carolina, J. K. Hall had been convicted of having made false reports and statements that violated the Espionage and Sedition Acts, and had threatened to inflict bodily harm upon the President of the United States. The threats, however, were wholly immaterial to the issues being tried. On February 6, 1919, this conviction was reversed by Judge Jeter C. Pritchard, Circuit Court of Appeals, Fourth District, because the introduction of the evidence of Hall's threats against the President tended to create a false impression upon the minds of the jury. Pritchard agreed with a colleague in a similar case who said that "In a time like this, when patriotism is at a high pitch and many people have to a certain extent lost their mental poise, courts and jurors should be extremely cautious when required to pass upon the rights of an individual charged with an offense affecting the welfare of the government."

Another case somewhat like that of Wolf in South Dakota, in that conviction of violating the Espionage and Sedition Acts for speech in private conversation was involved, was that of August Sandberg, consulting metallurgist of the Phelps-Dodge Corporation. He was convicted in Arizona of the charge of attempting to interfere with the success of the military and naval forces of the United States when he stated to a companion that our entry into the war was brought about by the Wall Street interests in order to protect our foreign loans to the Allies. Upon another occasion the defendant was said to have tried to bring about insubordination by saying that President Wilson was a weak character to allow England to dictate its policy, "and then the President coming out and making speeches to back up the British policies." In each instance, according to the Circuit Judge who reversed the conviction, there was a total lack of any showing in the evidence of any incriminating act on Sandberg's part other than the statements made by him to the persons named in the indictments, "in each instance in the course of private conversation and never in the presence of a third party."

On May 19, 1919, when the Judge of the Circuit Court of Appeals reversed the judgment of the District Court, he said of Sandberg's statements that they were mere expressions of opinion, and did not come within the provisions of the act upon which the indictment was based.

In another case the defendant's background, together with the occasion of his utterances, contributed to the acquittal of Theodore B. Pape of Quincy, Illinois. He was well educated, a member of the bar, and stood well among his neighbors, but he had not subscribed to the Liberty Loan or the Red Cross. A committee in charge of patriotic activities in Quincy noticed the absence of his name from all lists, and decided to appoint a special committee to wait upon him and ask him his reasons for "his omission of his patriotic duty." The members of the special committee met with Pape in his home where he told them that he would not subscribe to the Liberty Bonds; that it was a matter of principle with him; that he did not want the war to continue, and that the government was wrong in its position. Pape was said to have stated that he would not join the Red Cross "for that would be aiding the war and he was opposed to the war."

For those statements to the committee, Pape was indicted and charged "with intent to interfere with the operation and success of the military and naval forces of the United States, and to promote the success of its enemies."

In spite of the indictment, however, the defendant was discharged. The district attorney gave Pape's background, as well as the circumstances surrounding his statements that were the basis of the court action, to enable the court to consider a demurrer "in the light of all the facts surrounding the commission of the alleged crime." In sustaining the demurrer, the judge held that a citizen could not be prosecuted criminally under the Espionage Act for giving reasons for not subscribing to patriotic causes when requested for his reasons in the privacy of his own home. This was true particularly where the reasons were given in the presence of nobody but a duly authorized committee, "and especially when such reasons are mere matters of opinion, apparently honestly held."

Speech was the medium of communication involved in the first important case dealing with religious anti-war propaganda. This case arose in connection with the remarks of Clarence H. Waldron, pastor of the Baptist church of Windsor, Vermont. In his Bible class on different occasions, Waldron was said to have stated to men of draft age "a Christian ought not and should not fight; the boys will have to register, but if called upon it does not mean that they will have to go." And in front of a dry-goods store he told one member of the Bible class, after that person had enlisted, "I am sorry you have enlisted, and hope you will not go." For his remarks, he was convicted of sedition in the District Court of Vermont at Burlington in March 1918, and was sentenced to a fifteen-year term in the federal penitentiary at Atlanta.

The sentence imposed upon the Reverend C. H. Waldron by Judge Harlan B. Howe, of the United States District Court of Vermont, was one of the most severe imposed in the United States after war was declared on Germany. The *New York Times* recalled that Judge Howe had presided at the trial of Franz Rintelen, the German plotter, and his co-conspirators held in New York a few weeks before Waldron was sentenced. At the time that he sentenced Rintelen, Howe deplored the fact that under the law he could not send him and his fellow plotters to prison for life.

On March 5, 1919, the fifteen-year sentence imposed on Waldron was commuted to expire the following April. His case was one of fifty-two that received clemency at that time. The Department of Justice stated that in the cases thus acted upon the prisoners had been victims of wartime passion or prejudice, and had received long sentences not commensurate with their offenses.

For his alleged disloyal statements and false reports, another minister was sentenced to three years in the penitentiary. The Reverend John Fontana, a German Lutheran pastor in New Salem, North Dakota, was indicted for stating that President Wilson was a man who, after securing his election on the slogan " 'he kept us out of war,' turned squarely around and by the use of his high office of President whipped the members of Congress into line by threats of exposure of this one and that one, and in this way secured the authority to enter the war with Germany." The minister was said to have stated that the sinking of the *Lusitania* was justified, and that there was no reason whatever for the United States taking up arms against Germany; that he did not want to subscribe for Liberty Bonds, because it tended to encourage the administration; and that the purchase of those bonds would give the country more money to fight Germany and thus prolong the war.

Judge Charles F. Amidon, who presided at that trial, should be noticed for his remarks when he charged the jury and sentenced the pastor to three years in the penitentiary. The judge stated in his charge that there had been much evidence in the case about what the defendant did not do, namely, that he had not bought Liberty Bonds; that he did not subscribe to the Red Cross; he did not put up a flag in his church; and he did not sing patriotic songs. Amidon said this negative evidence was introduced to aid the jury in determining whether it found that the defendant used the language he was charged with using, and whether he was trying to make and convey false reports and thus interfere with the prosecution of the war. And when he sentenced Fontana, Amidon reminded the minister that the latter had received his final papers as a citizen in 1898, but, the judge stated "Every thought of your mind and every emotion of your heart through all these years has been German."

Fontana did not serve his three years, for on December 8, 1919, this conviction was reversed. Circuit Judge Walter H. Sanborn stated that the record in this case had been searched in vain for evidence that the defendant, before the indictment was filed, had ever made in public or in private five of the statements he was alleged to have uttered, and that only one person testified that Fontana had made the other statements with which he had been charged. At the same time, Judge Sanborn called attention to the many pages of the record which recited evidence permitted to be presented to the jury upon the question of the defendant's intent, which related to collateral issues, such as what the defendant had said about subscribing to the Red Cross.

Judge Sanborn examined all the issues, and reversed the decision of the lower court. He based his action upon the fact, according to him, that the statements alleged to have been made by Fontana had not been uttered where they would or could naturally and reasonably have affected the recruiting or enlistment service, nor were they indicative of any such intent, nor was any such result the necessary or legitimate consequence thereof.

The same judge who sentenced the Reverend C. H. Waldron to fifteen years in the Atlanta penitentiary, handed down a sentence of ten years to another minister, the Reverend Theodore Buessel, pastor of the German Lutheran church of Bristol, Connecticut. Buessel was suspected of disloyalty by persons in his community. To ascertain whether those suspicions were well founded, a female member of the American Protective League was assigned to the pastor "to get something on Buessel." That operative, according to the testimony at the trial, wined and dined the pastor, and engaged him in conversation about the war. As a result of the testimony of the member of the American Protective League, together with other witnesses, Buessel was said to have attempted to cause insubordination, disloyalty, and mutiny by stating that the war was nothing but a Wall Street war. Other incriminating remarks were to the effect that Germany was the most wonderful country in the world, and that all other nations could never crush it, and that it was unreasonable and unjust for the United States to have gone into the war. Buessel also was said to have stated that our soldiers and sailors were disloyal, and could be bought for small amounts.

As a result of the testimony, Buessel was found guilty on each of three counts. Judge Howe sentenced him to ten years on each of the three with the terms running concurrently. In passing sentence, the Court said that severe punishment was the only suitable sentence to impose upon a "counterfeit citizen." Buessel's term was commuted from ten years to expire April 1, 1919.

The socialists constituted one of the largest groups whose utterances were watched by the federal authorities for any violation of the Espionage or Sedition Act. The following cases illustrate the nature of the charges made against that group. For example, Frederick Krafft of Newark, New Jersey, secretary of the state Socialist Party, made a speech in Newark, August 9, 1917, in which he was reported to have stated that he did not see how the government could compel troops to go to France. Krafft was said to have remarked that if it was up to him, he would "tell them to go to hell." The secretary also remarked that he could not see why the socialists in America did not have the same rights as in Germany. For these and similar utterances before a crowd containing some men in the military service of the United States, Krafft was convicted of violating the Espionage Act, and was sentenced to five years in prison and ordered to pay a fine of $1,000.

Krafft was finally pardoned March 5, 1919. When he was pardoned, officials of the Department of Justice stated that consideration was given to the fact that in the Socialist National Convention at St. Louis early in the war, he was one of the pro-war leaders.

Another prominent official of the Socialist Party who had his sentence commuted the same day as did Krafft was Amos L. Hitchcock. On April 18, 1918, at Cleveland, Hitchcock, a member of the Board of Education of that city, was arrested on a warrant charging him with violating provisions of the Espionage Act by making remarks against the Liberty Loan. In a speech at Sandusky, Ohio, on April 6, he was alleged to have said that he did not believe in the Liberty Loan. Hitchcock was charged with saying that every dollar went into the pockets of profiteers, and that he would not contribute any of his money to those individuals. Moreover, by purchasing bonds, Hitchcock maintained that the purchasers were merely aiding the political ambitions of President Wilson. The socialist saw the whole war as a commercial scheme to make the rich richer and the poor poorer.

The case was tried before District Judge John M. Killits, who realized the emotional stress which wartime conditions placed upon the jury. In his charge to the jury, he stated that when matters were under consideration which tended to affect the patriotic feelings of citizens, and which tended to stir within persons the emotions of "reverence and love for our country, there is concurrent therewith a tendency to throw us off our balance of judgment, and to cause us to regard matters that are presented to our consideration with more or less heat." The jury found Hitchcock guilty and he was sentenced to ten years' imprisonment. On March 5, 1919, Hitchcock's sentence was commuted from ten years to two years.

Another ten-year sentence occurred in the more celebrated case of Mrs. Rose Pastor Stokes, at Kansas City, Missouri, June 1, 1918. The specific act upon which she was indicted was a letter she wrote the *Kansas City Star* in which she said "No government which is for the profiteers can also be for the people, and I am for the people, while the government is for profiteers." At the trial she was charged with obstructing the recruiting and enlisting service, attempting to cause insubordination, and of making certain false reports and false statements with the intent to interfere with our armed forces. She was convicted and received the ten-year sentence, but was allowed to be at liberty on $10,000 bond.

This case remained before the courts until 1920, when the earlier conviction was reversed by Circuit Judge Sanborn. Commenting upon the decision of the lower court, Sanborn said that its finding had taken place in the midst of war, when patriotic men "were particularly impatient of every interference and of every attempt to interfere with or cripple the universal efforts to win that war." When he considered the entire charge in the light of the time and circumstances surrounding the trial, of the extended discussion in the charge of the many side issues—these included discussions of whether England was a democracy, Bolshevism and internationalism—Judge Sanborn was unable to resist the conclusion that "the patriotic zeal of the court below led it to place too heavy a burden upon the defendant in her endeavor to meet the evidence which the government produced against her."

But the case that attracted the greatest attention of all was that of Eugene V. Debs. At Canton, Ohio, June 16, 1918, the three-times Socialist Party candidate for the Presidency, addressed a socialist convention, and stated that the purpose of the Allies in the war was the same as that of the Central Powers—plunder. He assured his hearers that they should know that they were fit for something better than cannon fodder. He declared himself, according to the *New York Times*, as guilty as the recently convicted Mrs. Rose Pastor Stokes. In addition, Debs praised the Bolsheviki and the I.W.W. He urged socialists to fight militarism wherever it was found.

For his speech at Canton, Debs was arrested in Cleveland, June 30, 1918, and charged with violation of the Espionage Act. The following were some of the charges made against Debs in the indictment: making false statements with the intent to interfere with the operation and success of our forces; attempting to promote the success of our enemies; attempting to cause insubordination, disloyalty, mutiny, and refusal of duty in our forces; attempting to obstruct the recruiting or enlistment service of the United States; opposing the cause of the United States by words; and for language that violated the Sedition Act. He was found guilty and sentenced to ten years in the penitentiary.

Debs was convicted of violating the Espionage and Sedition Acts, and during the next three years he spent most of his time in prison. An appeal to the Supreme Court in 1919 resulted in that court affirming the ten-year sentence, the famous decision of a united court having been written by Justice Holmes. Repeated requests for his pardon were refused by President Wilson, and it was not until December 25, 1921, that President Harding commuted his sentence, effective that day.

By the time that Debs was released from prison, the wartime restrictions upon freedom of speech had been removed. But the effects of those restrictions were to be felt by many individuals during the years that followed, and it is to that postwar heritage that we turn our attention in the closing chapter of this book.

Aftermath or Prologue

THE LASTING THREAT TO AMERICA'S DEMOCRATIC GOVERNMENT is in the carryover into peacetime of repressive measures instituted during war. In World War I there was an actual enemy whose defeat was necessary if this government was to continue to be able to guarantee citizens their freedom of speech, of assembly, and of the press. Also, during that struggle the government was a government of the people, by the people, "for the winning of the war." And the advent of peace did not result completely in replacing "for the winning of the war" with the traditional "for the people."

When peace came, the repressive measures, instead of being abolished, were used by federal, state and municipal officials, and were imitated by social, political and economic groups. These agencies employed censorship ideas and techniques against their domestic foes under the guise of protecting the institutions of the United States and the American way of life, without carefully defining the latter. As a result, in the years after 1918 many citizens discovered it was impossible for them to have pre-war freedom, but, at the same time they learned they could not be completely denied their constitutional rights.

In the post-war curtailments of civil liberties approximately the same groups received the attention of the censors. The only substitution was the Russian communist for the German spy. Except for that substitution, the other suspected groups remained the same, namely, those with radical ideas.

Evidences of suppression were everywhere as America faced the first full year of peace. Of paramount significance to the censors of 1919 was the spread of the anti-democratic and anti-capitalistic doctrines of communist Russia. Many officials classed as communists anyone with ideas of which the officials as individuals disapproved. In their drive against anarchists and radicals, the authorities used many different weapons. Those weapons varied from the Alien Law of October 16, 1918, to State Criminal Syndicalist and Red Flag Laws, as well as regulations controlling teachers and the curricula in public schools.

Since most of the agitation against the American form of government was thought to have come from a source outside the United States, the Alien Law seemed to solve the answer to that menace by providing for the deportation of undesirable aliens. Within three months after the Armistice, the first of the alien radicals whom the government planned to deport arrived in New York and were held at Ellis Island. In that initial group of fifty-seven men and one woman—the wife of a Finnish agitator—were disciples of Bolshevism, anarchy, terrorism, and members of the Industrial Workers of the World. The majority of them were ordered out of the country because they had been found to be members of an organization that advocated or taught the unlawful destruction of property.

Before the deportations were under way, two judges had disagreed as to whether membership in the Communist Party justified deportation. At the port of Boston, Judge Anderson ruled that such membership was not sufficient ground for that action. In the United States Court for the Southern District of New York, Judge John C. Knox held to the contrary, concluding that the aim of the Communist Party was to accomplish a definite end, namely, the capture and destruction of the state as now constituted, by force and violence.

All parts of the country contributed their share of deportees. From Seattle, members of the I.W.W. were shipped to Ellis Island. A student of the University of Minnesota was slated for deportation. He had served a year in prison as a conscientious objector in the days of conscription, and in 1919 had been arrested while delivering a public lecture on the subject, "Science is Revolution." And Fairmont, West Virginia, contributed sixteen radicals who had been arrested during a coal miners' strike in that state for their anti-government activities.

If deportation was not the fate of every alien radical, at least such a person's chances of becoming a citizen were lessened considerably in the years following the war. The Federal Circuit Court of Appeals, Third Circuit, sustained in 1930 the revocation of the citizenship of John Tapolesanyi, a Hungarian communist of Herminie, Pennsylvania. The court held that the principles of that party were so diametrically opposite to those embodied in the Constitution of the United States that a man could not be faithful to both. The interception of a letter from Tapolesanyi to his brother in Hungary in 1920 revealed his communistic beliefs, and led to the cancellation of his citizenship papers, according to the *New York Times*.

While Attorney General A. Mitchell Palmer, Assistant Attorney General Francis P. Garvan, and William J. Flynn, chief of the Secret Service were using deportation as one of their weapons against the Red menace, many states had passed or were passing laws "to keep Bolshevism and kindred lawlessness from gaining a foothold."

During the war many commonwealths had thought federal statutory restriction insufficient to cope with individuals and groups who were menacing the state and the nation. As a result, many states passed anti-pacifist and sedition laws to meet the emergency. With the return of peace, thirty states continued the main features of the Federal Espionage and Sedition Acts. They supplemented these regulations with statutes prohibiting individual acts having for their purpose incitement to destroy property, wreck the industrial system, overthrow the government, or advocate revolution by "general cessation of industry." And it was in the interpretation of these many laws that one of the real dangers to civil liberty lay.

Before considering those interpretations a few restrictive state laws of the post-war era should be noticed. Speaking of combating the Red menace in his state, the Governor of New Hampshire claimed that commonwealth had enacted the most drastic anti-Bolshevik law in the United States. Concerning that statute, the New York Times quoted Governor John H. Bartlett to that effect, and said that he had requested the Law Department "to rake the State with a fine-tooth comb to find evidence of their work. . . . No cost will be spared to suppress the social viper."

The various states hunted the "social viper" as an advocate of sedition or insurrection, a criminal syndicalist or as a displayer of the red flag. Kentucky, for example, in 1920 prohibited publication, assemblage or use of property for the promotion of criminal syndicalism and sedition under a penalty of imprisonment at hard labor for not more than twenty-one years or a fine of no more than $10,000, or both. The year before, Minnesota provided a punishment of not more than twenty years' imprisonment or a fine not in excess of $10,000, or both, for anyone indulging in seditious and disloyal speeches, acts or propaganda. From 1917 to 1920, fourteen states passed criminal syndicalism laws similar to those of Kentucky and Minnesota. In the matter of colored flags, persons in New Mexico had to refrain from displaying in public or private, a red or black flag, ensign, or sign of an organization opposed to organized government or urging the destruction of any and all government. Maximum penalties for violating that statute were $2,000 or fifteen years' imprisonment, or both. New Mexico was but one of thirty states that had enacted Red Flag Laws in 1919 and 1920.

It was not these various laws in themselves, however, that were dangerous to the citizens' enjoyment of civil liberty. It was in the interpretation that the danger lay. And the following cases show the manner in which those repressive laws were frequently interpreted. In many instances the power to punish far outran the ability to judge what was really dangerous to the American way of life.

Violation of one of these criminal syndicalism laws in California, in 1922, caused an Oakland clubwoman and social welfare worker to receive a sentence of from one to fourteen years in San Quentin. Charlotte Anita Whitney had come to the attention of the Oakland police force during the wartime agitation concerning criminal syndicalism and conscientious objectors. In 1920 she was arrested and found guilty of "aiding and abetting in the organization of a group having criminal syndicalism" as a belief. The organization referred to was the Communist Labor Party. In this case, Miss Whitney was convicted, "not for practising or teaching the tenets of syndicalism but for associating with those who proposed to teach it." At her trial, it was brought out that she had attended a meeting where the American flag had been draped with a red flag. After a fight of more than seven years to keep her out of prison, in which struggle the case was carried unsuccessfully to the Supreme Court, Miss Whitney was saved from serving that sentence by Governor Young of California, who pardoned her, June 20, 1927.

Another Californian, convicted of violating that state's red flag law, received more favorable attention from the Supreme Court. Yetta Stromberg, a young woman of nineteen, was one of the supervisors of a summer camp for children, between the ages of ten and fifteen, in the foothills of the San Bernardino mountains. The charge against her centered around a daily red flag raising ceremony in the camp. In connection with that exercise, the children saluted and pledged allegiance "to the worker's red flag, and to the cause for which it stands; one aim throughout our lives, freedom for the working class." For such activities the defendant was convicted in the Superior Court of San Bernardino County, and the decision was upheld by the District Court of Appeals of California. On May 18, 1931, the Supreme Court reversed that judgment.

Chief Justice Hughes delivered the opinion of the court in this case. It held that the verdict was a general one that did not specify the ground upon which it rested. The Chief Justice stated that a statute which was so vague and so indefinite as to permit the punishment of the use of the opportunity for free political discussion was "repugnant to the guaranty of liberty contained in the Fourteenth Amendment."

While Miss Whitney was being tried on charges of criminal syndicalism for associating with persons holding those opinions, Illinois was sustaining a similar law. William Bross Lloyd, a wealthy radical, had received an indeterminate sentence of from one to five years for alleged attempts to overthrow the government. The Supreme Court of Illinois, in 1922, affirmed the judgment of the lower court, and declared "Communists are a menace." The menace of Lloyd did not seem too great to Governor Len Small, who pardoned him. In pardoning Lloyd and his companions, the Governor was said to have stated, "These men are not criminals. Since their indictment and conviction in March 1921 they have suffered severely. . . . No great good can come from longer incarceration for them."

And in New York, Benjamin Gitlow, arrested in 1920, was indicted for criminal anarchy. He was charged with advocating and advising the overthrow of the government by certain ideas embodied in a publication entitled *The Left Wing Manifesto*. In addition, he was charged with printing and distributing a paper called *The Revolutionary Age* which advocated similar actions. For those sentiments, which Justice Sanford of the Supreme Court held "by their very nature involve danger to the public peace and to the security of the state," Gitlow was sentenced to from five to ten years in Sing Sing. In 1923, the case reached the Supreme Court where the decision of the lower courts was affirmed with Holmes and Brandeis dissenting. In his opinion, Holmes held that the small minority who shared Gitlow's views constituted no serious threat to the welfare of the government.

Michigan's anti-syndicalism law was invoked in 1922 in the case of Charles E. Ruthenberg, one of the leaders of the Workers' Party in the United States. He was convicted of attending the communist national convention which, according to the *New York Times*, had been held in a "wooded gorge in the wild and dune country twenty miles south of St. Joseph, on the shores of Lake Michigan." He was found guilty and was sentenced to five to ten years in the penitentiary. His appeal was pending before the Supreme Court when he died, nearly five years later.

Friends of Ohio's criminal syndicalism law seemingly outnumbered its foes. Early in 1931 an attempt was made to repeal it, but only ten state legislators voted for its repeal in the face of organized veterans' support of it. At Akron, however, Judge Walter B. Wanamaker, in Common Pleas Court held it was unconstitutional, stating that mere talk without evil consequences could not by law be made a crime in Ohio. And in the Ohio Supreme Court, December 21, 1932, it was pointed out that under this statute any person who quoted certain passages from the Declaration of Independence, or any printer who published it, was guilty of a felony.

But there was nothing wrong with that statute in the opinion of Judge George C. Canaga of Cadiz, Ohio. Two women communists were brought before him for distributing alleged anti-government literature during a so-called communist demonstration at Martins Ferry the preceding fall. Judge Canaga upheld the constitutionality of the state criminal syndicalist law, and sentenced both women to the state reformatory for from one to five and from five to ten years, and with fines of $2,000 and $5,000, respectively.

A similar law in Kansas drew objections from the United States Supreme Court. In that state the court held that the statute had been applied in a certain case to sustain the conviction of the defendant without any charge or evidence that the Workers' Industrial Union, a branch of the I.W.W., the organization for which he secured members, "advocated any crime, violence or other unlawful acts or methods as a means of effecting industrial or political changes or revolution."

In Oregon, possession of I.W.W. membership cards and assisting in the conduct of a communist meeting were sufficient to cause the indictment of various persons on charges of criminal syndicalism. At Portland fifty-seven men were indicted November 20, 1919, because of their membership cards. For presiding at, conducting, and assisting a meeting of the Communist Party, Dirk De Jonge was sentenced to serve seven years in the penitentiary, and the State Supreme Court upheld the verdict. This sentence was meted out although neither criminal syndicalism nor unlawful conduct was urged during the meeting.

The state and federal Supreme Courts disagreed about this case. The former upheld the conviction because, in its estimation, the Communist Party was an advocate of criminal syndicalism. Before the federal Supreme Court handed down its decision, argument before that body brought out the fact that if the Communist Party had a meeting in Oregon to discuss almost any political question, any person acting in the capacity in which De Jonge had served could be found guilty under that law. As a result of that argument the Supreme Court reversed the decision of the Oregon bodies in an opinion written by Chief Justice Hughes. The court held that notwithstanding the aims and objectives of the Communist Party, De Jonge still enjoyed his personal right of free speech.

Closely allied to the enforcement of criminal syndicalism laws were the instances of enforcement of the sedition acts passed by the various states. In Philadelphia, August 29, 1928, Israel Lazar, a communist speaker, was said to have stated that this government murdered Sacco and Vanzetti. After remarking that this was a strike-breaking government, he urged his hearers to teach "our young workers in time of war to shoot down people who ordered us to shoot other people." For his remarks, Lazar was sentenced to a term of two to four years. Also in Pennsylvania, two years later, allegations of communism were sufficient to cause indictment on a charge of sedition.

And in Pittsburgh a jury required only ten minutes to find Israel Blankenstein, an alleged communist organizer, guilty of sedition. At the trial it had been revealed that a large quantity of communist literature had been found in his room, and that he had been active in getting members for the party in the Pittsburgh district. Blankenstein was sentenced to from two to four years in the penitentiary.

Under the Illinois sedition law of 1919, this evidence against Blankenstein would have been unnecessary. According to a decision in that state in 1929, merely membership in the Communist Party was held to constitute a violation of that act.

While many states passed anti-communist measures, Georgia, for one, did not have any trouble finding a law to deal with that party. Georgia went back to a statute passed in Reconstruction days to sentence a Negro communist to a term of eighteen to twenty years.

With the coming of the depression, following the crash of 1929, communism and complaints concerning the scarcity of jobs brought new activity in the enforcement of these state sedition laws. The combination of the assemblage of a group of communists, and a discussion of unemployment was seditious in Newark, New Jersey, in 1930. According to the *New York Times*, eight communists were arrested after they had spoken at an unemployment meeting. They were said to have told the audience that President Hoover was only an office boy for the capitalists who were responsible for unemployment, and that the police were servants of the capitalists. The police said that the unemployed were urged to disregard the law, "take what they wanted," and shoot the police if the latter interfered.

Newark citizens were not kindly disposed toward the seditious. In 1920, Walter A. Gabriel had discovered that fact when he was under conviction for violating the state sedition law, and was required to furnish a $5,000 bail. The representative of one bonding company had signed the necessary papers when he noticed the charge against his client included hostility to the government. The representative tore off the signature, and announced that his company would not "bail a traitor."

Turning from law to education, the same desire for conformity and fear of alien influences caused scrutiny of teachers and texts. In Brooklyn, in May 1919, Benjamin Glassberg, a teacher of history, was dismissed because he had told his pupils that Bolshevism was not so bad as it had been painted. Six months later, Sonia Ginsberg, another Brooklyn teacher, had her license canceled when she admitted she belonged to the Communist Party.

In Cambridge, Massachusetts, a Radcliffe College graduate was temporarily suspended as a teacher. Miss Mary Peabody, whose name was on the lists seized when radical headquarters were raided in Cambridge, suffered that penalty when the contents of the lists became known to the school authorities. And in Ohio, one professor was discharged because he favored the cause of strikers.

Textbook sentiments were watched carefully. For example, in 1930, the volume *Modern History*, by Carlton Hayes and Parker Thomas Moon was reported barred as a textbook from the New York schools after seven years of use. This action followed complaints that the work was anti-patriotic, radical, and pro-Catholic.

By 1941, however, some schools could regard their faculty and students as being American. For example, President Robert G. Sproul of the University of California, in his biennial report to the Governor, said that classroom teaching in that institution compared favorably in quality with that of any American university. He stated, "It is free from subversive propaganda, loyal to the principles of democracy, and inspired by the highest ideals that the human mind and spirit are capable of conceiving."

The story of the attacks upon academic freedom in the decades following World War I is too extensive to admit of further treatment, but it may serve as the starting point for the examination of another field in which constitutional rights were interfered with—namely, with respect to the press—for in this field also special interests were able to see to continuation of wartime methods of suppression as necessary for national safety.

For instance, in New Mexico, July 13, 1923, the editor of the *Albuquerque Tribune* was sentenced to a year in jail, and his publishing company was fined $4,050 because his paper had charged that the judge, who later sentenced him, and various county officials were influenced by a political machine.

Six years later, in Cleveland, Newton D. Baker denounced contempt proceedings that had been brought against two executives of the *Cleveland Press*. The basis of this legal proceeding consisted of objection to two editorials that criticized a Cleveland judge for interfering with the sheriff's efforts to stamp out betting at the Thistledown race track.

Potentially, a Minnesota law of 1925, sponsored by a legislator who sought to silence an editor who was attacking him, offered the greatest obstacle to a free press. Commonly known as the "gag law," it gave the District Judge, sitting as a court of equity, power to suppress any publication printing "malicious, scandalous, and defamatory matter." Armed with this statute, officials followed the lead of County Attorney Floyd B. Olson, who had obtained a temporary injunction, and suppressed the *Saturday Press*, a Minneapolis weekly newspaper. This publication had attacked an alleged gambling and general racket business in that city, and had asserted that the situation was being tolerated by local officials and law enforcement heads.

The newspaper was quite direct in its charges. The offensive articles stated, in substance, that a gangster was in control of gambling, bootlegging, and racketeering in Minneapolis, and that law-enforcing officers and agencies were not performing their duties. The chief of police was charged with illicit relations with gangsters, and with participation in graft. One member of the grand jury was said to be in sympathy with the gangsters. Of the officials, the one to achieve most prominence was the County Attorney, Floyd B. Olson, whom the paper charged with knowing the existing conditions, and with failure to take adequate measures to remedy them.

Finally, June 1, 1931, the Supreme Court heard the case, and with a five-hour decision declared that "press gag" law unconstitutional. Because the district court had perpetually enjoined the defendants "from producing, editing, publishing, circulating, having in their possession, selling or giving away any publications whatsoever, which is a malicious, scandalous or defamatory newspaper, as defined by law," and also "from further conducting said nuisance under the name and title of said the *Saturday Press* or any other name," the Supreme Court held the statute to be an infringement of the liberty of the press guaranteed by the Fourteenth Amendment. This decision rested upon the operation and effect of the law without regard to the question of the truth of the charges against the *Saturday Press*. The impeccability of the officers named in the case, the Supreme Court stated, could not affect the conclusion that the statute imposed an unconstitutional restraint upon publication.

Without that statute, Minneapolis officials managed to exert some control over the press. For example, the *Public Press* had been forced to suspend publication in 1931, and more than a year later it resumed operation only to have its first edition confiscated by the police. The leading story in that issue dealt with the shooting of a man by a policeman in a quarrel over their feminine companion who accompanied them on a drinking party.

July 26, 1934 saw Governor Floyd B. Olson establish an even closer scrutiny of the Minneapolis press as well as of persons. A truck drivers' strike was in progress at that time, and the authorities considered the situation tense; consequently martial law was declared. One section of that edict stated that it was unlawful to print or distribute notices, handbills, or newspapers defaming the state of Minnesota or its national guard. According to the *Chicago Tribune*, anyone who criticized Olson's government or troops was defaming the state. The Chicago paper held that under the Governor's rule requiring permits for gatherings of more than one hundred persons it would mean that churches would have to hold their religious services by permit and military consent.

Governor Olson denied the existence of any censorship. He stated that there was no censorship of news nor was there any interference with speech or press. Olson was reported to have said that representatives of any publication could go to Minneapolis for the purpose of gathering news. The Governor stated that while criticism was invited, no defamation of the state or national guard would be permitted.

Just as communists and other radicals, more than any other individuals or groups, felt the force of the state criminal syndicalism and sedition laws, so did the communists and radical papers suffer more suppressions than did any of the reforming or sensational publications. Four editors and the business manager of the *Daily Worker*, New York communist labor paper, were prosecuted for publishing indecent matter. The obscene writing occurred in a poem entitled "America," printed March 12, 1927. The poem was a "violent attack upon the United States." And the *American Freeman* for June 25 and July 15, 1932, were pronounced unmailable by the postmaster of New York for an article "Why Don't the Workers Raise Hell." The article asked if a Texan, Kansan, or Kentuckian fifty years ago would have permitted himself to starve or his family to suffer from lack of food so long as there was food and his guns were in working order. Judge Robert P. Patterson upheld the postmaster's act, stating that while the article did not directly advise the readers to take weapons to obtain what they needed, the exhortation was there.

In the realm of press censorship, in the 1920's and 1930's, one New York editor discovered that communism and fascism were not accorded the same treatment by officials who did America's censoring. In August 1923, Carlo Tresca, anarchist, strike organizer, and editor of the anti-fascist New York weekly *Il Martello*, was arrested for sending obscene matter through the mails. One of the offensive articles, according to the *New York Times*, compared the Fascisti with the Ku Klux Klan. Ostensibly, it was said, he was arrested, indicted, and convicted for publishing a two-line advertisement of a book on birth control. He was sentenced to a year and a day in Atlanta, and served four months of that sentence. Four years later Tresca's paper was temporarily banned from the mails by the New York postal authorities. Whether it was a Christmas editorial or an article in which Italo Balbo, Italy's representative to the Aviation Congress in Washington, was called a murderer, the effect on the paper was the same.

This same respect for fascism was noticed thirteen years later in another American institution. In 1936, in the field of the cinema, fascist feelings were considered when Will Hays banned a film based on Sinclair Lewis's book, *It Can't Happen Here*. Both the German and Italian governments were reported pleased at the action against the work of Lewis whom one German spokesman called a "full-blooded communist."

Some local suppressions, also, centered about international relations. For instance, it was alleged that in the latter part of 1923, the board of regents of the University of Michigan refused George Wickersham the use of the Hill Auditorium for a speech on the League of Nations because University property could not be used for "political" purposes. On Americanization Day, April 27, 1927, after a celebration at which New York City was presented with forty American flags by the Veterans of Foreign Wars, Matthew Kirchner was arrested for distributing documents entitled *Hands Off China*. The offending publication said in part, "No American worker should accept the dirty job of being a mercenary for Wall Street to kill Chinese workers and farmers, fighting against foreign imperialist oppressors." For his efforts, Kirchner was charged with distributing pamphlets without permission, refusing to move on when ordered to do so by a policeman, and causing a crowd to gather. In 1928, when Nicaragua was attracting the attention of our government, mails bearing seals with the inscription "Protest against marine rule in Nicaragua" were barred by the Post Office Department. Proceeds from the sale of those seals were said to be used to aid General Sandino to carry on his rebellion in Nicaragua. And in Passaic, New Jersey, in 1935, when Italy was waging war against Ethiopia, anti-war meetings were prohibited, and the police halted a meeting on Ethiopia in the Bethel African Methodist church there.

Since the first World War, one channel of idea communication, relatively unimportant in 1917 and 1918, has received increasing attention. In the field of radio the Federal Communications Commission has licensing powers that are for the most part lacking in peacetime with respect to other channels. And in addition to this federal regulation, there are opportunities for censorship by broadcasting companies. For example, in 1926, officials of Station WEAF refused to allow Norman Thomas to broadcast a talk on the subject of compulsory military training. Officials of the station explained that in controversial subjects both sides had to be discussed, and when, in compliance with the station's request for a copy of the speech in advance, it was seen to be controversial, Thomas was informed it would not be allowed over WEAF.

Other instances of radio censorship occurred at WCAE, Pittsburgh, and WTCN, Minneapolis. The former refused to broadcast the speech of August 28, 1936, of Earl Browder, Communist candidate for President, after having broadcast speeches by Roosevelt and Landon. The Minneapolis station followed the same procedure concerning Browder's speech, and canceled its contract with the party to broadcast a series of speeches after $1,000 had been spent in advertising them.

For the last twenty-three years, however, most noticeable cases of censorship have been of local happenings which have occurred with respect to the rôle of the radical in the fields of politics and economics. In denying civil liberties in these spheres private citizens occasionally played the part of the censor. In New York, in November 1919, the Reverend Theodore Brown prevented Rose Pastor Stokes from addressing a group of communists in a New York hall. He had learned of the impending address and, after conferring with the Commissioner of Public Safety on police arrangements, had rounded up two hundred prominent citizens who agreed to seat themselves in the hall long before the time for the meeting, and thus crowd out as many as possible of the usual audience. When Mrs. Stokes attempted to deliver her address, Brown and his followers broke up the meeting by singing "The Star-Spangled Banner" and by giving three cheers for the United States.

An assemblage of alleged radicals in Passaic, New Jersey, was not broken up, but it proceeded under difficulties. On March 28, 1920, circulars announced a meeting of union workers in a certain hall that evening. The police notified the head of the union that the meeting could not be held without a permit, and that it was too late to issue one. Police also notified the owner of the hall not to allow the gathering. The union had expected this action, and had engaged another hall. When the police arrived there Norman Thomas was reading the Constitution of the State of New Jersey. When orders to stop the meeting failed, the police had the lights turned out, but with a candle in one hand Thomas continued until he had finished reading the State Constitution. Three more readings of the same document followed, and, according to the *New York Times*, the police stood by "and appeared interested in the organic law of the sovereign State of New Jersey." When a Pole, who had predicted that the red flag would float over the Passaic City Hall, repeated the performance in Polish, a police interpreter followed him closely to see that between sections of the Constitution the Pole "did not intersperse any Red doctrines to imperil the loyalty of the visiting speakers, detectives and newspapermen."

New Jersey furnished one example of rapid action on the part of the censor, so rapid in fact that it bordered on the prophetic. At a socialist meeting in Paterson, October 6, 1923, John Butterworth, a local socialist labor leader, was arrested after he had addressed the meeting to the extent of saying, "Fellow Citizens." Later he paid for those words at the rate of twenty-five dollars each, being fined fifty dollars for his effort.

Freedom of assembly was also restricted in Boston. For example, in October 1923, Mayor Curley barred Ku Klux Klan meetings in that city, and almost a year later Boston authorities were prohibiting a peace meeting called by the socialists on Defense Day, September 12.

In Dallas, Texas, in March 1931, two communists were jailed, not because of their Red affiliations, but because they mentioned racial equality. For that act, as was stated in the

New York Times, "They were jailed, on vagrancy charges, of course," and were kidnaped by a mob "that, the suspicion is strong, was tipped off by the police" as they were about to be spirited out of town. After their comrades had given them up for murdered they appeared in Kansas City.

A mass departure of radicals occurred from Weirton, West Virginia, in October 1919. There, more than one hundred fifty men, declared to have been members of the Red Guard of Finland, were rounded up, marched to the public square, forced to kneel and kiss the American flag, and then police and deputies drove them out of town. Each of the men treated in this manner had refused to buy Liberty Bonds, and all of them had been agitators in the steel strike that was then in progress. Weirton itself received a shower of handbills which read "Beware! This is America. No interference by the Finn Reds or I.W.W. will be tolerated." They were signed "Weirton Vigilance Committee." The following day the rest of the Finns were preparing to leave town after officials of the Weirton Steel Company announced that it would employ no more of that nationality.

Constitutional rights of labor agitators were circumvented in various ways. In New York in May 1930, three communists were arraigned in court on a disorderly-conduct charge because they had attempted to hold an outdoor street meeting without a license. When they had produced their April permit to speak, the police communicated with the Safety Commissioner who ordered it revoked. In Pittston, Pennsylvania, Powers Hapgood and his wife, in 1928, walked the street in front of a hall where a labor meeting had been banned by the mayor. On their arms they wore black arm bands bearing the legend "We Mourn Free Speech." They were arrested and charged with rioting, but were acquitted.

Near Fort McPherson, Georgia, strikers were interned in a concentration camp in 1934. The *New York Times* for September 20, 1934, carried a picture of the camp with the title "Women held in Concentration Camp," and the paper went on to relate that sixteen women strikers were being held indefinitely at that camp.

In the strike areas of Alabama and Oklahoma, in 1920 and 1925, respectively, meetings of various kinds were prohibited. In the former, the commander of the state guard posted notices throughout the troubled district forbidding public assemblies. In Oklahoma, in August 1925, the sheriff of Okmulgee County forbade the striking coal miners to pray publicly in outdoor groups near the mines to influence the non-union strikebreakers. For nearly a month before the order, the wives and children of the striking miners marched to the shafts singing hymns. Here they sang until the non-union workers came to work. At that time the group would cease singing and would pray for the souls of the men who had taken the strikers' places. These religious bands were supposed to have won away sixty workmen, and then came the sheriff's order.

Suppression, however, was not always in favor of the employer. In Boston, in February 1940, the Ford Motor Company agreed to comply with the order of the National Labor Relations Board to refrain from "disparaging" or "criticizing" labor organizations. That order applied to the company's Somerville plant, according to the *New York Times*, and "apparently dealt with an interview with Henry Ford . . . copies of which had been distributed to employees." In the interview, Mr. Ford was of the opinion that the employees were better off outside a union than in one.

With the present European War entering upon a period of activity, censorship has been of two kinds. The first consists of so crowding the channels and agencies of idea communication with the news and views of an approved sort that opposing ideas do not get a hearing; and second, suppression.

Censorship measures originating in World War I were used in one guise or another, and by one agency or another, for more than twenty years after the Armistice. They were used to stamp out evils that, in too many instances, were evils only in the opinion of groups applying the restrictions. In this connection, the plane upon which official wartime censorship was conducted was as far above the post-war repressions as Wilson's Fourteen Points were above Teapot Dome.

As this book is written censorship is once again commanding the anxious attention of America. Everyone with understanding of realities knows that censorship is necessary in wartime. But Americans, remembering the evils of the censorship carryover from World War I, should steadfastly resolve, in the midst of whatever crisis, that with the end of the crisis civil liberty in this country shall have a new birth. If repression continues after the war is over, we shall have lost the very ideal for which we fought. And Americans must always remember that nations, governments, and individuals usually receive the fate that they themselves have fashioned and that they deserve.

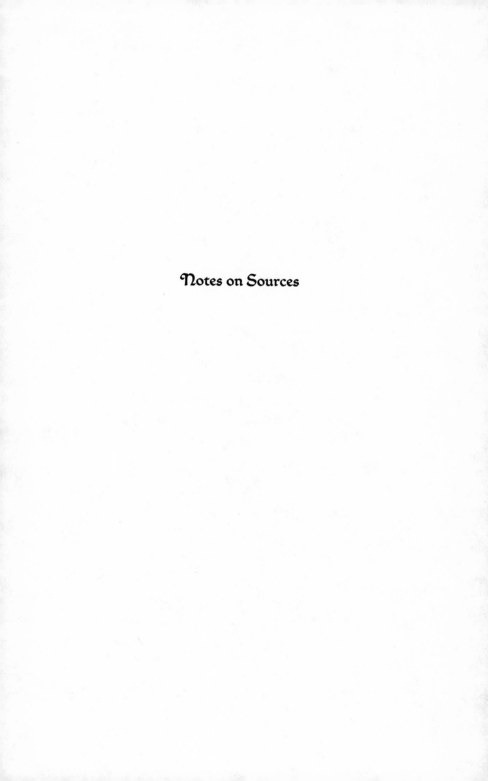

Notes on Sources

ͷotes on Sources

Documents in the files of various record groups in The National Archives constitute the greatest single source of information used in this volume. Groups of records used by the author include the following: the Committee on Public Information, United States Food Administration, United States Fuel Administration, Council of National Defense, United States Housing Corporation, Office of the Secretary of War, Office of the Secretary of the Navy, and the Adjutant General's Office.

To learn the attitude of the press and to gain an insight into the current events of the war years, the files of approximately fifty newspapers were read. In the selection of these newspapers an attempt was made to get a cross-section of the nation from as many different angles as possible.

Summaries of sources for each chapter are given below:

OUR CENSORSHIP HERITAGE

Duniway, C. A. *Freedom of the Press in Massachusetts* (Harvard Historical Studies, vol. 12. Cambridge, Harvard University Press, 1906).

Whipple, Leon. *The Story of Civil Liberty in the United States* (New York, Vanguard Press, 1927).

Van Tyne, Charles Halstead. *The Loyalists in the American Revolution* (New York, Macmillan, 1902).

Sharpless, Isaac. *History of Quaker Government in Pennsylvania.* 2 vols. (Philadelphia, T. S. Leach & Co., 1899).

Fiske, John. *The Critical Period of American History, 1783-1789* (Boston, Houghton, 1924).

Anderson, Frank Maloy. *Enforcement of the Alien and Sedition Laws* (In American historical association. Annual report, 1912. pp. 113-126, Washington, 1914).

Hildreth, Richard. *History of the United States.* 6 vols. (New York, Harper, 1880).

MacDonald, William, ed. *Select Documents of United States History* (New York, Macmillan, 1898).

Cheyney, Edward P. "Freedom and Restraint: A Short History" in *The Annals of the American Academy of Political and Social Science*, vol. 200, Nov. 1938.

Patterson, Giles Jared. *Free Speech and a Free Press* (Boston, Little, Brown and Company, 1939).

Smith, Charles William, Jr. *Public Opinion in a Democracy* (New York, Prentice-Hall, 1939).

Johnson, Gerald W. "Freedom of the Press" in *The Annals of the American Academy of Political and Social Science*, vol. 200, Nov. 1938.

Gibbs, George. *Memoirs of the Administrations of Washington and John Adams*, edited from the papers of Oliver Wolcott, Secretary of the Treasury. 2 vols. (New York, Printed for the subscribers. W. Van Norden, printer, 1846).

Alien and Sedition Laws. Sen. Doc. No. 873, 62 Cong., 2 Sess. (Washington, 1912).

Morison, Samuel Eliot and Commager, Henry Steele. *The Growth of the American Republic*. 2 vols. (New York, Oxford University Press, 1938).

The Virginia and Kentucky Resolutions of 1798 and '99, with Jefferson's Original Draught Thereof. Also, Madison's Report, Calhoun's Address, Resolutions of the Several States in Relation to State Rights. With Other Documents in Support of the Jeffersonian Doctrines of '98 (Washington, Published by Jonathan Elliot, 1832).

Channing, Edward. *A History of the United States*. 6 vols. (New York, Macmillan, 1932-1937).

Beard, Charles A., "The Great American Tradition" in *The Nation*, 123:8-9, July 7, 1926.

Hall, James Parker. "Free Speech in War Time" in 21 *Columbia Law Review* 526.

Jones, Robert William. *The Law of Journalism* (Washington, Washington Law Book Co., 1940).

A Sermon of War Preached at the Melodeon, on Sunday, June, 1846, by Theodore Parker, Minister of the Twenty-eighth Congregational Church of Boston (Printed by I. R. Butts, 1846).

Rhodes, James Ford. *History of the United States*. vols. 3-6 (New York, Macmillan, 1928).

Official Records of the Union and Confederate Armies. Series II, vols. 1 and 2.

Randall, James Garfield. *Constitutional Problems Under Lincoln* (New York, Appleton, 1926).

Office of the Secretary of War, Military Book, No. 48. 1862.

Office of the Secretary of War, Book 295. Orders War Dept. Jan. 28, 1862 to Telegrams Received by the Secretary of War. vol. 13. 1862.

Office of the Secretary of War, Telegrams Received by the President. vol. 5. 1866.

Claghorn, Charles Eugene. *The Mocking Bird* (Philadelphia, The Magee Press, 1937). Thanks are due to the author and to the publisher who have permitted quotations from this book.

For all events subsequent to the Civil War the sources used are the files of the Office of the Secretary of War and of the Old Files Section, Old Records Division, Adjutant General's Office. Both of these record groups are now in The National Archives.

THE SEED OF CENSORSHIP

Sources for this chapter were largely legal, newspaper and documentary. For state regulations concerning civil liberties, the laws of the various states enacted from 1915 to 1919 were examined. The instances of economic control are to be found in the files of the United States Food Administration, United States Fuel Administration, United States Housing Corporation. The records of all these agencies are to be found in The National Archives.

From the vast newspaper collection in the Library of Congress, the author obtained the accounts of the incidents showing local censorship. The papers consulted most frequently were: *Pittsburgh Post, Pittsburgh Dispatch, Des Moines Register, Atlanta Constitution, Anaconda Standard, Nebraska State Journal* (Lincoln), *Daily Patriot* (Concord, N.H.), *Newark* (N.J.) *Star-Eagle, Emporia Gazette, Saint Paul Dispatch, New York Times, Topeka Daily State Journal, Kansas City Star, Evening Journal* (Wilmington, Del.), *Every Evening* (Wilmington, Del.), *Daily Herald* (Vicksburg, Miss.), *St. Louis Republic, St. Louis Globe Democrat, Idaho Daily Statesman, Boise Capital News, Bismarck Evening Tribune, Argus and Patriot* (Montpelier, Vt.), *Wisconsin State Journal* (Madison), *Providence* (R.I.) *Journal, Albany Evening Journal, Helena* (Mont.) *Daily Independent, Christian Science Monitor, Boston Transcript, Minneapolis Journal, Minneapolis Morning Tribune, Santa Fe New Mexican, State Gazette* (Trenton, N.J.), *Illinois State Register* (Springfield), *Chicago Tribune, Chicago Daily News, Cleveland Plain Dealer, Cincinnati Enquirer, San Francisco Examiner, Times-Picayune* (New Orleans), *Arizona Republican* (Phoenix).

Other sources include the following:

O'Brian, John Lord, "Civil Liberty in Wartime" in New York State Bar Association Report, vol. 42 (1919). pp. 275-313.

Chafee, Zechariah, *Freedom of Speech* (New York, Harcourt, Brace and Company, 1920).

School and Society. 1917, 1918, 1919, 1938.

Bureau of Education. Report of the Commissioner of Education. 1917, 1918, 1919, 1920.

"LAWS AGAINST SPIES AND TRAITORS"

The sources for this chapter are: Chafee, *Freedom of Speech*; the previously mentioned files of the Adjutant General's Office and of the Secretary of the Navy in The National Archives; the Congressional Record of the 64th and 65th Congresses; *Editor and Publisher*, the *New York Times*; the file of Executive Orders now in the custody of the Federal Register, The National Archives.

In addition to the *New York Times*, the same newspapers were scanned that have been listed in the preceding chapter.

The Espionage Act is found in C. 30, 40 *Stat.* 217, while the Sedition Act appears in C. 75 Sec. 1, 40 *Stat.* 553. For the Trading-with-the-Enemy Act see C. 106, 40 *Stat.* 411.

THE CENSORSHIP BOARD

For the background and organization of the Censorship Board the most information was obtained from the following: the files of the Secretary of the Navy, mentioned above, contain the account of radio and cable censorship. In the records of the Committee on Public Information are copies of the bulk of the minutes of the Censorship Board, as well as copies of the reports of Military and Naval Intelligence.

Supplementing this information, the author corresponded or conversed with several members of the Censorship Board. Persons thus approached were George Creel, Edgar Sisson, Paul Fuller, Jr., Captain Frederic Bulkley Hyde, Eugene Russell White, and Major General Frank McIntyre.

Of special value for this and subsequent chapters was Navy Department, Office of Naval Intelligence. *Cable Censorship Digest* (Washington, Government Printing Office, 1933).

CABLES AND TELEGRAMS

Material in this chapter was derived from the following sources. The files of the Secretary of the Navy, in the custody of The National Archives, provided the account of the censorship activities of the Navy. Other incidents and cases cited are to be found in the records of the Committee on Public Information, and in those of the Old Files Section of the Old Records Division of the Adjutant General's Office, also in The National Archives.

In this as in the preceding chapter, the *Cable Censorship Digest* was useful. Of the newspapers consulted for material relating to this chapter, the *New York Times* was most helpful.

SOLDIERS, SAILORS, AND CENSORS

Information relating to censorship bearing directly upon the armed forces is in the General Orders of the War Department, and of the General Headquarters, A.E.F., as well as in the Special Regulations of the War Department, 1918.

Other records of value here, but already mentioned, were those of the Committee on Public Information, and of the Secretary of the Navy.

The file of *The Stars and Stripes* used was that of the Library of Congress.

PROTECTIVE CUSTODY IN THE POST OFFICE

The records of the Committee on Public Information, and of the Secretary of the Navy provided the greater part of the material relating to Postal Censorship. Other sources were the *Annual Report of the*

Postmaster General, 1917, 1918, 1919, and the *Cable Censorship Digest.*

AT THE EDITOR'S ELBOW

The bases of this chapter consisted of the records of the Committee on Public Information, the files of the paper or publication treated in the text, and Chafee, *Freedom of Speech.*

Cases cited appear in the following: *The Federal Reporter, United States Reports, Annual Report of the Attorney General,* 1917, 1918, 1919, and the Department of Justice, *Interpretations of War Statutes,* Bulletins Nos. 1-204.

BANNED BOOKS

This chapter was written from the records of the Committee on Public Information, the files of the newspapers previously listed, and from an examination of the banned books themselves in the light of the censors' comments.

SCISSORS AND FILMS

The *Exhibitor's Trade Review* provided much of the background for this chapter. Other sources were the Old Files Section, Old Records Division of the Adjutant General's Office and the records of the Committee on Public Information.

For the account of the cinema *The Spirit of '76* see, Chafee, *Freedom of Speech,* the files of the *Chicago Tribune, New York Times, Los Angeles Times,* 258 Fed. 908, 252 Fed. 946, and Department of Justice, *Interpretation of War Statutes,* Bulletin No. 33.

President Wilson's attitude toward the picturization of Ambassador Gerard's *My Four Years in Germany* is revealed in Ray Stannard Baker's *Woodrow Wilson, Life and Letters* vol. 7 (New York: Doubleday, Doran, 1938).

"NO MORE SOAP-BOXES"

Again the records of the Committee on Public Information were valuable for the subject of censoring speech, and the *New York Times* provided much additional information.

For specific instances of censorship the files of the paper or periodical referred to in the text were examined, or the individual cited was approached by the author, either through correspondence or conversation.

Schoberg's case is to be found in 264 *Fed.* 1 and in 253 *US* 494. The *Cincinnati Enquirer* covered the trial.

The action relating to Enfield is in 261 *Fed.* 141.

The *Annual Report of the Attorney General,* 1918, treated the suit of U.S. *v.* Daniel H. Wallace, and also that of Kate Richards O'Hara. The case of the latter is the subject of Department of Justice, *Interpretation of War Statutes,* Bulletin No. 49, and of 253 *Fed.* 540.

Bulletin No. 56 relates to W. B. Tanner, while *Bulletin No. 69* and 255 *Fed.* 301 deals with H. E. Kirchner. *Bulletin No. 103* and 257 *Fed.* 639 concerns W. E. Mead. Louis B. Nagler's alleged violation of the Espionage Act is related in *Bulletin No. 127*. *Bulletin No. 160* is the source of information about Wm. Madison Hicks.

For Deason see 258 *Fed.* 259.

Bulletin No. 78 and 253 *Fed.* 481 relate to Leonard Foster, while *Bulletin No. 81* and 259 *Fed.* 388 give the evidence concerning Wolf. Hall's case is given in 256 *Fed.* 748, and that of Sandberg in *Bulletin No. 151* and 253 *Fed.* 270 considered U.S. *v.* Theodore B. Pape. Arguments for and against Clarence H. Waldron are given in *Bulletin No. 79*. Reverend John Fontana's case is treated in *Bulletin No. 148* and in 262 *Fed.* 283. Sources for information about Buessel are *Bulletin No. 131* and 258 *Fed.* 811. U.S. *v.* Krafft is the subject of 249 *Fed.* 919. Hitchcock's case may be read in *Bulletin No. 122*.

This list of sources is completed with the citations for the Stokes and Debs cases. The former is in *Bulletin No. 106* and 264 *Fed.* 18 with the latter in *Bulletins No. 155* and 196, and in 249 *U.S.* 211.

Aftermath or Prologue

Sources for this chapter include: The previously mentioned records of the Secretary of the Navy in The National Archives; session laws of the several states; files of the newspapers mentioned in the text, especially those of the *New York Times*; Morris L. Ernst and Alexander Lindley, *The Censor Marches On*, Doubleday, Doran, New York, 1940; publications of the American Civil Liberties Union; *Seven Campuses*, University of California, Berkeley, California, vol. 3 No. 2, April 1941.

In addition to newspaper accounts of the law cases treated in this chapter, those concerning Miss Whitney, Stromberg, Gitlow and De Jonge are found in 274 *U.S.* 357; 283 *U.S.* 359; 268 *U.S.* 652; and 299 *U.S.* 353 and 57 *Sup. Ct.* 255, respectively. For the case of *The Saturday Press* see 283 *U.S.* 697 and 51 *Sup. Ct.* 625.

Index